D0556101

PRIVACY LAW
IN A NUTSHELL®

SECOND EDITION

by

JOHN T. SOMA
Professor of Law
University of Denver Sturm College of Law
Executive Director—Privacy Foundation

STEPHEN D. RYNERSON
Bryan Cave LLP
Denver, Colorado

ERICA KITAEV
Baker Hostetler LLP
Denver, Colorado

WEST
ACADEMIC
PUBLISHING

Mat #41498848

Nutshell Series, In a Nutshell and the Nutshell Logo are trademarks registered in the U.S. Patent and Trademark Office.

444 Cedar Street, Suite 700
St. Paul, MN 55101
1-877-888-1330

West, West Academic Publishing, and West Academic are trademarks of West Publishing Corporation, used under license.

Printed in the United States of America

ISBN: 978-0-314-28942-1

ACKNOWLEDGMENTS

We owe our thanks to those who have helped us on this Nutshell. University of Denver, Sturm College of Law, research associate Jonathan Gray, assisted us in numerous drafts, as well as the final draft, by suggesting many revisions, as well as organizing and tracking the normal plethora of last minute changes. Law students Alexandra Molina and Morgan Batcheler greatly assisted with early drafts. Thanks go to Associates Tina Amin and Aaron Thompson, with Baker Hostetler LLP, Denver, for their extensive research and editing. Our thanks also go to Cindy Goldberg, Administrative Assistant to the Privacy Foundation for her ever-present support and helpful comments.

JTS
SDR
EGK

OUTLINE

TABLE OF CASES

References are to Pages

PRIVACY LAW

SECOND EDITION

CHAPTER ONE

INTRODUCTION

We live in a world where information is the foundation of modern society. Federal, state, and local governments, as well as intergovernmental organizations, assemble near-limitless amounts of personal information concerning individuals' birth, marriage, divorce, property, court proceedings, driving records, political activities and affiliations, criminal transgressions, professional licensing, travel, and countless other activities. Private businesses also gather personal information for marketing purposes, to prepare credit histories, or to sell to various other entities, both private and public. This collection of personal information by its very nature implicates the concept of privacy—a concept of central importance in today's technological world.

Before venturing into the complex and difficult task of defining privacy one must understand why the topic is important and why privacy law is one of the most exciting developing fields of legal study. Professor Roger Clarke, a pioneer in the field of privacy and information technology, describes individual privacy as consisting of four dimensions: the psychological, the sociological, the economic, and the political. Psychologically, people need private space to preserve a sense of individual identity. Sociologically, people require the opportunity to connect and interact with others, but without the continual threat of being observed. These dimensions of privacy have long been recognized. Indeed, as the Eighteenth Century British philosopher Jeremy Bentham wrote in describing his vision of the ultimate prison (the "Panopticon"), "the most important point [is] that the persons to be inspected should always feel themselves as if under inspection . . . ."[1] More recently, the economic and political dimensions have come to be recognized as critically important as well. Economically, people must be able to plan and innovate without their efforts being subject to continual scrutiny by others who might seek to appropriate their ideas. Politically, if representative governments are to be functional, people need to be able to think, argue, and act without fear of their identities being exposed. For a free political system to function successfully, people must be able to vote without the fear of retribution from others who hold a different viewpoint. Individuals must have privacy in their choice to engage in the political process, as well as in their decision of what causes to support. All four of these dimensions inform the study of the law of privacy.

It is vital that both lawyers and the public in general become familiar with the study of privacy law. First, with the increasing rapidity of technological advancement and ever-greater exchanges of information, notions of privacy are being challenged as never before. Through the

---

[1]   JEREMY BENTHAM, PANOPTICON OR THE INSPECTION HOUSE, Letter V (1787), *available at* http://cartome.org/panopticon2.htm.

collection, manipulation, and dissemination of personal information, commercial and government entities are gaining more influence over individual autonomy and decision making. As members of a democratic society we have the choice, through studying and understanding privacy laws, to shape the kind of society we desire as we move ever deeper into the Information Age. Second, and flowing in large part from the first trend, public concern over invasions of privacy has grown tremendously in the last few decades. Privacy concerns appear with increasing frequency on the legislative agendas of Congress and state legislatures, and garner increased media attention with each subsequent revelation about theft or misuse of personal information. Third, at the nexus of the first two trends, we find an increasing amount of litigation which implicates privacy law, either directly or indirectly. Lawyers are faced with drafting privacy policies for businesses, litigating privacy issues, and helping a variety of industries and government agencies conform to ever more complex and pervasive privacy regulations.

Most law students will receive only tangential schooling on the subject of privacy law. Criminal procedure discusses the constitutional limits on where police can go and what evidence the police can collect in criminal investigations under Fourth Amendment searches and seizures; reproductive, sexual and family privacy is deemed a subset of First and Fourteenth Amendment jurisprudence; and privacy in cyberspace is often treated as a subset of intellectual property or communications law. None of these particular courses, however, are aimed at providing students with a systemic framework through which broader debates about privacy issues can be examined. As a result, privacy problems are often not well articulated and we, who are being affected by privacy intrusions, are faced with the lack of a convincing account of what is at risk when privacy is threatened and what exactly the law must do to solve these problems. Rather than using a narrow, topical framework that isolates specific sub-types of privacy protection, privacy law is best understood by first approaching it from a broad conceptual perspective before moving to an examination of particular sub-topics.

In this Nutshell, we divide the study of privacy into four parts. First, we begin by examining the history of privacy law. More specifically, we explore the definitions of privacy from a wide array of jurists, philosophers, legal scholars, psychologists, economists, and sociologists. This is followed by a discussion of the historical trends in privacy, including: a general discussion of the development of international privacy rights; the European Union's view on privacy; the United States' view on privacy; the Organization for Economic Co-operation and Development (OECD) guidelines; and the collection, retention, accuracy, and use of privacy information. The first part concludes with a discussion of the technological impact on privacy.

Second, we have selected representative examples of court decisions, federal statutes and legislation, agency decisions, state constitutions and statutes, and professional ethical rules. These authorities are the root of claims brought on behalf of those who demand privacy against government officials, business entities, and private individuals in the United States.

Third, we provide an overview of international privacy law for comparison with the United States' standards and views on privacy. Canada, the European Union, Mexico, Japan, South Korea, China, and India are all analyzed. Notwithstanding the philosopher Ayn Rand's observation that, "[c]ivilization is the progress toward a society of privacy,"[2] privacy does not have a universal meaning that is the same across all cultures. Indeed, the significance of privacy in a particular nation depends on the social importance attached to the context in which privacy concerns are raised. Also in this chapter, we review legal developments, business perspectives, and concerns regarding transborder privacy data flows. Transborder data flows include the transfer of data containing personal or sensitive information from an entity in one nation to an entity in another. This is an area of both increasing economic significance and regulation around the world.

Finally, we explore a variety of current and developing challenges to privacy. This chapter focuses primarily on the challenges new technologies pose to the legal concepts discussed in earlier chapters.

---

[2]   AYN RAND, *The Soul of an Individualist*, *in* FOR THE NEW INTELLECTUAL 84 (1961).

This Nutshell is by and large not structured around traditional legal categories such as torts or constitutional law. Rather, it provides an overview of legal theories, principles, doctrines, statutes, rules, policies, and international norms and customs, which define and inform the term "privacy," as well as where the challenges to individual privacy are likely to be in the future based upon developing technologies. The broad structure of this book is intended to allow individuals to develop a legal and logical framework to understand potential implications for privacy concerns in a variety of contexts.

CHAPTER TWO
HISTORY AND DEFINITIONS

I.   A BRIEF HISTORY OF PRIVACY

Constitutional scholar William Beaney remarked in an article shortly after the U.S. Supreme Court's landmark privacy decision in *Griswold v. Connecticut*, "even the most strenuous advocate of a right to privacy must confess that there are serious problems of defining the essence and scope of this right."[1] Indeed, the only certainty in defining privacy is that it is a concept that is highly malleable depending on the experience, interests, and agenda of the person interpreting it and the socio-political context the definition is offered in. For most individuals, however, privacy's definition does not depend on some philosophical underpinning, but rather is a simple, even intuitive concept. This Nutshell does not provide an exhaustive list of philosophical definitions of privacy; rather, it uses some of the common philosophical positions to illustrate the fluidity and complexity of this concept. By declining to endorse any of the particular definitions, we attempt to provide an objective and comprehensive account of what exactly "privacy" is to certain individuals.

---

[1]   William M. Beaney, *The Right to Privacy and American Law*, 31 LAW & CONTEMP. PROBS. 253, 255 (1966).

A.   HISTORICAL EVOLUTION OF PRIVACY

Although not defined explicitly as "privacy," it is clear that some idea of an individual need for separateness from the public sphere has existed since the mythic era of the earliest human civilizations. In the Sumerian *Epic of Gilgamesh*, composed over four thousand years ago, the human, but immortal, Utnapishtim lives as a hermit and does not reveal his identity to his visitor, Gilgamesh, until the wandering king has explained the reason for his trip to Utnapishtim's home. In the Old Testament of the Bible one of the signs that humans have learned the distinction between good and evil is that Adam and Eve make clothing for themselves to conceal their nakedness.

More formally, privacy concerns appear in the Code of Hammurabi, one of the earliest legal texts. Drafted in the Babylonian Empire in approximately 1760 B.C.E., paragraph 21 of the Code made it a crime to break a hole through the wall of another's house. Privacy concerns are also reflected in the Laws of Manu, codified in India in approximately 200 B.C.E. That text included a provision under which if an individual deposited goods or money with a storehouse in secret, the custodian was obliged to likewise return such goods or money to the owner in secret.

In Greek and Roman societies, philosophers increasingly recognized the significance of the distinction between the private and public realm. At his trial for corrupting the youth of Athens, one of the accusations Socrates defended himself against was the claim that if his teachings were not illegitimate then he should have entered the realm of politics and spoken publicly instead of privately instructing students. Socrates rebuked his accusers, stating that to openly declare his teachings would have simply incited the public against him even sooner and "he who will fight for the right, if he would live even for a brief space, must have a private station and not a public one."[2] Meanwhile, the Roman Stoic philosopher Epictetus explained that logic dictated that human thoughts are inherently private—even the threat of imprisonment or death could never force an individual to truly disclose what his or her thoughts were.

Over the ensuing centuries, one can see the slow but steady movement toward the recognition of what most Twenty-First Century Americans would call "privacy." In 1361, the Justices of the Peace Act in England provided for the arrest of peeping toms and eavesdroppers. At his trial in 1535 for allegedly denying the legitimacy of Henry VIII's status as head of the Church of England, Thomas More rejected the suggestion that his silence in the face of the charges against him could be sufficient evidence to support a conviction. Echoing Epictetus's observations from more than a thousand years earlier, More stated, "[F]or this my taciturnity and silence neither your law nor any law in the world is able justly and rightly to punish me, unless you may

---

[2]   2 PLATO, THE DIALOGUES OF PLATO 125 (Benjamin Jowett trans., Macmillan & Co. 3d ed. 1892).

besides lay to my charge either some word or some fact in deed."[3]

As Europe moved into the era of the Enlightenment, the distinction between public and private spheres became ever more important as people sought to limit the increasing powers of government. In the late Seventeenth Century, John Locke, one of the most influential political philosophers in history, emphasized the point repeatedly in his works that the state must necessarily be restrained from invading the property or person of its citizens. As he explained, "Though the earth . . . be common to all men, yet every man has a 'property' in his own 'person.' This nobody has any right to but himself."[4] In 1765, British Lord Camden, striking down a warrant to enter a house and seize papers wrote, "We can safely say there is no law in this country to justify the defendants in what they have done; if there was, it would destroy all the comforts of society, for papers are often the dearest property any man can have."[5] In 1776, the Swedish Parliament enacted the Access to Public Records Act, which required that all government-held information be used for legitimate purposes. In 1789, the French Declaration of the Rights of Man and the Citizen declared, "No one should be disturbed on account of

---

[3]   ERNEST EDWIN REYNOLDS, THE TRIAL OF ST. THOMAS MORE 84 (1964).

[4]   JOHN LOCKE, TWO TREATISES OF GOVERNMENT 204 (George Routledge & Sons 2d ed. 1887).

[5]   Entick v. Carrington, 95 Eng. Rep. 807, 817 (C.P. 1765).

his opinions, even religious, provided their manifestation does not upset the public order established by law."[6]

These are just some examples of the origins of the idea of privacy. Although privacy as a concept existed, it did not receive formal acknowledgment in the American legal community as a protectable "right" until the publication of Samuel D. Warren and Louis D. Brandeis's "The Right to Privacy."

B. THE MODERN ERA: WARREN AND BRANDEIS'S "THE RIGHT TO BE LET ALONE"

As far back as 1834, the U.S. Supreme Court stated that a "defendant asks nothing—wants nothing, but to be let alone until it can be shown that he has violated the rights of another." *Wheaton v. Peters*, 33 U.S. 591, 634 (1834). It was here where the American legal system first acknowledged an individual interest in being let alone; however, the context was different from how Warren or Brandeis used it. Equally, the "right to be let alone" first appeared in T.M. Cooley's *A Treatise on the Law of Torts* as part of the phrase the "right to enjoy life and be let alone." Although Cooley coined the term, it did not receive widespread recognition until Warren and Brandeis's article.

Much debate surrounds the motivation of Warren and Brandeis to write an article devoted to the topic of privacy. Some scholars speculate it was a

---

[6]   Déclaration de Droits de l'Homme ét du Citoyen, art. X (Fr. 1789).

response to the increased sensationalism of the press in general or, perhaps more cynically, in reaction to media attention focused on the lavish social parties the Warren family was known for hosting in the 1880s. Whatever their motivation for writing the article, its impact was, and continues to be, undeniable. The article's key phrase, "the right to be let alone," continues to dominate privacy discourse, not just in the U.S. legal system, but abroad as well. Warren and Brandeis stated:

> Gradually the scope of these legal rights broadened; and now the right to life has come to mean the right to enjoy life,—*the right to be let alone*; the right to liberty secures the exercise of extensive civil privileges; and the term 'property' has grown to comprise every form of possession—intangible, as well as tangible.[7]

Almost forty years later, Brandeis echoed this right to be let alone in his dissent in *Olmstead v. United States*, 277 U.S. 438, 478 (1928) (emphasis added):

> The makers of our Constitution undertook to secure conditions favorable to the pursuit of happiness. They recognized the significance of man's spiritual nature, of his feelings, and of his intellect. They knew that only a part of the pain, pleasure and satisfactions of life are to be found in material things. They sought to protect Americans in their beliefs, their

---

[7]   Samuel Warren & Louis Brandeis, *The Right to Privacy*, 4 HARV. L. REV. 193, 193 (1890) (emphasis added).

thoughts, their emotions and their sensations. They conferred, as against the Government, *the right to be let alone*—the most comprehensive of rights, and the right most valued by civilized men. To protect that right, every unjustifiable intrusion by the Government upon the privacy of the individual, whatever the means employed, must be deemed a violation of the Fourth Amendment. And the use, as evidence in a criminal proceeding, of facts ascertained by such intrusion must be deemed a violation of the Fifth.

Though the right to be let alone has become a catch-all definition of privacy today, the specific definition lies in its context. Warren and Brandeis used the term in proposing a new tort: the invasion of privacy. The invasion of privacy was a more profound harm than mere injury to reputation, one that damaged a person's sense of his or her own independence, distinctiveness, dignity, and honor. The right to be let alone is the freedom from unwanted intrusions into the person. Warren and Brandeis's right to be let alone is not a concept developed out of a constitutional right, but in tort.

Warren and Brandeis did not demand the recognition of an absolute right to privacy, in part because the word privacy does not appear in the U.S. Constitution. Rather they sought to ground privacy in the common law right to life, a right enunciated in the Declaration of Independence, and formally recognized by the Fifth Amendment to the Constitution. Warren and Brandeis, recognizing this potential inconsistency, articulated six limitations on the right to privacy. First, the right to privacy generally permits publication of public material. Matters of general or public interest do not facilitate an unwarranted invasion of individual privacy—the very event Warren and Brandeis sought to protect. Second, "the right to privacy does not prohibit the communication of any matter, though in its nature private, when the publication is made under circumstances which would render it a privileged communication according to the law of slander and libel."[8] "Circumstances" entail courts of justice, legislative bodies, municipal assemblies, or any public body formed as a voluntary association. Third, there must be special damages suffered by the invasion of privacy through oral publication. Like the elements of many present day laws, an individual must have suffered a specific redressable personal damage. Fourth, the right to privacy terminates upon the publication of the facts by the individual, or with consent of the individual. If an individual chooses to publish any facts detrimental to his or her person or consents thereto, no action will lie in tort. Fifth, according to the authors, truth is not a defense. Sixth, the lack of "malice" in the publisher is not a defense. The intent of the individual publishing materials intruding on someone's privacy is irrelevant because privacy is to be protected, rather than a particular state of mind punished. These six limitations serve to provide some limits on a concept revolutionary for its time.

---

8   *Id.* at 216.

As commentators have pointed out, the right to be let alone, although revolutionary in its impact, was in many ways simply the logical culmination of earlier work and, as some would argue, it suffers a number of significant defects.

Critics suggest the right to be let alone is fundamentally flawed in two respects: it is either too broad or too narrow. "Too broad" means the definition counts as violations of privacy things that intuitively are not; while "too narrow" fails to count as violations of privacy things that intuitively are. Professor Judith Thomson of M.I.T. illustrates the problem of a broad definition with the following example:

> If I hit Jones on the head with a brick I have not let him alone. Yet, while hitting Jones on the head with a brick is surely violating some right of Jones', doing it should surely not turn out to violate his right to privacy. Else, where is this to end? Is every violation of a right a violation of the right to privacy.[9]

Conversely, Thomson's example of a too narrow definition is:

> The police might say, "We grant that we used a special X-ray device on Smith, we grant we trained an amplifying device on him so as to be able to hear everything he said; but we let him

---

[9]   Judith Jarvis Thomson, *The Right to Privacy*, 4 PHIL. & PUB. AFF. 295 (1975) (emphasis omitted).

strictly alone, we didn't even go near him—our devices operate at a distance."[10]

Although their definition is open to criticism, whether one is a critic or advocate of Warren and Brandeis's definition, it is undeniable that their article opened the floodgates to privacy as a legitimate legal concern and continues to be at the heart of a variety of different philosophical definitions.

II.   DEFINITIONS

As the idea of privacy has become more important to human societies over the past century or so, philosophers and other scholars have increasingly wrestled with the difficult question of what, exactly, is "privacy"? Below we discuss a few of the major schools of thought on the subject and their disagreements with each other.

A.   CONCEPTUAL VS. INTERPRETIVE WAYS TO VIEW PRIVACY

Privacy definitions can be analyzed two different ways: interpretively and conceptually. Interpretively viewing privacy concentrates on examining the evolution of privacy jurisprudence in the common law and the courts' explorations of the concept—particularly Brandeis's dissent in *Olmstead* and forward. A purely conceptual analysis focuses on the search for a privacy definition whose foundation rests on general philosophical grounds

---

[10]   *Id.*

and hence, can be used to evaluate and make sense of privacy debates arising not just from a particular legal tradition, but within any political or legal system. In this Nutshell, privacy is approached with both interpretive and conceptual analysis in an effort to provide an explanation of the numerous definitions currently pervading privacy discourse.

B.   ANTI-REDUCTIONISM/LIMITED ACCESS TO SELF VS. REDUCTIONISM

Conceptual analysis of privacy leads to a variety of different philosophical definitions. Several scholars define privacy broadly as limited access to the self or "anti-reductionism." Anti-reductionists assert that a diverse set of invasions of, or interferences with, an individual should be understood under the basic heading of privacy. Even within the anti-reductionist camp, definitions differ as to what interferences include. For most, interferences with personal information, secrecy, repose, reserve, bodily integrity, anonymity, solitude, seclusion, and decisions are treated as separate dimensions of privacy. While at first glance it appears privacy as limited access is identical to the right to be let alone because solitude appears in both definitions, limited access definitions are a more complex formulation of that right. Anti-reductionists acknowledge that privacy extends beyond simply being apart from others. Under this view, individuals are afforded much greater privacy protection because the definitions are extremely expansive.

E.L. Godkin, a contemporary of Warren and Brandeis who was trained as an attorney and later became an influential magazine editor, was the first theorist to advance privacy as a limited access theory by observing that "nothing is better worthy of legal protection than private life, or, in other words, the right of every man to keep his affairs to himself, and to decide for himself to what extent they shall be the subject of public observation and discussion."[11] Godkin's definition did not expressly provide for limited access. As a result, later anti-reductionist theorists sought to advance a more concise definition of accessibility. Legal philosopher Anita Allen stated that, "a degree of inaccessibility is an important necessary condition for the apt application of privacy."[12] Perhaps the most compelling limited access definition of privacy is advanced by Professor Ruth Gavison. Gavison believes an individual's interest in privacy is related to accessibility to others. Accessibility in Gavison's theory is parsed into three facets: "the extent to which we are known to others, the extent to which others have physical access to us, and the extent to which we are the subject of others' attention."[13] Privacy in this view is not understood as a psychological state or as a form of control over personal information; rather it is a combination of

---

[11]   E.L. Godkin, *Libel and its Legal Remedy*, 12 J. OF SOC. SCI. 69, 80 (1880).

[12]   ANITA L. ALLEN, UNEASY ACCESS: PRIVACY FOR WOMEN IN A FREE SOCIETY 10 (1988).

[13]   Ruth Gavison, *Privacy and the Limits of Law*, 89 YALE L.J. 421, 422–24 (1980).

three separate and irreducible elements: secrecy, anonymity, and solitude. A violation of any one of these elements infringes upon accessibility and is a violation of privacy. Many anti-reductionists characterize the primary virtue of their approach to analyzing privacy as being that it is relatively unconstrained by narrow cultural and legal issues and thus promotes a more universal view of privacy.

Some critics accuse limited access definitions of over-emphasizing a form of individual control over access to the self as opposed to a state of existence. As explained by Professor David O'Brien, the weakness of the limited access definition is that, "privacy is not identical with control over access to oneself, because not all privacy is chosen . . . some privacy is accidental, compulsory, or even involuntary."[14] Limited access definitions also fail to articulate what violations of access implicate privacy. Although limited access theorists or anti-reductionists can catalog a variety of interferences with privacy, their definition provides no guidance as to the degree of access necessary to constitute a violation of these accessibility interferences.

Reductionists believe the more expansive conceptions of privacy are vague, ambiguous, or indeterminate. Motivated by views of what ought to be protected from intrusion through the recognition of rights, reductionists assert that privacy can be reduced to other concepts and rights. An argument in favor of this theory is that it affords greater

---

[14]   DAVID M. O'BRIEN, PRIVACY, LAW, AND PUBLIC POLICY 15 (1979).

protection of privacy rights within existing legal frameworks than anti-reductionist theory. By viewing privacy as being the sum of a broad collection of already acknowledged rights, a violation of privacy is actually the violation of another right, which is clearly redressable.

Professor Thomson, the most well-known of reductionists, has studied numerous cases which are usually considered to represent violations of the right to privacy, and concluded that all of the cases can be sufficiently and equally explained in terms of violations of liberty, property rights, or rights over the person. As she states, the "right to privacy is everywhere overlapped by other rights."[15] In a sense, a privacy violation is better understood as a violation of a more basic right. Legal decisions that implicate remedies for privacy violations can be analyzed most effectively and consistently by reference to some other corresponding violation of a basic right, not privacy as a standalone right. It would be an error, however, to conclude that Thomson and other reductionists are trying to eliminate the right to privacy. Rather, reductionists conclude from this analysis that the protection of privacy can be better accomplished by ensuring basic rights are not violated. Many reductionists would argue that the advantage to this approach is that by relying on extensions of more concretely

---

[15]   Judith   Jarvis   Thomson,   *The   Right   to   Privacy*, PHILOSOPHICAL DIMENSIONS OF PRIVACY 284 (Ferdinand David Schoeman ed. 1984).

established rights the validity of a right to privacy is bolstered.

Critics of reductionism suggest that by conceding the non-existence of a true right to privacy and, instead, attempting to derive it from a cluster of other rights, the reductionists are undermining the overall goal of protecting privacy. In this view, deriving a privacy remedy as a result of some other right's violation obscures the extent of current legal protection for privacy *qua* privacy. Reductionism is also criticized as giving the erroneous impression that the concern with privacy is a modern, and particularly Western, phenomenon. By treating privacy only as a label for selected aspects of other basic rights, reductionism is seen as threatening to undermine belief in the distinctness and importance of privacy for privacy's sake, as well as exposing privacy protections to the risk of being eroded by collateral changes in the law governing the underlying rights reductionists are otherwise trying to ground their definition on.

C.   CONTROL VS. CONDITION DEFINITIONS OF PRIVACY

Legal scholars debate whether privacy is best understood as a capacity for control or description of a condition. A number of theorists conceive of privacy as a form of control over personal information. Control definitions associate privacy with an individual's control over access to some characteristic of the self. Professor Charles Fried of Harvard Law School stated that privacy "is not simply an absence of information about us in the minds of others; rather it is the control we have over information about ourselves."[16] It is irrelevant whether the information is a general fact or a detailed account; if the person seeks control over the information, it is private information that should be protected. Under this definition of privacy, the emphasis is on guarding as private all information over which individuals want to preserve control.

"Informational privacy," a term coined by political scientist Dr. Alan Westin, is an example of a control definition of privacy. Informational privacy is the interest an individual has in managing the handling of his or her own personal information. In other words, privacy is not a first principle, but rather is a function of the claim and ability of a party to determine why, when, how, and to what extent information about it is shared with others. From this definition, Westin concludes that personal information would be best thought of as a form of property right.[17] Control over information is ownership in the information.

Advocates of conditional privacy definitions are the staunchest critics of control definitions and informational privacy. The scholars argue control definitions are too narrow because they exclude those aspects of privacy that are not informational, e.g., a right to make determinations about reproduction or how one's children should be raised.

---

[16]   Charles Fried, *Privacy*, 77 YALE L.J. 475, 482 (1968).

[17]   *See* ALAN F. WESTIN, PRIVACY AND FREEDOM 324 (1967).

Proponents of the control definition rebut this point by noting that it can encompass protection of all information over which individuals want to preserve control. The *facts* of such things as reproductive decisions and child rearing are clearly informational in nature; individuals may seek to retain control over those facts and thereby protect the underlying decisions and activities. As with most legal theories, however, it is vulnerable to attack on the basis of a word's meaning. Theorists relying on control definitions often fail to define what is meant by "control" over information, and the word can plainly range from extremely narrow to extremely broad. Legal philosopher Tom Gerety has pointed out that the most popular definition used by control theorists "includes *all* control over *all* information about oneself, one's group, one's institutions. Surely privacy should come, in law as in life, to much less than this."[18] Even if one were to limit the definition of control to the exertion of management power over specific information, the concept is still arguably overbroad because individuals lose control over information in manners not involving anything most people would consider an invasion of privacy. For example, if an individual is observed walking down a public street and then enters a particular building, the information that the individual visited that particular building is now beyond his or her control because it is known to the observer. Other critics argue control is not a necessary condition for the existence of informational privacy because a

---

[18]   Tom Gerety, *Redefining Privacy*, 12 HARV. C.R.-C.L. L. REV. 233, 262–63 (1977).

person can lose control over information but still retain privacy.

"Condition" definitions define privacy as a condition or state of affairs in which it is possible to describe changes that may be considered losses of privacy. If the condition changes, that alteration in the state of affairs is seen as a diminution of an individual's privacy. A loss of privacy in this view is contingent on a change in the conditions of the privacy definition. This approach obviously simplifies the process of finding a privacy violation because one no longer needs to focus on normative arguments. Instead, the question of whether privacy has been lost becomes a pure question of fact. The aim of condition definitions is to explain what a "loss of privacy" consists of, without addressing either the circumstances that led up to that loss or otherwise attaching any particular legal, moral, or political significance to the change in condition.

While some theorists suggest limited access definitions are a subset of control definitions, these definitions are not identical to control definitions because privacy is often accidental or involuntary. Indeed, limited access definitions are better viewed as an example of condition definitions. Limited access definitions define privacy as a condition of limited access to one or more aspects of a person; therefore, the loss of privacy is recognized as a loss of inaccessibility. Two prominent limited access theorists discussed above, Anita Allen and Ruth Gavison, define privacy with a set of conditions— Allen's relies on accessibility, while Gavison's focuses on solitude, secrecy, and anonymity. A violation of these conditions results in a corresponding privacy loss, but a loss depends on the asserted condition. This inevitably leads to the question: what are the conditions for a privacy loss? Conditions are those dictated by whoever is articulating the definition. As a result, condition definitions ultimately become particularized to each individual. While offering opportunities for flexibility in policy-making, this approach also makes it difficult for two different individuals to determine whether they are actually advocating the same scope for privacy.

D.   PRIVACY AS INTIMACY AND SOCIOLOGICAL PERSPECTIVE

A more recent privacy definition that has drawn increasing interest argues that "intimacy" properly defines what information or matters are private. Many of these theorists stress the significance of developing various interpersonal relationships with others. This theory views privacy as consisting of some form of limited access or control, and it locates the value of privacy in the development of personal relationships. Charles Fried, also a control definition theorist, argues that privacy has inherent value because privacy is essential for one's development as an individual, with a moral and social personality, able to form intimate relationships involving respect, love, friendship, and trust. Privacy as intimacy allows one to define oneself and freely choose which social relationships to develop. Justifications for defining privacy as intimacy vary. In the view of Professor Jeffrey Rosen of George Washington University Law School, "when intimate information is removed from its original context and revealed to strangers, we are vulnerable to being misjudged on the basis of our most embarrassing, and therefore most memorable, tastes and preferences."[19] While intimacy is a narrow concept, it is classified as a sociological perspective because intimacy affects how social relationships are developed. Privacy allows us to vary our behavior with different people so that we may maintain and control our various social relationships.

Critics claim intimacy definitions merely serve to privilege embarrassing or otherwise awkward information individuals want to keep away from others. Philosopher Jeffrey Reiman provides an example of this inadequacy. Reiman observes that individuals reveal information to psychoanalysts that they would not reveal to close friends or family members, but the same individuals would not say that they had intimate relationships with their psychoanalysts. As an intimacy theorist himself, Reiman argues that the definition may be nuanced by placing greater emphasis on qualitative aspects of intimacy.[20] Yet this attempt to bolster the theory of privacy as intimacy reveals that it can also be too narrow a definition. The theory centers almost

---

[19]   JEFFREY ROSEN, THE UNWANTED GAZE 9 (2001).

[20]   See Jeffrey H. Reiman, *Privacy, Intimacy, and Personhood*, PHILOSOPHICAL DIMENSIONS OF PRIVACY 304–06 (Ferdinand David Schoeman ed., 1984).

exclusively on interpersonal relationships and the feelings produced by them; minimizing by omission concerns about the confidentiality of financial information, political activity, and other subjects frequently considered private from a lay perspective. As Professor Julie Cohen noted in further critiquing the intimacy definition of privacy, for many modern individuals economic concerns are paramount in their daily lives, not preserving or deepening their intimate associations.[21] The intimacy definition can also be criticized for arguably discarding the notion that an individual may have a privacy interest in his or her internal thoughts or acts taken in solitude because of its emphasis on person-to-person communications.

E.   ECONOMIC PERSPECTIVE ON PRIVACY

While most theorists believe privacy is an important democratic right that the state has some duty to protect through regulatory policy, scholars arguing from an economic perspective believe privacy is better protected through individual responses and market-based mechanisms. One of the most well-known advocates of the economic perspective on privacy is Judge Richard Posner of the U.S. Court of Appeals for the Seventh Circuit. For Posner, many approaches to defining privacy lead to economically inefficient results. The emphasis in defining privacy should instead be on identifying those circumstances in which access to

---

[21]   *See* Julie E. Cohen, *Privacy, Ideology, and Technology: A Response to Jeffery Rosen*, 89 GEO. L.J. 2029, 2031–32 (2001).

information diminishes its economic value.[22] Where shielding information maximizes economic gain, the information should be protected; conversely, where the dissemination of information maximizes these gains, the information should not be protected from public exposure. While this approach to defining privacy has the virtue of prioritizing objective criteria, thus making it easier to establish what constitutes privacy and the loss thereof, it does have two major weaknesses. First, as Professor Cohen has noted, it is clear that a free market is able to find some means of wringing value from almost any piece of information. While the fact that any given individual prefers a particular brand of toothpaste is nearly valueless in isolation, when this information is aggregated from millions of individuals it can be worth vast sums to businesses interested in marketing toothpaste or complimentary goods. Balancing those relative interests across literally billions of transactions every day in the United States is in practice impossible. Second, as has been explored above, the concept of privacy (however defined) has a strong psychological component, which is not easily susceptible to quantification in market transactions.

F.   THE FEMINIST CRITIQUE OF PRIVACY

Many feminist theorists believe privacy is used as a shield to conceal domination, degradation, and abuse of women and others who are viewed as being

---

[22]   RICHARD A. POSNER, THE ECONOMICS OF JUSTICE 232–35 (1981).

outside the power structure of modern societies. Professor Catharine MacKinnon of the University of Michigan Law School believes privacy can be dangerous for women because it is used to conceal repression and physical harm of women in the domestic sphere, while discouraging intervention by state actors. She suggests traditional concepts of privacy should be abandoned because they have at root been developed to privilege those with power over those without power.[23] The challenge for feminists is drawing the appropriate line between government invasions of privacy and protecting the notion of privacy without letting this protection lead to the abuse of women in the private domestic realm. A critique of the view espoused by Professor MacKinnon and related theorists is that they have fundamentally misapprehended the definitions of privacy other modern theorists have been working on. In most of the other theories discussed here, individuals can only unilaterally privilege information concerning themselves; where two or more individuals are involved ordinarily each of them is considered to be free to separately determine whether information is shielded.

G.   PROBLEMS WITH PHILOSOPHICAL DEFINITIONS OF PRIVACY

Despite the insight and understanding these philosophical definitions bring to privacy discourse, as with all theories, there is an inherent criticism.

---

[23]   *See generally* CATHARINE MACKINNON, TOWARD A FEMINIST THEORY OF THE STATE (1989).

Most definitions successfully enhance our ability to understand the moral basis for privacy; however, few of these definitions account for the privacy issues that have developed in the wake of information technology advancements or offer specific guidance on questions of public policy. Philosophical definitions are, in the end, shaped as much by these developments as they influence our view of these developments. As a result, modern expectations of privacy may not be satisfied unless a new philosophy of privacy develops which accounts for technological advancements. Professor Helen Nissenbaum, a Senior Fellow at the Information Law Institute, argues philosophical definitions bring with them the implication that privacy is an interest we need to defend in the private sphere alone and that privacy in public information makes no sense at all. Put another way, Professor Nissenbaum explains, "these theories lack mechanisms to deal with conflicts involving privacy in public and have generally not taken up hard questions about surveillance in nonintimate realms."[24] For example, data warehousing companies often explain that their collection of personal information has no troubling implications for personal privacy because the information has been drawn from the public domain, thus no individual's expectation of privacy was violated. This is exactly the question philosophical theories

---

[24]   Helen Nissenbaum, *Protecting Privacy in an Information Age: The Problem of Privacy in Public*, 17 Law & Phil. 559, 576 (1998), *available at* http://www.nyu.edu/projects/nissenbaum/papers/privacy.pdf (last visited Oct. 3, 2013).

largely fail to confront: when is such surveillance in public acceptable and when is it an invasion of privacy? Answering this question is part of the ultimate challenge of privacy law as it seeks to convert esoteric theories into legal concepts. The other part to that challenge is conforming those legal concepts to the practical realities of day-to-day human existence and real life expectations of privacy. The next section considers the primary way the U.S. legal system has sought to reconcile the elegant philosophies of privacy and the messy facts of the real life—tort law.

III.   TORT HISTORY

A right to privacy or its ensuing definition differs greatly from how the law of privacy is applied in the legal world. Although privacy is an important value, it is not protected without some sort of enforcement mechanism or redressability. In the U.S. legal system, torts, civil wrongs that will support an action for damages, are the broadest means of protecting against breaches of privacy.[25] Most people acknowledge Warren and Brandeis's article

---

[25]   Privacy rights may also be established by contracts and statutes. Constitutional protections exist as well and will be discussed at length below. Each of these methods is typically narrower than the protections of tort law. Contracts typically only provide protection to the actual parties to the agreements. U.S. Statutes most often guard only specific pieces of information held by individuals or entities that fall within narrowly drafted criteria. The U.S. Constitution and most state constitutions only cover privacy violations by state actors. By way of comparison, the European Union has a broad privacy Directive, with many supplemental Directives and rules.

as first articulating a privacy tort. The identification and elaboration of four major privacy torts followed, and is best understood by examining William Prosser's categories individually: appropriation, false light, intrusion, and disclosure.

A. APPROPRIATION

Appropriation, the longest recognized privacy tort, is the act of appropriating an individual's name or likeness for the appropriator's advantage. Violations of this right often involve a defendant's use of a person's name on a product label or in advertising a product or service without consent. The rationale of this tort is to prevent unjust enrichment by the theft of "goodwill" associated with a particular individual's identity and to prevent the psychological discomfort that can result from unexpectedly becoming an object of public attention. The first signs of appropriation are found in the cases *Roberson v. Rochester Folding Box Co.*, 64 N.E. 442 (1902), and *Pavesich v. New England Life Ins. Co.*, 50 S.E. 68 (1905).

In *Roberson*, a picture of a young woman was printed on a flier advertising a baking flour company, which used the picture without permission or compensation. The woman's family claimed the unwanted attention caused her severe embarrassment and humiliation. The New York Court of Appeals surveyed a number of earlier cases which dealt with possible appropriations of people's likenesses and concluded:

An examination of the authorities leads us to the conclusion that the so-called "right to privacy" has not as yet found an abiding place in our jurisprudence, and as we view it, the doctrine cannot now be incorporated without doing violence to settled principles of law by which the profession and the public have long been guided.

64 N.E. at 447. In a sharply worded dissent, Judge Gray disagreed. Drawing on what can be recognized as reductionist and control theories of privacy, Judge Gray concluded, "I think that this plaintiff has the same property in the right to be protected against the use of her face for defendant's commercial purposes as she would have, if they were publishing her literary compositions." *Id.* at 450.

Three years later, the Georgia Supreme Court, expressly rejecting the majority decision from *Roberson*, reached an opposite conclusion in *Pavesich*. In *Pavesich*, an insurance company used a man's picture to sell insurance without his authorization. After reviewing the history of efforts to litigate questions of privacy law and quoting at length from Judge Gray's dissent, the Georgia court explained:

The knowledge that one's features and form are being used for such a purpose and displayed in such places as such advertisements are often liable to be found brings not only the person of an extremely sensitive nature, but even the individual of ordinary sensibility, to a realization that his liberty has been taken away from him, and, as long as the advertiser uses him for these purposes, he can not be otherwise than conscious of the fact that he is, for the time being, under the control of another, that he is no longer free, and that he is in reality a slave without hope of freedom, held to service by a merciless master; and if a man of true instincts, or even of ordinary sensibilities, no one can be more conscious of his complete enthrallment than he is.

So thoroughly satisfied are we that the law recognizes within proper limits, as a legal right, the right of privacy, and that the publication of one's picture without his consent by another as an advertisement, for the mere purpose of increasingly the profits and gains of the advertiser, is an invasion of this right, that we venture to predict that the day will come when the American bar will marvel that a contrary view was ever entertained by judges of eminence and ability. . . .

50 S.E. at 80–81. While *Pavesich* laid the groundwork for the tort of appropriation and acknowledged a right to privacy, it also recognized the tension that this right could have with other long-established principles of both contract law and free speech. *See id.* at 72, 74. This tension has led to the development of affirmative defenses to the tort.

The most common defense, and one necessarily implicated by the First Amendment to the U.S. Constitution, is that the subject's personality is of public interest. News agencies can use the name, likeness, or identity of an individual in news stories, even though they have a commercial motive in publishing, broadcasting, or distributing the information. In most jurisdictions, a news organization must show the material published was "newsworthy." Almost any information about a well-known public figure or a public official will be considered newsworthy, as well as any person's recent involvement in criminal behavior. As with each privacy tort, a right against appropriation can be waived by either explicit or implied consent. A final defense to appropriation is that the individual is not identifiable. This defense is rarely raised because, logically, the person who could bring the claim will rarely learn their likeness has been improperly appropriated.

B.   FALSE LIGHT

False light concerns placing an individual in a "false light" in the eyes of the public, typically by publicly misrepresenting statements as being attributed to the individual. These misrepresentative statements are usually highly offensive to the person or otherwise may expose them to danger of retribution by other parties that have learned of the statements. At first glance, this appears similar to defamation, and some commentators have indeed suggested that courts are migrating away from what would otherwise be difficult defamation cases into the more lenient realm of the false light tort. This is inconsistent with the purpose behind false light. A successful defamation action requires that the information be false; whereas in a privacy action for false light, the information is usually accurate or non-falsifiable, but creates a misleading impression about the alleged speaker. According to § 652D of the *Restatement (Second) of Torts*, false light occurs when the publication by the actor would be highly offensive to a reasonable person and the actor undertook the publication with knowledge or a reckless disregard as to the falsity of the publicized matter and the false light in which the other would be placed.[26]

False light tort violations emerged in *Hinish v. Meier & Frank Co.*, 113 P.2d 438 (1941), where the plaintiff's name was falsely signed to a telegram to the governor urging defeat of certain legislation. The Oregon Supreme Court found, based on an extension of the appropriation tort, that the defendants had taken the plaintiff's name "and whatever influence he may have possessed, and injected them into a political controversy in which . . . he had no interest." *Id.* at 448. Interestingly, unlike Judge Gray and the *Pavesich* court, the *Hinish* court reached this conclusion based on explicitly anti-reductionist grounds in reaction to technological advancements:

---

[26]   False light does not appear in the Restatement (Third) of Torts. Despite this, the tort of false light is still recognized by some states. *See, e.g.*, Gill v. Curtis Pub. Co., 239 P.2d 630 (1952) (recognizing the tort of false light). *But see, e.g.*, Costanza v. Seinfeld, 719 N.Y.S. 2d 29 (2001) (holding that the tort of false light is not a separate claim, but is "within the domain of Civil Rights Law").

. . . [W]e deem it unnecessary to search for a right of property, or a contract, or a relation of confidence. The question is whether a right of privacy, distinct and of itself and not incidental to some other long recognized right, is to be accepted by the courts and a violation of the right held actionable . . . .

Our consideration of the subject leads us to the conclusion that natural justice and the needs of the society in which we live should prevail over objections based upon the novelty of the asserted cause of action. It is time that fictions be abandoned and the real character of the injury be frankly avowed. When Brandeis and Warren wrote in 1890, it was the unseemly intrusions of a portion of the press into the privacy of the home that was emphasized as the main source of evil; since then motion pictures and the radio have been perfected and have taken their places among our great industries, while instantaneous photography today accomplishes miracles scarcely dreamed of fifty years ago. Thus, the potentialities for this character of wrong are now greatly multiplied. A decision against the right of privacy would be nothing less than an invitation to those so inclined who control these instrumentalities of communication, information and education, to put them to base uses, with complete immunity, and without regard to the hurt done to the sensibilities of individuals whose private affairs might be exploited, whether out of malice or for selfish purposes.

Id. at 446–47.

There are several defenses to a false light tort claim. False light is the only privacy tort that allows accuracy as a defense. If the public statement was correctly attributed to the plaintiff, then there is, by definition, no false light claim. Other defenses include that the individual was not identified, the conduct was not offensive to a reasonable person, and consent to the use of the individual's name. Whether the tort of false light will eventually evolve from its privacy roots into a watered down defamation tort remains to be seen. For now it continues to be important to view the two concepts separately, with false light being a true privacy tort.

C.   DISCLOSURE

Disclosure (sometimes called "wrongful publication of private facts") is the act of publicizing embarrassing facts about an individual that were otherwise not widely known. For example, sexual relations, contents of personal letters, family quarrels, medical treatment, and photographs of a person in their home have all been classified as "private facts" by courts. One can break down this tort into four elements: (1) dissemination of true information; (2) offensive to a reasonable person; (3) not of public concern; and (4) so intimate that publication outrages the public's sense of decency.

The first signs of the disclosure tort appeared in *Melvin v. Reid*, 297 P. 91 (1931). The plaintiff was a former prostitute who, following a trial and acquittal on murder charges, had reformed herself and had taken up "an exemplary, virtuous, honorable, and righteous life," and whose criminal past was not widely known. *Id.* at 91. The defendants produced a motion picture based on the plaintiff's earlier life in which they used her real name and advertised the film as being a true account of the plaintiff's life. Following a review of the law of other states, the California court concluded that while the defendants were entitled to produce a film based on the facts of the plaintiff's life, the use of the plaintiff's real name was "not justified by any standard of morals or ethics known to us . . . ." *Id.* at 93. The court specifically declined to say that it was devising a new tort, instead basing its decision on the California state constitution's protection of the right of "pursuing and obtaining safety and happiness." *Id.* Relying in part on *Melvin*, the Florida Supreme Court formally recognized a tort of disclosure in *Cason v. Baskin*, 20 So. 2d 243 (1945).

Disclosure is the privacy tort that most closely butts up against the First Amendment's guarantee of freedom of speech and press. In *Cox Broadcasting Corp. v. Cohn*, 420 U.S. 469 (1975), a television station obtained details about the rape and murder of a seventeen year-old girl from court records and subsequently broadcast her name and other truthful information about her. The victim's father, claiming his privacy was invaded by the use of his daughter's

name, sued the station pursuant to a Georgia
statute banning the release of rape victims' names
and also in tort for wrongful disclosure of private
facts. In a decision that effectively overruled the
prototypical disclosure case, *Melvin v. Reid*, the U.S.
Supreme Court held that, given the information had
been obtained from official court records, the First
and Fourteenth Amendments precluded a claim
based on the tort of disclosure. *Id.* at 492–96. The
Court concluded by observing:

> If there are privacy interests to be protected in
> judicial proceedings, the States must respond
> by means which avoid public documentation or
> other exposure of private information. Their
> political institutions must weigh the interests
> in privacy with the interests of the public to
> know and of the press to publish. Once true
> information is disclosed in public court
> documents open to public inspection, the press
> cannot be sanctioned for publishing it.

Id. at 496. The decision in *Cox Broadcasting*
significantly limited the growth of the disclosure
tort and, to some extent, has forced it into a
hybridization with the tort of intrusion discussed
below.

Although most courts had presumed
newsworthiness and use of information from public
records were defenses to the tort of disclosure, the
Cox Broadcasting ruling made clear that these
defenses were not merely prudential, but
constitutionally required. Consequently,
newsworthiness is generally an extremely successful

defense because courts have broadly construed what information is of legitimate public concern. Furthermore, because courts have recognized that certain individuals are hypersensitive, a requirement that the disclosure outrage community notions of decency or be patently offensive to a reasonable person has been required since the earliest cases. *See, e.g., Cason*, 20 So. 2d at 251 ("The protection afforded by the law to this right must be restricted to 'ordinary sensibilities,' and cannot extend to supersensitiveness or agoraphobia."). Finally, courts have long taken into account a plaintiff's character as a public figure when determining whether the disclosure was tortious.

D. INTRUSION

Appropriation, false light, and disclosure are all torts that require publicity; intrusion, on the other hand, is unwanted information gathering in someone's private space. Intrusion is the act of invading an individual's private affairs or solitude. Legal wrongdoing occurs at the time of the intrusion, not at publication as in the other three torts. Intrusion on an individual's solitude encompasses not only physical intrusion into their presence, but also audio and visual intrusions via artificial means.

Identifying the exact point at which the tort of intrusion formed is difficult given that many of the cases that first explored this tort concerned facts that would suggest other types of privacy torts or perhaps not even be recognized as privacy torts at all under modern jurisprudence. One of the early cases which stands out as recognizing the key distinction of the harm flowing from the intrusion itself, rather than the publication, is *Rhodes v. Graham*, 37 S.W.2d 46 (Ky. 1931). In *Rhodes*, the defendants tapped the telephone lines of the plaintiffs and made recordings of their conversations. There was no indication that the defendants publicized the contents of the recordings or otherwise disseminated them beyond the circle of conspirators involved in the wiretapping. Citing Warren and Brandeis's article and analogizing the situation to that of the common law trespass tort of eavesdropping, the Kentucky Court of Appeals concluded:

> The evil incident to the invasion of the privacy of the telephone is as great as that occasioned by unwarranted publicity in newspapers and by other means of a man's private affairs for which courts have granted the injured person redress. Whenever a telephone line is tapped the privacy of those talking over the line is invaded and conversations, wholly proper and confidential, may be overheard.

Id. at 47.

It also bears mention that intrusion differs from the tort of disclosure in that it extends protection even over public figures whose personal affairs might otherwise be considered sufficiently newsworthy to merit publication. In *Galella v.*

Onassis, 487 F.2d 986 (2d Cir. 1973), a freelance photographer followed Jacqueline Kennedy Onassis for purposes of photographing her at inopportune times, but claimed he was permitted to do so because she was a public figure. The Second Circuit thought differently, stating, "[t]here is no constitutional right to assault, harass, or unceasingly shadow or distress public figures." *Id.* at 991.

The primary defense to a claim of intrusion is that the alleged tortfeasor's conduct actually took place in a public space. Claims generally will not lie for intrusive actions in public spaces, with the exception of harassment, but in such situations other non-privacy torts, *e.g.*, assault, battery, or intentional infliction of emotional distress, are more likely to be invoked. Freedom from intrusion can also be waived by either explicit or implied consent. A narrower defense occurs through recognition of a right for individuals pursuing news stories to go on property with law enforcement and fire officials. In *Florida Publishing Co. v. Fletcher*, 340 So. 2d 914 (Fla. 1976), a newspaper photographer accompanying fire investigators took a picture of a silhouette left on a floor by a girl's body who had been trapped in the fire. The girl's mother sued, claiming trespass and an invasion of privacy. The Florida Supreme Court did not find there was a trespass or invasion of privacy because the fire was a disaster of public interest and it was customary for journalists to accompany public officials to the scene of disasters. *Id.* at 915. Ultimately, the tort of intrusion frequently disappears in a sea of reductionism because it is a rare occasion that a putative commission of the tort will not be accompanied by other, better-established torts relating to the protection of person and property.

IV.   TODAY'S PRIVACY LANDSCAPE

Examining the development of privacy definitions allows one to understand how flexible the concept of "privacy" is. Our review so far has focused primarily on U.S. law. It is important, however, to become familiar with the international privacy environment in comparison to the generally held U.S. view of privacy. The issues individuals consider private are formed by culture and history, and vary across cultures and historical eras. Equally, technological advancement is both an endogenous and exogenous driver of change in expectations regarding privacy. There is also a common denominator underlying both cultural and technological concerns regarding privacy: the commoditization of information and, by necessary implication, privacy. Successful privacy laws must be reactive to both social and technological reality, while simultaneously facilitating and restraining the use of personal information in market transactions. This precarious troika describes the modern state of privacy.

A.   PRIVACY AND GLOBALIZATION

A majority of countries throughout the world recognize some form of a right to privacy in their

constitutions.[27] These provisions include at least
rights of inviolability of the home and secrecy of
communications. In countries including the United
States, where no explicit right to privacy is found in
the Constitution, the right is often implied through
other provisions. In the 1960s, protecting personal
information became an increasing concern because
of the digitization of personal information and the
increased reliance by both public and private
entities on the collection, use, storage, and exchange
of personal information. In the early 1970s,
countries began adopting laws to protect the privacy
of information within their countries and, by the
late 1980s, most advanced industrial countries had
adopted some form of privacy law.[28] There is a

---

[27]   In 2006, the US-based Electronic Privacy Information
Center and the UK-based Privacy International have completed
the most comprehensive survey of global privacy to date. The
survey, titled "The Privacy & Human Rights Report," tracked
developments in 70 countries, assessing the state of surveillance
and privacy. The purpose of the report is to recognize countries
where privacy protection is of high priority and those countries
whose privacy efforts have lagged behind in privacy protection.
This global report, along with country specific privacy reports,
can be found at https://www.privacyinternational.org/reports.

[28]   Major national laws in order of their passage include:
Swedish Data Act (1973); U.S. Privacy Act (1974); German Data
Protection Act (1977); Canadian Privacy Act (1977); French Law
on Informatics and Liberties (1978); Norwegian Personal Data
Registers Act (1978); Danish Private Registers Act (1978);
Austrian Data Protection Act (1978); Luxembourg's Data
Protection Act (1979); Iceland's Act on the Systematic recording
of personal Data (1981); New Zealand's Official Information Act
(1982); British Data Protection Act (1984); Finish Personal Data
File Act (1987); Irish Data Protection Act (1988); Australian
Privacy Act (1988); Japanese Personal Data Protection Act
(1988); and the Netherlands's Data protection Act (1988).

general shift towards the development and adoption of comprehensive privacy laws that establish a mechanism for protection. The idea of protecting the right to privacy continues to gain strength across the globe. The number of countries recognizing some form of data privacy laws has steadily increased from 76 in 2011 to 101 by mid-2013.[29] These laws vary with particular governments, with some advocating more stringent laws like the European Union and others placing less importance on privacy including, perhaps surprisingly, the United States.

1. The European Union's View on Privacy

Due to Europe's historically greater distrust of corporations than in the United States, European privacy law has focused most heavily on protecting consumers' personal information from being improperly collected or misused by commercial entities. In most European nations, personal information cannot be collected without consumers' permission and they have the right to review the data and correct inaccuracies. Companies that process data must register their activities with the government and personal information cannot be shared by companies or across borders without express permission. Even intrusions into privacy that most Americans take for granted, including employers monitoring their employees' private communications or checkout clerks requesting

---

[29]   Graham Greenleaf, *Global Tables of Data Privacy Laws and Bills* (Univ. of N.S.W., Research Paper No. 2013–39, 2013), *available at* http://papers.ssrn.com/sol3/papers.cfm?abstract_id= 2280875.

addresses and telephone numbers from patrons, are restricted in many European countries. To a large extent, these rights stem from the E.U. Directive on Data Protection of 1995 (Data Protection Directive).[30] The Directive's purpose is to provide for analogous protections for personal information throughout the European Community.

Central to the Data Protection Directive is enforceability. The European Union wants to ensure that individuals have rights enshrined in explicit rules, and that they can go to a governmental authority that can act on their behalf to assist in the preservation of those rights. Indeed, the Data Protection Directive is in many ways a classical example of "positive law"—it creates broad obligations for private entities to protect the personal information of individuals and strongly proscribes how such information, once collected, can be used or disseminated.

2. The United States' View on Privacy

In the United States, privacy is most often equated with liberty from an intrusive government. Traditionally, Americans have been, if not necessarily trusting of the business sector, then at

---

[30] The European Commission is considering reforming the Data Protection Directive to "strengthen privacy rights" in order to keep up with "[t]echnological progress." The new directive, if passed, would establish a single law across the entire European Union and include a "right to be forgotten." A draft of the proposed directive can be found at http://www.europarl. europa.eu/meetdocs/2009_2014/documents/libe/pr/922/922387/ 922387en.pdf.

least not highly skeptical of it; instead reserving their deepest distrust for the institutions of government, and particularly the Federal government. Illustrative of the United States' position on privacy is a statement from Senator George McGovern: "One way to attack a nation such as the United States which depends heavily on information and communications is to restrain the flow of information—cutting off contact between the headquarters and the overseas branches of a multinational firm; taxing telecommunications crossing borders; building information walls around a nation." Thus, the United States has mainly focused not so much on the protection of personal privacy in day-to-day affairs, but instead at the point where individuals most directly come into conflict with government—criminal law.

When the United States has addressed privacy concerns beyond the criminal context, it most often has sought to do so in a manner that would have the least possible impact on economic activity beyond what was perceived as being necessary to address a particular immediate concern. The United States uses what is typically called a "sectoral approach" that relies on a mix of legislation and self-regulation. The United States avoids general data protection rules in favor of specific laws governing, for example, video rental records and information collected during certain types of financial transactions. A variety of mechanisms enable enforcement, but there is a strong bias toward self-regulation, where companies and industry bodies establish codes of practice. In most day-to-day situations in the United States, unlike in the European Union, the default position will be that either no privacy protection applies beyond the privacy torts (not all of which are even recognized in every state), or a limited amount of protection flowing from contractual agreements.

3. The OECD Guidelines and International Harmonization on Privacy

In 1977, the Organization for Economic Cooperation and Development (OECD) convened an international conference to discuss the problems of "transborder data flows"—the ability to manage the international movement of personal information. Over 300 representatives from various governments, private industry, and intergovernmental organizations determined that national legislation on privacy of personal data should be harmonized. In an effort to mitigate what it feared might be an overly restrictive approach to the subject, the United States government formed an interagency task force that drafted the proposed guidelines, and in 1980, the OECD adopted guidelines that included most of the United States' proposals. Realizing the changing technological landscape, and new challenges presented in today's global economy, the OECD revised these guidelines in 2013, marking the first update to the guidelines since their inception in 1980.

The 2013 OECD guidelines introduced several new concepts, including a focus on coordinating privacy strategies at the government level, privacy management programs to ensure appropriate safeguards are implemented, and the need for effective notice procedures for those affected by a privacy breach. Rather than add to the 1980 principles, the 2013 guidelines attempt to act as more of a blueprint on how to best implement the 1980 principles in practice. For example, the new concepts noted above are discussed in a new section, titled "Implementing Accountability," and a revised section, titled "National Implementation." These sections stress the importance of these new concepts in adhering to the privacy principles by recommending member countries, and those that control the data, to implement these new concepts in their overall privacy protection schemes. So despite the first update to the guidelines since their inception in 1980, the 2013 guidelines remain committed to the original eight principles, which have become the touchstone of modern privacy law in the international context.[31]

> 1. The Collection Limitation Principle: "There should be limits to the collection of personal data and any such data should be obtained by lawful and fair means and, where appropriate, with the knowledge or consent of the data subject."

---

[31]   Organization for Economic Cooperation and Development [OECD], OECD Guidelines Governing the Protection of Privacy and Transborder Flows of Personal Data C(80)58/FINAL, as amended by C(2013)79 (July 11, 2013), *available at* http://www.oecd.org/sti/ieconomy/2013-oecd-privacy-guidelines. pdf.

2. The Data Quality Principle: "Personal data should be relevant to the purposes for which they are to be used, and, to the extent necessary for those purposes, should be accurate, complete and kept up-to-date."

3. The Purpose Specification Principle: "The purposes for which personal data are collected should be specified not later than at the time of data collection and the subsequent use limited to the fulfillment of those purposes or such others as are not incompatible with those purposes and as are specified on each occasion of change of purpose."

4. The Use Limitation Principle: "Personal data should not be disclosed, made available or otherwise used for purposes other than those specified in accordance with Paragraph 9 except: a) with the consent of the data subject; or b) by the authority of law." Paragraph 9 refers to the purpose specification principle.

5. The Security Safeguards Principle: "Personal data should be protected by reasonable security safeguards against such risks as loss or unauthorized access, destruction, use, modification or disclosure of data."

6. The Openness Principle: "There should be a general policy of openness about developments, practices and policies with respect to personal data. Means should be readily available of establishing the existence and nature of personal data, and the main purposes of their

use, as well as the identity and usual residence of the data controller."

7. The Individual Participation Principle: "An individual should have the right: a) to obtain from a data controller, or otherwise, confirmation of whether or not the data controller has data relating to him; b) to have communicated to him, data relating to him within a reasonable time; at a charge, if any, that is not excessive; in a reasonable manner; and in a form that is readily intelligible to him; c) to be given reasons if a request made under subparagraphs (a) and (b) is denied, and to be able to challenge such denial; and d) to challenge data relating to him and, if the challenge is successful to have the data erased, rectified, completed or amended."

8. The Accountability Principle: "A data controller should be accountable for complying with measures which give effect to the principles stated above."

A proposal by several countries following the enactment of the 1980 guidelines to adopt them as a legally enforceable treaty was rejected. This meant adherence to the 1980 guidelines was completely voluntary, however, in the years following the adoption of the 1980 guidelines many nations enacted legislation or regulations that in some manner tracked them. The most notable example of this is the E.U.-U.S. Safe Harbor, which seeks to reconcile the European and American approaches to privacy described above.

The "Safe Harbor," which is analyzed at length in Chapter 4, incorporated the 1980 OECD Guidelines as regulations administered primarily by the Federal Trade Commission. U.S. businesses voluntarily certify that they will comply with provisions of the Safe Harbor and are thereby allowed to continue receiving data transfers from the European Union. The precise means of complying with the Safe Harbor are left to the discretion of the businesses registering with it, but the Federal Trade Commission, under its authority to punish deceptive trade practices, enforces compliance with those standards once enunciated. The 2013 guidelines present another opportunity for countries to act, and we will have to wait and see what, if any, changes occur as a result of the updated guidelines.

B.   PRIVACY AND TECHNOLOGY

Whether altering the definitions of privacy or causing greater collection, retention, and use of personal information, technology challenges and reshapes privacy law and policy on a daily basis. Indeed, courts recognized almost as a matter of course when adopting the privacy torts that technological advancements have altered traditional expectations of privacy. These advancements assist the aggregation, storage, and analysis of immense amounts of information about people; breed an extraordinary capacity to track and monitor people; and permit access to, communication, and publication of this information at ever-greater volumes and speeds.

Specific fields of technological development that impact privacy will be discussed in Chapter 5, but it is useful to first contemplate the point that, as the U.K. Royal Academy of Engineering suggests, all information technologies can be divided into three major categories: connection, processing, and disconnection. "Connection" technologies are those which affect how organizations transfer information both internally and externally, whether to or from other organizations or individuals. While improvements in connection technologies lower transaction costs while permitting broader distribution of goods and services, they also lead to greater collection and retransmission of personal information. "Processing" technologies are addressed to the problems of how organizations internally handle information. Effectively, they represent the ability to add value to the raw data collected and moved through connection technologies. "Disconnection" technologies are means to control access to personal information. These may be employed by parties utilizing connection or processing technologies, or both, to shield already collected information in their possession, or by parties that wish to prevent the collection and processing of their information in the first place. It is useful to keep these three categories of technology in mind while reviewing efforts to protect privacy, as they give context to regulatory schemes.

C.   PRIVACY AND ECONOMICS

It is unquestionable that "information," broadly construed, has had value for as long as sentient life has existed on Earth. Having exclusive knowledge of the location of a prime hunting ground was a survival advantage over other tribes. Knowing the healing properties of particular herbs conferred status and a position of power over others who lacked this information. As civilization advanced, information became more easily quantified in value, whether as drachmas, shekels, or wen, but the type of information still largely concerned the exterior world—what trade goods were available where, what the physical properties of certain materials were, and so forth.

The revolution that has happened over the past century or so, and most particularly in the post-World War II era, is the economic significance of personal information, *i.e.*, information unique to a particular individual. While personal information was always an exploitable resource, for example to be able to curry favor with a particular noble, it was rarely worth systematically collecting because the vast majority of humanity lived at bare subsistence levels.

The development of mass production flowing from the Industrial Revolution and the corresponding rise of living standards began to alter this equation. As the average person gained disposable income and leisure time, they became more appealing subjects for marketing purposes. This drove the development of marketing into a science, as manufacturers, distributors, and retailers increasingly sought to understand the consumer preferences of the general public. While the ability to predict the specific preferences of a particular individual remained elusive, marketers discovered that preferences were generally tied to more easily quantifiable demographic data: sex, age, race, education level, and income. Given the high cost of collecting, storing, and processing this information manually, however, marketers were constrained to conducting surveys of limited numbers of individuals, and long-term storage of the raw data was out of the question except for particularly valuable information.

The invention and refinement of computers and computer networking solved the marketers' problem. Personal information equivalent to trillions of hardcopy pages of text is now stored and routinely transmitted at minimal cost. Driver's licenses, motor vehicle records, voter registration lists, medical records, court records, credit card activity reports, financial transfers, and personalized shopping data collected from "loyalty cards" join traditional demographic information in these databases. Each of these data points enables companies to predict future behavior and consumer preferences on an ever more individualized level. Indeed, not only is information used that has been directly collected, but interpolation from that information is increasingly possible as well. For example, purchasing a house in one neighborhood as compared to another will trigger different direct marketing based on census tract information. As computer processing power continues to grow, the marketers' need for additional personal information to provide more data points likewise increases.

This process is, of course, value neutral in and of itself. Humans, by nature, are consumers and generally aspire to do so in a manner that best satisfies their wants and needs, and marketers do not specifically aspire to compromise individual privacy. As Professor Cohen has noted:

> The colonization of private spaces by cookies, web bugs, smart microchips, and self-enforcing licenses is an entirely predictable consequence of the market-driven search for more and better information. If information is money, there is no reason to expect that the desire for more information should stop politely at the residential doorstep or its virtual equivalent.[32]

Ironically, if, as political philosopher Chris Sciabarra has suggested, capitalism was the driving force in developing the modern concept of privacy by enabling people "to produce, earn, and keep the product of their efforts, and to acquire private estates within which to pursue private joys,"[33] it may also pose the most pervasive threat to privacy.

---

[32]   Julie E. Cohen, *Privacy, Ideology, and Technology: A Response to Jeffery Rosen*, 89 GEO. L.J. 2029, 2041 (2001).

[33]   Chris Matthew Sciabarra, *Privacy and Civilization*, THE FREE RADICAL, at 6 (Sept.–Oct. 2003).

CHAPTER THREE
U.S. LEGAL BASIS OF PRIVACY

I.   U.S. CONSTITUTION

Constitutional privacy is generally understood to mean the right of persons to be free from unwanted and unwarranted governmental intrusions. These rights or "autonomy interests" have been found to include reproductive freedom; family relationships; sexuality; personal autonomy; decisions about dying and death; and informational privacy. Constitutional privacy also embraces the right of the individual not to have certain private information gathered, preserved, or disseminated by the government. Constitutional law accordingly restricts intrusions into certain areas or communications.

As was discussed at length in Chapter 2, there are many different philosophical approaches to defining privacy. In U.S. constitutional law, however, scholars find that there are two primary definitions that courts concern themselves with: (1) individual privacy or autonomy; and (2) data privacy or control of information. As Professor Raymond Nimmer of the University of Houston Law Center explains, the "autonomy" definition refers "to the ability of an individual to prevent others from knowing, discovering, or disclosing sensitive generally confidential information pertaining the private life of the individual or to recover damages from their having done so . . . ." The "control" definition refers to "what right an individual has to prevent or control another party's use of data that is personally identifiable to the individual, but was lawfully obtained by the other party."

A. PRIVACY AND AUTONOMY

Neither the U.S. Constitution nor any of its amendments specifically mentions the right to privacy. The First, Third, Fourth, and Fifth Amendments, however, all contain some privacy components. The First Amendment guarantees freedom in both religious and political matters, including the freedom of association. These rights have historically been understood to contain an element of privacy. In his famous *Commentaries on the Constitution of the United States*, Justice Joseph Story noted that these freedoms were intended to secure the rights of "private sentiment" and "private judgment." The Third Amendment protects the privacy of the home in peacetime from soldiers seeking quarters without the owner's consent. Justice Story explained that that the purpose of this provision was "to secure the perfect enjoyment of that great right, of the [English] common law, that a man's house shall be his own castle, privileged against all civil and military intrusion." The Fourth Amendment prohibits intrusions into dwellings, specifically providing that persons have the right to be secure in their persons, houses, papers, and effects, against unreasonable searches and seizures. Judge Thomas Cooley likewise considered this an extension of the common law principle that "a man's house is his castle" and that in this castle, persons were to be free from "the prying eyes of the government." The Fifth Amendment, by prohibiting compulsory self-incrimination and thereby guaranteeing the right to silence, protects the privacy of one's thoughts. This can be seen as an affirmation of Sir Thomas More's remark to his prosecutors two centuries earlier that silence cannot be taken as an admission of guilt.

Arguably, privacy was always highly valued by American society; however, the U.S. Supreme Court did not specifically recognize an independent right to privacy until the latter half of the Twentieth Century. In the landmark privacy case, *Griswold v. Connecticut*, 381 U.S. 479 (1965), Justice Goldberg, joined by Chief Justice Warren and Justice Brennan (in their concurring opinion) found the Ninth Amendment to be the source of the right to privacy, starting a line of privacy cases that continue to dominate all analysis of individual privacy rights vis-à-vis federal and state governments.

1. Griswold v. Connecticut

Sixty years after Georgia became the first state to recognize a right to privacy,[1] the Supreme Court announced an independent right to privacy under the U.S. Constitution in *Griswold*. The Supreme Court held unconstitutional a Connecticut law that prohibited the use and distribution of contraceptives. The state law also made it a crime to assist, abet, or counsel a violation of the law. The

---

[1]   Pavesich v. New England Life Ins. Co., 50 S.E. 68 (Ga. 1905).

Court, in an opinion by Justice Douglas, found that the right to privacy was a fundamental right. Choosing to avoid questions of substantive due process (a form of constitutional jurisprudence which many considered discredited), the Court expressly rejected the proposition that the right was derivable from the due process clause of the Fourteenth Amendment. Instead, the Court found that privacy was implicit in many of the specific provisions of the Bill of Rights, including the First, Third, Fourth, and Fifth Amendments.

The forgoing cases suggest that specific guarantees in the Bill of Rights have penumbras, formed by emanations from those guarantees that help give them life and substance. Various guarantees create zones of privacy.

. . . .

We have had many controversies over these penumbral rights of privacy and repose. These cases bear witness that the right of privacy which presses for recognition here is a legitimate one.

Id. at 484–85.

In a concurring opinion, Justice Goldberg, joined by Chief Justice Warren and Justice Brennan, suggested that the Ninth Amendment could be a source of authority to protect privacy rights absent an express textual reference to the concept. Meanwhile, Justices Harlan and White, concurring in the judgment, postulated in separate concurrences that if there was a right to privacy that protected individuals against action by state governments it would be independently derived from the Fourteenth Amendment.

In the dissenting opinion, Justices Black and Stewart argued that there was no right to privacy mentioned in the Constitution and that they believed the Court was at risk of following in the steps of the substantive due process decisions by enforcing values that had no textual basis in the Constitution.

The *Griswold* Court's approach has been heavily criticized and, while its conclusion that a constitutional right to privacy exists has been influential, its legal analysis has not been followed by subsequent cases. Constitutional scholars generally have noted that the penumbral approach is ultimately a form of substantive due process analysis. Regardless of such criticism though, numerous subsequent U.S. Supreme Court cases have extended the right of privacy first established in *Griswold*.

2. Roe v. Wade

Roe v. Wade, 410 U.S. 113 (1973), is best known for recognizing a constitutional right to abortion. But this conclusion flowed from the Court's analysis of a right to privacy. In an effort to avoid the fractured concurrences of *Griswold*, Justice Blackmun's opinion paved over the question of where precisely a right to privacy could be found in the Constitution:

This right to privacy, whether it be founded in the Fourteenth Amendment's conception of personal liberty and restrictions upon state action, as we feel it is, or, ... in the Ninth Amendment's reservation of rights to the people, is broad enough to encompass a woman's decision whether or not to terminate her pregnancy.

Id. at 153. Ultimately, while the *Roe* Court decline to articulate the exact source of a right to privacy, it concluded that such a right was protectable via the Fourteenth Amendment's due process clause.

3. Bowers v. Hardwick

In *Bowers v. Hardwick*, 478 U.S. 186 (1986), the Supreme Court upheld a state sodomy law that criminalized private homosexual activity between consenting adults. Justice White, writing the majority opinion, stated that the fundamental right to privacy in the Court's earlier decisions did not have "any resemblance to the claimed constitutional right of homosexuals to engage in acts of sodomy." *Id.* at 190. Elaborating on this point, Justice White explained that homosexual activity could not be considered a fundamental right because it was not part of the United States' history and traditions and it was not a form of individual liberty that must be defended in the democratic process, thus the statute was upheld. The majority rebuffed the defendants' privacy argument, suggesting that *Griswold* and *Roe*, among other cases, did not actually create a broad right to privacy but rather were to be viewed as part of a line of cases dealing with limitations on government interference with child rearing.

The four dissenting Justices, however, sharply argued that a right of privacy was at issue in the case:

> This case is no more about "a fundamental right to engage in homosexual sodomy," . . . than *Stanley v. Georgia*, 394 U.S. 557 (1969), was about a fundamental right to watch obscene movies, or *Katz v. United States*, 389 U.S. 347 (1967), was about a fundamental right to place interstate bets from a telephone booth. Rather, this case is about "the most comprehensive of rights and the right most valued by civilized men," namely, "the right to be let alone." *Olmstead v. United States*, 277 U.S. 438, 478 (1928) (Brandeis, J., dissenting).

478 U.S. at 199. The dissenters concluded that the ability of adults to engage in private voluntary sexual conduct that did not result in physical harm was an essential part of personal autonomy that could be appropriately protected under the Court's earlier privacy decisions.

4. Lawrence v. Texas

Seventeen years after *Bowers*, the Court invalidated a Texas state law that prohibited persons from engaging in sodomy with a person of the same sex. In *Lawrence v. Texas*, 539 U.S. 558 (2003), the Court held that the state law violated the due process clause of the Fourteenth

Amendment. Justice O'Connor concurred in the judgment of the Court, but instead argued that the Court should have invalidated the law based on the equal protection clause. This would have accomplished the same result without overturning *Bowers*, by instead deciding a question left open in the earlier case—whether the state could punish sexual activity outside of marriage only by a group of persons defined by some trait that was disliked by the majority of persons in the political process. The dissenting Justices believed that the *Lawrence* Court's ruling could not be justified in terms of the Supreme Court's prior cases, nor from the Court's role in the definition of fundamental rights based on the United States' history and traditions.

B.   PRIVACY AND CONTROL OF INFORMATION

Although numerous proponents of privacy rights have argued over the years that the Constitution should be interpreted to create an individual right to control information regarding one's self, there has been little support for such a right from the Supreme Court. *Whalen v. Roe*, 429 U.S. 589 (1977), was the first case in which the Court squarely faced the question of whether the constitutional right to privacy encompasses the collection, storage, and dissemination of information in government databases. *Whalen* was also the first decision in which the Court acknowledged that the constitutional right of privacy consists of two branches: informational privacy and privacy-autonomy.

1. Whalen v. Roe

Whalen addressed a New York law that required physicians to identify patients receiving prescription drugs that had a potential for abuse. Challengers noted that the resulting state-maintained database infringed on the right to privacy, arguing that individuals have a right to avoid disclosure of personal matters. *Id.* at 598–99. In balancing privacy interests against the police powers, the Court noted that the government had an important interest in monitoring the use of prescription drugs that might be abused, and a particular responsibility for the health of the community, which did not automatically amount to an impermissible invasion of privacy. The Court, however, did not reject the possibility that the right to privacy might be recognized in the future to include a right to control information:

> We are not unaware of the threat to privacy implicit in the accumulation of vast amounts of personal information in computerized data banks or other massive government files. The collection of taxes, the distribution of wealth and social security benefits, the supervision of public health, the direction of our Armed Forces, and the enforcement of the criminal laws all require the orderly preservation of great quantities of information, much of which is personal in character and potentially embarrassing or harmful if disclosed. . . . We therefore need not, and do not decide any question which might be presented by the

unwarranted disclosure of accumulated private data-whether intentional or unintentional-or by a system that did not contain comparable security provisions. We simply hold that this record does not establish an invasion of any right or liberty protected by the Fourteenth Amendment.

Id. at 605–06.

Whalen is a major example of judicial recognition that constitutional protection for limiting government access to personal, confidential, or intimate information about individuals is not confined to unreasonable searches and seizures in violation of the Fourth Amendment.

2. Katz v. United States

For many years, the major source of law on informational privacy arose under federal constitutional cases dealing with invasions of privacy in the form of personal searches or literal intrusions into physical places. The most litigated issue concerned judicial review of search and seizure actions by government entities, most often municipal police or federal law enforcement agents, engaged in collecting information for purposes of criminal prosecutions. Developments in this area of the law led to the landmark case of *Katz v. United States*, 389 U.S. 347 (1967), which still underlies most modern constitutional privacy jurisprudence.

In *Katz*, the Supreme Court considered electronic eavesdropping on a telephone conservation in a public telephone booth. The petitioner asked the Court to approach the issue as presented in two separate questions: first, whether a telephone booth can be an area subject to protection against government searches under the Fourth Amendment; and second, whether the fact that the eavesdropping was accomplished by a non-physically invasive method avoided turning the surveillance into a "search" of the telephone booth. *Id.* at 349–50. The Court rejected both of these formulations, finding them overly narrow and overbroad:

> [T]he Fourth Amendment cannot be translated into a general constitutional "right to privacy." That Amendment protects individual privacy against certain kinds of governmental intrusion, but its protections go further, and often have nothing to do with privacy at all. Other provisions of the Constitution protect personal privacy from other forms of governmental invasion. But the protection of a person's general right to privacy—his right to be let alone by other people—is, like the protection of his property and of his very life, left largely to the law of the individual States.

Id. at 350 (footnotes omitted).

As the Court explained, both Katz and the Federal government placed far too much emphasis on the question of exactly which types of physical locations are the sort that should be protected against searches:

> [T]he Fourth Amendment protects people, not places. What a person knowingly exposes to the public, even in his own home or office, is not a subject of Fourth Amendment protection. But what he seeks to preserve as private, even in an area accessible to the public, may be constitutionally protected.

Id. at 351 (citations omitted). The Court likewise rejected the argument over whether the use of electronic surveillance was a form of trespass within the scope of earlier Supreme Court decisions regarding searches. Recognizing that it had formerly found physical trespass was necessary, the Court acknowledged that it was discarding that approach and instead pursuing what could be identified as an anti-reductionist methodology:

> It is true that the absence of such penetration [into a physical space] was at one time thought to foreclose further Fourth Amendment inquiry . . . . But the premise that property interests control the right of the Government to search and seize has been discredited.

> We conclude the underpinnings of [those earlier cases] have been so eroded by our subsequent decisions that the trespass doctrine there enunciated can no longer be regarded as controlling. The Government's activities in electronically listening to and recording the petitioner's words violated the privacy upon which he justifiably relied while using the telephone booth and thus constituted a search and seizure within the meaning of the Fourth

Amendment. The fact that the electronic device employed to achieve that end did not happen to penetrate the wall of the booth can have no constitutional significance.

Id. at 352–53 (parentheses, quotation marks, and citations omitted). Despite the broad reach of this holding, the majority opinion expressly declined to find that the ruling encompassed surveillance for purposes of national security.

The *Katz* decision produced two concurrences of particular significance. First, Justice Douglas, joined by Justice Brennan, warned that the deliberate limitation of the holding to regular criminal cases gave "a wholly unwarranted green light for the Executive Branch to resort to electronic eavesdropping without a warrant in cases which the Executive Branch itself labels 'national security' matters." *Id.* at 359. Douglas explained that there was nothing in the Fourth Amendment that could be read to distinguish "searches" made for purposes of national security from those made for purposes of ordinary criminal investigations. Second, Justice Harlan used his concurrence to explore under what circumstances an individual can expect to enjoy protection against unreasonable searches. It was here that the famous term "reasonable expectation of privacy" was coined. *Id.* at 360. Justice Harlan articulated the rule as requiring a two part analysis, "first that a person have exhibited an actual (subjective) expectation of privacy and, second, that the expectation be one that society is prepared to recognize as 'reasonable.'" *Id.* at 361.

3. United States v. White

In *United States v. White*, 401 U.S. 745 (1971), the Supreme Court considered whether certain conversations between the defendant and a government informant, overheard by police by use of a radio transmitter, were constitutionally protected. The Court noted:

Inescapably, one contemplating illegal activities must realize and risk that his companions may be reporting to the police. If he sufficiently doubts their trustworthiness, the association will very probably end or never materialize. But if he has doubts, or allays them, or risks what doubt he has, the risk is his. In terms of what his course will be, what he will or will not do or say, we are unpersuaded that he would distinguish between probable informers on the one hand and probable informers with transmitters on the other. Given the possibility or probability that one of his colleagues is cooperating with the police, it is only speculation to assert that the defendant's utterances would be substantially different or his sense of security any less if he also thought it possible that the suspected colleague was wired for sound. At least there is no persuasive evidence that the difference in this respect between the electronically equipped and the unequipped agent is substantial enough to require discrete constitutional recognition, particularly under the Fourth Amendment which is ruled by fluid concepts of "reasonableness."

Id. at 752–53. The principle emanating from *United States v. White* is that a person has no constitutionally protected expectation of privacy in information voluntarily disclosed to someone else, absent some recognized form of privilege. While the Court's analysis on its face appears uncontroversial under most of the definitions and philosophies of privacy discussed in Chapter 2, the breathtaking scope of this rule was revealed five years later in *United States v. Miller*.

4. United States v. Miller

In *United States v. Miller*, 425 U.S. 435 (1976), building on *United States v. White*, the Supreme Court held that a bank customer had no reasonable expectation of privacy in canceled checks and other transaction records held by his bank. The Court held that the otherwise personal information contained in records was under control of his bank, and not the customer, notwithstanding that the records were in part held by the bank because a Federal statute compelled their retention. The specific ruling in *Miller* has been superseded in the Federal context by the Right to Financial Privacy Act,[2] as well as by numerous state statutes and state court decisions. The *Miller* decision has been interpreted by some scholars to give private entities

---

[2]   12 U.S.C. § 3401 *et seq.* (2012). The Right to Financial Privacy Act pertains to disclosures by banks to federal agencies. *See infra* Chapter 3, Part II(A)(5) for further discussion.

that collect data in a proper and legal manner co-equal ownership of the right to use and disclose the data.

5. Smith v. Maryland

In *Smith v. Maryland*, 442 U.S. 735 (1979), the Supreme Court synthesized its rulings in *Katz* and *Miller*. In *Smith*, local police apprehended a man wanted for questioning in a robbery and series of stalking incidents by placing a "pen register" at the local telephone company's central office for purposes of monitoring which telephone numbers he was dialing. No warrant was obtained prior to installing the pen register. After the police confirmed the suspect was the individual calling the victim, they obtained a warrant for his house, where incriminating evidence was recovered and he was subsequently convicted.

On appeal, the defendant argued that the installation of the pen register without a warrant violated the rule set forth in *Katz* because he possessed a reasonable expectation of privacy. The Court rejected this argument on three major grounds. First, it observed that "a pen register differs significantly from the listening device employed in *Katz*, for pen registers do not acquire the *contents* of communications." *Id.* at 741 (emphasis in original). Second, the Court found that there was no reasonable expectation of privacy in the information as to which numbers were dialed because, "[a]ll telephone users realize that they must 'convey' phone numbers to the telephone company, since it is through telephone switching equipment that their calls are completed. All subscribers realize, moreover, that the phone company has facilities for making permanent records of the numbers they dial . . ." *Id.* at 742. Finally, relying on *Miller*, the Court explained that "a person has no legitimate expectation of privacy in information he voluntarily turns over to third parties. . . . When he used his phone, petitioner voluntarily conveyed numerical information to the telephone company and 'exposed' that information to its equipment in the ordinary course of business." *Id.* at 744. Thus, the defendant could not avail himself of the protections of *Katz* and his conviction was affirmed.

The two *Smith* dissents highlighted important problems with the majority's analysis, which have become even more significant in the age of ubiquitous Internet usage. Justices Stewart and Brennan took issue with the majority's view that telephone numbers are effectively unconnected to the contents of the communication. Instead, Justice Stewart wrote, "that information is an integral part of the telephonic communication that under *Katz* is entitled to constitutional protection." *Id.* at 747–48. Meanwhile, Justice Marshall, with whom Justice Brennan also joined, emphasized that the majority ruling set up an inevitable conflict between privacy and technology, unlike the *Katz* ruling which had sought to make constitutionally protected privacy coextensive with technological change. Justice Marshall warned that once privacy rights became dictated by technology then "unless a person is prepared to forgo use of what for many has become a personal or professional necessity, he cannot help but accept the risk of surveillance." *Id.* at 750. Despite these trenchant criticisms, lower Federal courts have effectively interpreted *Smith* to mean that routing information on any sort of electronic communication is not "private" for Fourth Amendment purposes.[3]

II.   FEDERAL STATUTES

Due to the incomplete nature of constitutional privacy protection in the United States, numerous statutory schemes have been enacted to fill perceived gaps in those protections. As is the inherent nature of the legislative process, these statutes represent a compromise between the demands of diverse constituencies. The following section surveys the development of privacy protections in certain subject areas and provides brief overviews of other significant pieces of legislation.

---

[3]   *See, e.g.,* United States v. Forrester, 512 F.3d 500, 504 (9th Cir. 2008) ("Alba challenges the validity of computer surveillance that enabled the government to learn the to/from addresses of his e-mail messages, the Internet protocol ('IP') addresses of the websites that he visited and the total volume of information transmitted to or from his account. We conclude that this surveillance was analogous to the use of a pen register that the Supreme Court held in *Smith v. Maryland,* 442 U.S. 735 (1979), did not constitute a search for Fourth Amendment purposes.").

A.   FINANCIAL PRIVACY

1. Introduction

Customers of financial institutions desire, and even presume, that their financial records are private. Law enforcement, on the other hand, presses a legitimate need for access to financial records to assist in performing its duties. Prior to 1970, the law was largely implicit. Various courts held that customers had an implied right of financial privacy at common law, established by the contract between bank and customer. Starting with the Bank Secrecy Act and the Fair Credit Reporting Act, both passed in 1970, Congress began to define and limit the scope of financial privacy in the face of law enforcement pressure for ever-greater access. In 1976, the U.S. Supreme Court handed down the landmark case *United States v. Miller*, establishing the constitutional boundary for financial records protection and disclosure.

Since 1976, three new laws have variously contracted and expanded the ability of third parties to share or subpoena, or both, financial records both with and without consent of the individual being targeted. The Right to Financial Privacy Act of 1978 established, in part, circumstances under which financial records may be disclosed to third parties without individual consent. Fearing the pendulum had swung too far in the direction of financial information sharing, the Gramm-Leach-Bliley Financial Modernization Act of 1999 established an individual's option to limit the sharing of financial information among affiliated institutions and with third parties. On the heels of the September 11, 2001 terrorist attacks, in an effort to enhance law enforcement's ability to "follow the money" as a means of thwarting future terrorist activity, Congress passed the USA PATRIOT Act of 2001.

2. Bank Secrecy Act

In 1970, with an eye toward preventing money laundering, Congress passed the Bank Secrecy Act (BSA).[4] The BSA requires banks and other financial institutions to keep certain records and to report certain transactions as authorized by the Secretary of the Treasury. The act formalized the definition of "financial institution."[5]

Upon becoming law, the United States Treasury Department promulgated regulations requiring financial institutions to report any deposit, withdrawal, currency exchange, or other payment or transfer involving more than $10,000.[6] As became immediately apparent after passage, the BSA was easily thwarted by simply limiting the size of any single transaction to less than $10,000. As a result, Congress and the Treasury Department have adjusted the regulations to require reporting of

---

[4]   Pub. L. No. 91–508, 84 Stat. 1114 (1970) (codified as amended in parts of 12 U.S.C., 15 U.S.C., 18 U.S.C., and 31 U.S.C.).

[5]   31 U.S.C. § 5312(a)(2) (2012).

[6]   31 C.F.R. § 103.11 (2012).

related transactions that, combined, exceed $10,000.[7]

3. Fair Credit Reporting Act

If the BSA was all about financial disclosure, the Fair Credit Reporting Act (FCRA), simultaneously passed in 1970,[8] was all about not disclosing financial information. Targeted at credit bureaus, the FCRA restricted the use of consumer credit reports to specific purposes and required credit bureaus to respond to consumer complaints.[9] The stated objective was to meet the commercial need for credit and other financial information in a fair and equitable way for the consumer, while assuring confidentiality, accuracy, and relevancy.[10]

Consumer credit reports contain highly sensitive personal information. When an individual applies for a charge account, personal loan, insurance, or job, a file is created about that individual. The file contains information on where the individual works and lives, how bills are paid, and whether the individual has ever been sued, arrested, or filed for bankruptcy. Companies that gather and sell this information are called Consumer Reporting Agencies (CRAs). The most common type of CRA is the credit bureau. The activities of other CRAs—

---

[7]   *See* 31 U.S.C. § 5324 (2012) (criminalizing transactions made for the purpose of evading reporting requirements).

[8]   Pub. L. No. 91–508, 84 Stat. 1114 (1970) (codified as amended at 15 U.S.C. §§ 1681–1681t).

[9]   *See* 15 U.S.C. § 1681–1681t (2012).

[10]   15 U.S.C. § 1681b.

including tenant or employment screening services, or agencies whose data is limited to an individual's check-writing history—that offer reports on consumers in specific situations are also governed by the FCRA. CRAs may sell information about individuals to creditors, employers, insurers, and other businesses in the form of a consumer report. In addition to credit reports on file with credit bureaus, the FCRA may govern other files of information collected and maintained on consumers, depending on their content and use. Medical information and information used to prevent and detect fraud are sometimes governed by the FCRA.

a. FCRA Remedies

The FCRA provides some remedies for breaches of financial privacy. The FCRA regulates credit information and provides for the investigation and correction of disputed accounts in an effort to ensure the accuracy of consumers' creditworthiness. The FCRA imposes certain duties upon credit agencies, such as Experian, Equifax, and TransUnion, and places duties upon commercial entities as well as furnishers of information to those credit reporting agencies including banks and credit card companies. If a consumer alleges discrepancies exist in their credit report, then the credit reporting agency is required to investigate the complaint to ensure accuracy.[11] If the agency finds that the consumer information is in fact inaccurate, the agency must delete or correct the inaccurate information and

---

[11]   *See* 15 U.S.C. § 1681i(a)(1).

notify the consumer of the decision. Also, those who furnish credit information have a duty to investigate disputed consumer information, correct any inaccuracies, and then notify the reporting agency of any changes that resulted.[12]

If entities governed by the FCRA willfully or negligently disregard its terms, then a private cause of action against those violators may exist.[13] Furthermore, entities that furnish credit information, or credit reporting agencies that fail to abide by the FCRA obligations are liable for actual damages, which can include mental damages, as well as attorney fees. Punitive and statutory damages may be levied against those who commit a willful violation of the FCRA.

b. FCRA Amendments of 2003

The prevalence of privacy breaches and identity theft issues were responsible for driving amendments to the FCRA in 2003.[14] If consumers, in good faith, believe they have been, or are about to become, the victim of identity theft, the amendments require reporting agencies to place a "fraud alert" on the consumers' file. Once the fraud alert has been filed, the creditors are required to take additional steps to verify the identity of the applicant before taking any action regarding

---

[12]   15 U.S.C. § 1681s-2(b).

[13]   15 U.S.C. § 1681n–o.

[14]   The amendment was formally titled the Fair and Accurate Credit Transactions Act of 2003, Pub. L. No. 108–159, 117 Stat. 1952 (2003).

accounts for that consumer. In addition, identity theft victims are entitled to receive a free credit report.[15] If a credit reporting agency receives verification of consumer identity theft, it must also prevent the reporting of such information.

To ensure that incorrect information about identity theft victims is not redistributed, furnishers of credit information must establish and follow reasonable procedures to ensure that, when they are notified by credit reporting agencies of a disputed account, they take the necessary steps to prevent inaccurate redistribution. If the furnisher of credit information learns that the information is in fact correct, then it can report negative credit information.[16]

c. Individual Claims under the FCRA

The FCRA does not impose liability on a defendant for actually stealing the victim's identity or for a theft that resulted because of inadequate supervision or security. Instead, FCRA claims usually focus on the manner in which third parties, such as those who furnish credit information or credit agencies themselves, have investigated and reported the information and facts involving the incident of identity theft, which in turn negatively impacted the victim's credit report.

In some cases, however, the defendant may be liable for both FCRA violations and common law

---

[15]   15 U.S.C. § 1681c–1.

[16]   15 U.S.C. § 1681s–2(a)(6)(A)–(B).

negligence. If a bank issued a credit card to an identity thief, for example, the bank could be liable for negligence or other common law theories. If the account subsequently went into default and the bank then incorrectly reported any negative information about the victim to a credit reporting agency, a claim under the FCRA may arise.

In a recent case involving an identity theft claim, the plaintiff was able to establish a violation of the FCRA under 15 U.S.C. § 1681c-1 when the credit reporting agencies ignored her complaints of identity theft as they published her credit report.[17] The claim was allowed even though the plaintiff did not identify which of the credit reports was inaccurate, could not specify which of the defendant credit reporting agencies had violated the FCRA, and did not identify which provision of the FCRA the defendants had violated. The plaintiff's complaint alleged that the defendants had her supposed signature but could not verify that it was actually hers, and that when the plaintiff told the defendants that the credit card bill did not come to her address, the plaintiff received no response from the defendants. She also notified the defendants that she had been a victim of identity theft, but they failed to notify the creditor of the identity theft. These actions by the plaintiff were found by the court to have sufficiently informed the defendants of the plaintiff's claims under the FCRA identity theft provisions.

---

[17]   Collins v. Experian Credit Reporting Serv., No. 3:04CV1905(MRK), 2005 WL 2042071 (D. Conn. Aug. 24, 2005).

Those who furnish credit information, and credit reporting agencies, are obligated to investigate consumer disputes, and these actions are usually judged by a standard of reasonableness. In a case involving a plaintiff who was victimized by an identity theft resulting in a fraudulent student loan in the plaintiff's name, the defendant credit reporting agency did have procedures in place to deal with issues arising from identity theft, and upon following those procedures, did in fact remove the inaccurate information, but only temporarily.[18] An error in the defendant's computer system allowed the adverse information to reappear on the plaintiff's credit report, thus giving doubts about the reasonableness of the credit reporting agency's procedures. The company servicing the loan transferred the plaintiff's account to another servicer, but failed to ensure that the loan was appropriately categorized to reflect that it had been the result of identity theft. The loan servicer changed the account number and, despite being notified that the loan was fraudulently obtained via identity theft, continued reporting the loan as a "charge off," thus giving rise to noncompliance actions under the FCRA.

In another case, a court ruled that the plaintiff's lack of action, coupled with only her denial that a fraudulent account was hers, was not sufficient to oblige the defendant to take further investigation

---

[18]   Jordan v. Equifax Info. Servs., LLC, 410 F. Supp. 2d 1349 (N.D. Ga. 2006).

under the FCRA.[19] The plaintiff's boyfriend allegedly used her Social Security number to obtain a credit account and then forged her signature on a personal guarantee letter to secure the account. The plaintiff did not file a police report regarding the matter, nor did she provide the defendant with any evidence that her supposed signature was forged, nor did she ever indicate that the account was the result of fraud, identity theft, or forgery. As such, the defendants owed her no duty to investigate her simple denial.

In a case involving a reasonableness standard, the defendant was entitled to summary judgment because its investigation of an identity theft allegation was determined to have been sufficiently reasonable.[20] The plaintiff discovered that a former friend had stolen his identity and had opened an account with the defendant credit bureau using the plaintiff's information. The plaintiff filed a statement with the credit reporting agency, TransUnion, regarding the fraud, along with information concerning the identity thief. Upon receipt of this information, TransUnion produced a Consumer Dispute Verification Form (CDV) and sent it to the defendant credit bureau for investigation. The CDV form, however, did not mention identity theft or fraud, and did not provide any information about the identity thief that the

---

[19]   Robinson v. Equifax Info. Servs., LLC, No. Civ.A. CV 040229 RP, 2005 WL 1712479 (S.D. Ala. July 22, 2005).

[20]   Westra v. Credit Control of Pinellas, 409 F.3d 825 (7th Cir. 2005).

plaintiff had provided. The lack of information did not enable the defendant to make a quick assessment as to whether the account was indeed fraudulent. In fact, it took several months for the defendant to determine the account was actually fraudulent. Before the defendant had concluded its investigation, the plaintiff refinanced his home, and alleged that he was denied the most advantageous interest rate because the defendant had failed to conduct a reasonable investigation as required by the FCRA. Considering the lack of information provided to the defendant from TransUnion, the court reaffirmed that the defendant was entitled to summary judgment. If TransUnion had provided additional information, the defendant would have been obligated to conduct a more thorough investigation. Furthermore, the court held that the defendant, under these circumstances, was not required to contact the plaintiff directly as part of its investigation because requiring direct contact between every entity who furnishes credit information with every consumer who disputes an account would create inefficiencies and an undue burden upon the entity.

4. United States v. Miller

The BSA and FCRA left financial privacy headed in two seemingly opposite directions. On one hand, any transaction or aggregate of related transactions over $10,000 was reported to the Treasury Department. On the other hand, credit report use was restricted. The rationale for limiting use of one type of information, while opening the door on another related type, was somewhat ambiguous. In 1976, the U.S. Supreme Court sought to clarify the scope of financial privacy.

Although the holding of *United States v. Miller* has been briefly discussed before, a deeper exploration of the facts is necessary in understanding its specific impact on financial privacy. The case was rooted in the operation of an illegal still. On December 18, 1972, a deputy in Georgia, acting on a tip, stopped a van, occupied by two of three co-conspirators, containing a distillery apparatus and raw material. On January 9, 1973, while fighting a fire in a warehouse rented to Mitch Miller, the third co-conspirator, firemen and sheriff department officials discovered a 7,500–gallon-capacity still and 175 gallons of non-tax-paid whiskey.

Two weeks later, agents from the Treasury Department's Bureau of Alcohol, Tobacco and Firearms presented blank grand jury subpoenas to the presidents of two banks where Miller maintained accounts. The subpoenas instructed the presidents to appear on a specified day with all records of any savings, checking, loan, or other accounts in Miller's name.

On February 12, 1973, Miller and the other co-conspirators were indicted, based in part on the information provided by the banks, which tied various incriminating purchases to Miller. Miller argued that the bank documents were illegally seized. Although convicted at trial, the Fifth Circuit Court of Appeals agreed with Miller, indicating that compulsory production of "private papers" for the purpose of establishing a criminal charge was prohibited.[21] Because it concluded that Miller's Fourth Amendment right against unreasonable search and seizure had been circumvented by requiring a third party to produce the records without sufficient legal process, the appellate court reversed the conviction.[22]

On appeal, the United States Supreme Court, with Justice Powell writing for the majority, dealt with the scope of the Fourth Amendment in relation to financial privacy, which the government argued did not extend to financial records. Powell began by noting that, when the government is involved in investigative activities, the Fourth Amendment is not implicated unless the investigation intrudes into the "zone of privacy." 425 U.S. at 440. The zone of privacy establishes the security relied upon when an individual is properly within a constitutionally protected area.

While "private papers" arguably fall within the "zone of privacy," the bank records provided to the investigating agents and the grand jury were not private papers because Miller could not assert either ownership or possession. Instead, the bank records, required to be kept under the BSA, pertained to transactions to which the bank was a party, making the records not "private papers," but business records.

---

[21]   See United States v. Miller, 500 F.2d 751, 757 (5th Cir. 1974) (citing Boyd v. United States, 116 U.S. 616, 622 (1886)).

[22]   See id. at 757–58.

Miller, however, argued that the combination of the BSA recordkeeping requirement and subpoena power enabled investigators to circumvent the Fourth Amendment by setting up a way to obtain private records without complying with the legal requirements of proceeding against Miller directly. The question, then, became whether or not the compulsion to keep and produce records contained in the BSA created a Fourth Amendment right where one did not otherwise exist.

Miller contended that the bank records were not business records, but copies of personal records made available to the bank for a limited purpose and for which Miller had a reasonable expectation of privacy. Justice Powell responded, however, that the checks were not personal records; rather, they were negotiable instruments used in commercial transactions. In fact, all of the documents obtained, including the financial statements and deposit slips, contain only information Miller voluntarily shared with the banks and their employees in the ordinary course of business.

Further, Congress, in enacting the BSA, which requires records be maintained because they are highly useful in criminal, tax, and regulatory investigations, creates a presumption that there is no legitimate privacy expectation in financial records. The bank customer then, in revealing his financial transactions to another, willingly and knowingly takes the risk that the information will be shared with the government. The BSA records retention and production requirements, therefore, are not aimed at circumventing Fourth Amendment protections, but are merely an attempt at ensuring these records are available when needed by law enforcement. As a result, Miller was left only with the general rule that a third party records subpoena does not violate a defendant's rights, even if the subpoena is in anticipation of a criminal prosecution.

The ruling in *United States v. Miller* established four principles relating to financial privacy that remain highly relevant today:

1. Records of an individual's bank accounts, maintained by a bank in compliance with the record keeping requirements of the BSA, are not Fourth Amendment protected "private papers," but are the bank's business records.

2. Checks, deposit slips, and financial statements are not confidential communications, but either negotiable instruments used in commercial transactions or information voluntarily conveyed to the bank and bank employees in the ordinary course of business.

3. BSA requirements that a bank permanently retain account information is merely an attempt to ensure the records are available when needed by law enforcement.

4. There is no legitimate privacy expectation in bank records.

In short, following *United States v. Miller*, the needs of law enforcement largely take precedence over the individual right to financial privacy.

5. Right to Financial Privacy Act

Partly in response to *United States v. Miller*, Congress turned its attention to better defining and narrowing the circumstances under which financial records could be discovered, and establishing notice requirements to affected individuals. The result was the enactment of the Right to Financial Privacy Act of 1978 (RFPA).[23]

The RFPA focuses primarily on notice requirements where a government agency seeks financial records. In general, individual financial records may not be disclosed to a government authority without the individual's consent. Consent is not required, however, if the disclosure is sought subject to a judicial subpoena, search warrant, or administrative subpoena. Similarly, consent is not required where the information sought is not individually identifiable, when the financial institution itself is the subject of the investigation, or when disclosure is necessary to comply with Internal Revenue Code provisions or the provisions of other federal regulations or statutes. If consent is obtained, an individual may later choose to revoke that consent.

---

[23]   Pub. L. No. 95–630, 92 Stat. 3697 (1978) (codified as amended at 12 U.S.C. §§ 3401 to 3422).

Whether consent is required or not, if the government agency seeks financial records, notice to the affected individual is required before release of the information to the requesting authority. In turn, the individual has the right to challenge the disclosure. The RFPA does, however, contain important notice requirement exceptions. Pursuant to a court order, for example, notice may be delayed until after the financial information has been obtained if the government agency demonstrates that notice will result in a serious investigative compromise or lead to flight from prosecution, evidence destruction, or witness intimidation. The RFPA is limited in application to individuals and small partnerships and, therefore, its protections do not extend to corporations or other organizations.

6. "Know Your Customer"

With the balance between the individual right to financial privacy and Government right to effective investigation set by the confluence of the BSA, FCRA, and RFPA operating within the Fourth Amendment parameters established by *United States v. Miller* and related decisions, financial privacy regulations remained relatively unchanged until 1998.

In 1998, federal banking regulators put forth a series of proposed regulations under the heading "Know Your Customer."[24] The regulations sought to reduce the barriers to law enforcement seeking

---

[24]   *See* Know Your Customer, 63 Fed. Reg. 67,536 (1998).

financial records. For example, Know Your Customer would require financial institutions: (1) to determine a customer's identity, (2) identify the source of a given customer's funds, and (3) establish an expected and normal level and type of transactions for monitoring accounts inconsistent with expectations to determine if the transactions were suspicious.

Know Your Customer essentially proposed a framework for circumventing the notice and consent requirements of the RFPA by expanding the recordkeeping and reporting requirements of the BSA to include the kinds of activity actual individual records, if obtained, would disclose. Due to an overwhelming response opposing the rules, regulators withdrew the proposal in 1999. While the Know Your Customer proposal failed, the exercise ignited Congressional interest in strengthening the right to financial privacy by formally preventing the type of notice and consent "workaround" Know Your Customer attempted to establish. The result was a new piece of landmark legislation.

7. Gramm-Leach-Bliley Financial Modernization Act

The Gramm-Leach-Bliley Financial Modernization Act (GLB),[25] passed in 1999, repealed various provisions of the Glass-Steagall Act.[26] The Glass-Steagall Act was a New Deal

---

[25]   Pub. L. No. 106–102, 113 Stat. 1338 (1999) (codified in scattered sections of 12, 15, 16 & 18 U.S.C.).

[26]   Pub. L. No. 73–66, 48 Stat. 162 (1933) (formerly codified at scattered sections of 12 U.S.C.).

regulation that restricted certain bank and securities firm affiliations. Broadly, GLB lifted the restrictions, making bank, stock brokerage, and insurance company mergers and affiliations permissible. In turn, GLB raised the specter of previously unimagined volumes of financial information sharing among these entities, which are now permitted to affiliate with each other. As a result, Title V of GLB addresses the sharing of financial information, referred to as nonpublic personal information.[27] Title V is divided into two subtitles.

a. GLB Subtitle A

In general, Subtitle A establishes specific obligations for financial institutions relative to disclosing nonpublic personal information to unaffiliated third parties. Financial institutions are required to establish and implement procedures that ensure the confidentiality of nonpublic personal information, and to protect nonpublic personal information from unauthorized access. As part of the protection process, financial institutions are required to provide customers with an annual notice explaining the policies and procedures for protecting nonpublic personal information. The annual notice must further describe the financial institution's policies for disclosing nonpublic personal information with both affiliated and non-affiliated entities. In turn, financial information may not be disclosed without first giving customers the

---

[27]   See 15 U.S.C. §§ 6801–09 (2012).

opportunity to "opt-out" of the disclosure. The opt-out is not absolute. Nonpublic personal information, for example, may be disclosed to credit reporting agencies and particular regulatory agencies.

b. GLB Subtitle B

Subtitle B establishes federal criminal penalties for either fraudulently obtaining or fraudulently using nonpublic personal information.[28] The target is information brokers that obtain nonpublic personal information, which they use to defraud either individuals or financial institutions.

c. GLB Scope

Recalling that the BSA established a formal definition of "financial institution," GLB refines the definition to include any institution that section 4(k) of the Bank Holding Company Act[29] describes as engaging in financial activities. The Bank Company Holding Act describes financial activities as any activity that the Federal Reserve Board determines—by order or regulation—which closely relates to banking, managing or controlling a bank, or incident to banking.[30]

A number of institutions have sought clarification as to whether or not they are closely enough related to banks or banking to make them subject to the requirements of GLB. As a result, the courts have

---

[28] *See* 15 U.S.C. §§ 6821–27 (2012).

[29] Pub. L. No. 84–511, 70 Stat. 133–146 (codified as amended at 12 U.S.C. sections 1841 to 1850).

[30] 15 U.S.C. § 6809.

been asked to particularly address the scope of GLB in at least three instances concerning organizations not traditionally thought to be "financial institutions." Specifically, credit-reporting agencies and credit counseling services are covered by GLB; however, law firms are not covered.[31]

Beyond issues defining "financial institution" and what entities fall within GLB's scope, GLB has resulted in challenges regarding whether or not GLB preempts state law, and how GLB impacts litigation discovery, which helps to further illuminate the scope of GLB.

d. GLB and State Law Preemption

The U.S. Congress and Supreme Court are not the only players on the privacy stage. Individual states have also exhibited a keen interest in striking the right balance between keeping financial information private and providing access where needed for law enforcement or regulatory oversight. As a result, state and federal law inevitably come into contact. GLB in particular has been a source of contention in determining if, and when, state law is preempted. States have sought to regulate the sharing of nonpublic personal information among affiliated entities, and have taken differing views on whether individualized customer consent is required for sharing with unaffiliated entities.

---

[31]   *See* American Bar Ass'n v. FTC, 430 F.3d 457, 468 (D.C. Cir. 2005); Trans Union LLC v. FTC, 295 F.3d 42, 48 (D.C. Cir. 2002); FTC v. AmeriDebt, Inc., 343 F. Supp. 2d 451, 461–62 (D. Md. 2004).

GLB specifically provides that state statutes are not preempted as long as the state law is consistent with GLB. In addition, GLB provides that state statutes are not preempted unless the state law is less protective than GLB. The challenge is determining when a state statute is consistent with or more protective, or both, than GLB. For example, California enacted the California Financial Privacy Act (California Act) in 2004.[32] Like GLB, the California Act restricted the use of nonpublic personal information by targeting information sharing among affiliated and unaffiliated entities. The California Act was explicitly intended to provide greater protection than GLB.

Recalling that under GLB nonpublic personal information may be shared with both affiliated and unaffiliated entities unless the individual customer opts-out of the sharing, the California Act required, instead, that nonpublic personal information may not be shared with unaffiliated entities unless the individual customer "opts-in" to the sharing. On the other hand, affiliated entities may share nonpublic personal information subject to the individual customer "opting-out."

In *American Bankers Ass'n v. Lockyer*, 412 F.3d 1081 (9th Cir. 2005), three financial services industry trade associations sued arguing that the California Act was preempted by GLB, and that the California Act was incorporated in the FCRA information sharing restrictions. The United States

---

[32]   CAL. FIN. CODE §§ 4050 to 4060 (2004).

District Court for the Eastern District of California found that GLB, in expressly allowing states to pass laws consistent with GLB, and to pass more restrictive information sharing laws, made the California Act not only permissible but anticipated by GLB. The decision was appealed to the United States Court of Appeals for the Ninth Circuit.

The Ninth Circuit analyzed the California Act primarily in light of the FCRA, framing the issue simply as whether or not the FCRA preempted the California Act. The Ninth Circuit began by noting that the FCRA regulates the use of "consumer reports" by "consumer reporting agencies." A consumer report is any communication of any information that reflects on a consumer's credit worthiness, credit standing, credit capacity, character, general reputation, personal characteristics, or mode of living.

Communication among entities, whether related by common ownership or corporate control, of information that only shows transactions or experiences between a customer and the person making the report is not considered part of a "consumer report." A consumer report also does not include any other information sharing among entities related either by common ownership or corporate control if the customer receives clear and conspicuous disclosure that such information may be shared along with an opportunity to opt-out of such sharing before sharing occurs. In other words, the FCRA sets out exceptions for "experience" information and "non-experience" information, which, then, would not fall within FCRA protections. A consumer reporting agency is an entity regularly engaged in assembling or evaluating consumer credit information or other information on consumers for the purpose of providing the information to third parties.

The FCRA contains a specific preemption clause, which provides that no State law may impose restrictions respecting the exchange of information among entities affiliated by either common control or common ownership. The preemption clause precludes any state "requirements" and "prohibitions" on the communication of information among affiliated entities. "Information" has a specific meaning in the statute, including only that information described in the consumer report definition of the FCRA.

Taken together, Congress, through the FCRA, specifically precludes states from regulating the sharing of information, as defined by the FCRA. As a result, the Ninth Circuit concluded that the California Act was preempted to the extent of the FCRA—*i.e.*, information relating to credit worthiness, credit standing, credit capacity, character, general reputation, personal characteristics, or mode of living. The Ninth Circuit remanded the case for determination if, in fact, the California Act did regulate sharing of information that the FCRA preempts. On remand, the California Act was found to be preempted by the FCRA.[33]

While the Ninth Circuit is the highest court to address the scope of federal preemption of state law protecting nonpublic personal information, courts in Massachusetts and Vermont have dealt with the scope of GLB state law preemption from different angles. The Massachusetts Consumer Protection Act Relative to the Sale of Insurance by Banks[34] prohibited bank referrals to insurance agents without the customer having first inquired about insurance. The Act further prohibited the payment of referral fees to the referring banker, and required that any insurance solicitation be conducted in a physically separate area of the bank. The Massachusetts Bankers Association challenged the Act on the grounds that the law was preempted by GLB.[35] The issue was whether GLB preempted laws aimed at interfering with the ability of banks to cross-market. GLB was found to preempt the referral, referral fee, and separation requirements of the Massachusetts law because the requirements "significantly curtailed" banks' ability to cross-market.

On the other hand, a Vermont Department of Banking, Insurance, Securities, and Healthcare Administration regulation creating "opt-in"

---

[33]   *See* American Bankers Ass'n v. Lockyer, No. Civ. S 04–0778MCE KJM, 2005 WL 2452798 (E.D. Cal. Oct. 5, 2005).

[34]   MASS. GEN. LAWS ch. 167F, § 2A (1998).

[35]   *See* Massachusetts Bankers Ass'n v. Bowler, 392 F. Supp. 2d 24 (D. Mass. 2005).

provisions for the sharing of nonpublic personal information, similar to those in the California Act, was not preempted by GLB.[36] GLB set a floor with the opt-out provision, and the opt-in provision of the Vermont regulation provided greater protection than GLB, which is permitted by GLB, and thus the Vermont regulation is not preempted.

Given the various interpretations of GLB found in the California, Massachusetts, and Vermont examples, the extent and scope of preemption is unclear and likely ripe for a unifying interpretation by the U.S. Supreme Court.

e. GLB and Litigation Discovery

Is GLB violated when a financial institution discloses nonpublic personal information during discovery in a court proceeding? As with the state law preemption issue, the courts are split, but a majority view has emerged. The U.S. District Court for the Southern District of West Virginia reasoned that, even though GLB does not contain an explicit exception for discovery, the general prohibition against financial information disclosure does not create a right to circumvent the discovery process.[37] When a party responds to a discovery request, the response is to the "judicial process," which requires the disclosure of non-public personal information. A

---

[36] *See* American Council of Life Insurers v. Vermont Dept. of Banking, No. 50–1–02 Wncv, 2004 WL 578737 (Vt. Super. Ct. Feb. 12, 2004).

[37] Marks v. Global Mtg. Group, Inc., 218 F.R.D. 492, 496 (S.D. W. Va. 2003).

majority of those courts reviewing the issue have adopted the judicial process exception.[38]

f. GLB Summary

In repealing the New Deal prohibition of bank, insurance, and securities firm affiliations, GLB opened nonpublic personal information to the possibility of disclosure across a broad spectrum of consumer financial service organizations. Recognizing the potential to decimate real financial privacy, GLB contains specific rules about sharing such financial information:

1. Financial institutions are required to establish and implement procedures keeping nonpublic personal information confidential and protecting the information from unauthorized use;

2. Customers must receive an annual notice detailing how nonpublic personal information is protected and on what basis information is shared;

3. Customers must be given the right, though not absolute, to opt-out of information sharing;

4. Fraudulently obtaining or using nonpublic personal information is a federal crime;

5. While the courts are split, states may not regulate the sharing of information included in

---

[38] *See, e.g.,* McGuire v. Rawlings Co., No. CV000375212S, 2005 WL 895870 (Conn. Super. Ct. Mar. 14, 2005); Ex parte Mutual Savings Life Ins. Co., 899 So.2d 986 (Ala. 2004); Martino v. Barnett, 595 S.E.2d 65 (W. Va. 2004).

the definition of consumer report contained in the FCRA;

6. A financial institution, despite GLB restrictions, is expected to respond to information requests made as part of the judicial process.

8. USA PATRIOT Act

As codified by the BSA, anti-money laundering law traditionally aimed at tracing criminal proceeds. In the period following the terrorist attacks of September 11, 2001, the Federal government sought to expand the use of financial information from merely tracking the result of crime to intercepting criminal financing in order to prevent crime. In October 2001, the Uniting and Strengthening America by Providing Appropriate Tools Required to Intercept and Obstruct Terrorism Act, or USA PATRIOT Act (Patriot Act) was signed into law.[39] Among hundreds of pages of provisions, the Patriot Act significantly altered the rules regulating financial privacy in three main areas.

a. *"Financial Institution" Redefined*

The Patriot Act reached back to the BSA and expanded the definition of financial institution to include entities ranging from traditional ones, such as commercial banks or trust companies and credit unions, to logical newcomers, including issuers of travelers' checks and money transfer agencies, to

---

[39]   Pub. L. No. 107–56, 115 Stat. 272 (2001) (codified as amended at scattered sections of 12, 15, 18, and 31 U.S.C.).

organizations whose possible connections to international terrorism are obscure, such as persons involved in real estate closings and settlements. Furthermore, the Secretary of the Treasury may expand the definition to include any other business or agency "whose cash transactions have a high degree of usefulness in criminal, tax, or regulatory matters."[40] In other words, the definition of financial institution is now so broad that criminals may not simply avoid the old BSA restrictions by using non-traditional financial channels. In turn, law enforcement may now cast a stunningly wide and diverse net in gathering financial information.

b. The Return of "Know Your Customer"

Reviving the "Know Your Customer" rules attempt of 1998, the Patriot Act directed the Secretary of the Treasury to establish regulations setting standards for financial institutions regarding customer identity. The resulting regulations require a financial institution to establish and implement procedures for verifying the identity of any person seeking to open an account. In addition, financial institutions must maintain records of the information used to verify identity, including name and address and any other identifying information. Government agencies are in turn to provide financial institutions with lists of known or suspected terrorists and terrorist organizations, which financial institutions are to compare to each customer identity for a match.

---

[40]   31 U.S.C. § 5312(a)(2)(Z).

In contrast, prior to the Patriot Act, the then-narrower list of entities considered financial institutions were only required to identify customers when the BSA reporting requirements were triggered by transactions exceeding $10,000, singly or in a related series. In addition, the BSA required reporting transactions if "suspicious" and more than $3,000, or any transaction when selling cashier's checks and money orders, or when transferring money by wire. Although not formally repealed, these provisions of the BSA have been largely mooted by the Patriot Act's more stringent requirements.

A transaction or related series of transactions greater than $10,000 triggers the requirement that the financial institution file a Currency Transaction Report (CTR). A suspicious transaction results in filing a Suspicious Activity Report (SAR). A CTR or SAR is filed with the Financial Crimes Enforcement Network (FinCEN).

c. Information Sharing

The pivot point for the sharing of financial information in the Patriot Act is FinCEN. Law enforcement agencies may gather information about the financial arrangements of any person under investigation for either terrorist activity or money laundering. FinCEN responds to the request by disclosing information provided by financial institutions or by requiring financial institutions to search their records to see if a given institution has conducted transactions or maintained an account for an identified individual. Then, records may be requested that do not follow from the usual CTR or SAR transactions. Law enforcement may request any financial record for any individual under investigation.

Procedurally, the Patriot Act only requires that the requesting agency provide FinCEN information identifying the individual under investigation and a certification that the target of the investigation is engaged in, or reasonably suspected of, engagement in terrorist activity or money laundering. Put another way, the Patriot Act does not require that law enforcement, in requesting financial information, have a search warrant, grand jury subpoena, or even an administrative subpoena, provided that the request is capable of being couched in those categories.

The financial institution, upon receipt of a FinCEN information request, is required to "expeditiously" search for any records related to the named individual. If a record is found, the financial institution is to report to FinCEN the name, Social Security number, date of birth, account number, and any other identifying information provided when the account was opened or a transaction was performed. A financial institution is prohibited from disclosing to anyone that a request was received from FinCEN, or that information was provided to FinCEN, unless disclosure of the information request is necessary to provide the information.

The Patriot Act includes an incentive for financial institutions to comply with FinCEN requests. When a financial institution seeks regulatory approval for a merger or acquisition, banking regulators are required to consider the institution's record of combating crime by responding to FinCEN. The implication is that the regulators will look favorably on those financial institutions that are more forthcoming with requested information.

If, after a financial institution has reported the identifying information indicating a match for an individual under investigation and the investigating agency wants the actual documents, then the agency must comply with regular procedural safeguards for securing the documents. The investigating agency may, for example, request a search warrant, which issues only upon a showing of probable cause to a judge. In the alternative, a grand jury subpoena may be requested through a prosecutor's office. Here, the showing required is not probable cause but virtually any information the prosecutor deems adequate. Unlike with a search warrant, however, the receiver of the subpoena may challenge the request, before the documents are provided, on the basis that compliance is unreasonable, oppressive, or requests privileged information. In turn, a court may modify or quash the subpoena.

An investigative agency may, however, elect to forgo the search warrant or grand jury subpoena, with the accompanying required showing and right to challenge, in favor of an administrative subpoena issued by a federal or state agency. An administrative subpoena does not require a showing of probable cause or court order, but a showing only of relevance. In 1989 the Office of Thrift Supervision (OTS) was created to regulate the safe and sound operation of savings and loan associations. The OTS is authorized to subpoena information relevant to the affairs or ownership of any bank, financial institution, or affiliate.[41]

During a routine examination in 1990, the OTS discovered that the subject Bank was nearly insolvent.[42] Upon further investigation, OTS discovered that two of the Bank's directors owned a mortgage company and law firm. Large overdrafts in the law firm deposit accounts were covered by overnight transfers from the mortgage company escrow accounts, suggesting violation of fiduciary duties of the Bank and Mortgage Company Act, as well as a violation of OTS regulations regarding loans to affiliated parties and overdraft restrictions on director maintained accounts.

As a result, OTS issued a subpoena to each director seeking personal financial documents belonging to them, spouses, and any entity owned, controlled by or through which either director or their spouse did business. Included in the subpoena was a request for financial statements, tax returns, and bank account statements. The directors refused to comply.

---

[41]   12 U.S.C. § 1820(c) (2006).

[42]   The factual background is found at *In re* Sealed Case, 42 F.3d 1412, 1414–15 (D.C. Cir. 1994).

Arguing in district court, OTS claimed three reasons for the subpoena. First, OTS wanted to determine if either director benefited from the use of the escrow funds to cover the law firm overdrafts. Second, it was seeking to determine the extent to which the directors could pay civil money penalties. Third, the agency wanted to determine if there was any other as yet unknown wrongdoing. The district court found that the information sought was reasonably relevant, not too burdensome, and within OTS's authority to request. The directors appealed on the basis that the Fourth Amendment limited the ability of OTS to obtain personal financial documents.

The test for deciding whether a subpoena should be enforced is three pronged: (1) is the request within the authority of the agency; (2) is the request not too indefinite; and (3) is the information sought reasonably relevant.[43] The directors argued that the first and third prongs were not met.

The D.C. Circuit found the first and second prongs were met because the requested information would facilitate OTS's statutory duty to assess civil penalties, issue orders of removal, and determine liability.[44] Because the subpoenas satisfied the first and second prong, the directors were left with their argument that the information requested was not relevant. The test for relevance is simply that the requested information is "reasonably relevant" to

---

43   *Id.* at 1415.

44   *Id.* at 1416.

the general purpose of the agency investigation, thus there was no question the requested information, including personal financial and banking records, was relevant to the OTS's investigation to determine if the directors benefited personally and were able to pay a civil penalty.[45]

The subject of an administrative subpoena, therefore, must comply unless they can overcome the relatively low agency burden of showing relevance to the investigation. The only practical protection afforded the recipient of an agency subpoena is to refuse to comply. An agency may not enforce the subpoena, but must seek enforcement through the courts, as demonstrated by *In re Sealed Case*. The subpoena power only comes into play, however, when an agency wants actual documents. After all, through FinCEN and the authority granted in the Patriot Act, a vast amount of information may be collected without notice.

d. The Patriot Act at Work

In practice, the Patriot Act authority has not been limited to terrorist or money laundering investigation, but has been used in relatively routine criminal investigations. For example, the financial transactions of particular individuals targeted by law enforcement agencies in an investigation called "Operation G-Sting," who were suspected of bribing public officials in exchange for votes changing the regulations for a Las Vegas strip

---

[45]   *Id*. at 1419.

club, were tracked under authority of the Patriot Act.

A Honduran lobsterman was also convicted of illegally importing lobster into the United States in violation of Honduran size regulations.[46] The Lacey Act prohibits the importation of fish caught in violation of United States or any foreign law.[47] The investigation was enabled in part due to the use of the Patriot Act to gather financial information on the basis that money from the proceeds of the lobster sales was deposited in banks.

e. The Patriot Act and the Future

The Patriot Act liberalizes the ability of law enforcement to gather financial information and relaxes the safeguards imposed by prior laws, such as the BSA and GLB. There is a constant stream of proposed amendments to the Patriot Act, some of which would create greater privacy protections. Much has been written about safeguards that should be considered. Congress or the courts could be given an oversight role in monitoring FinCEN activity. In turn, FinCEN could be required to make periodic reports to a designated judge or adjunct of Congress in order to ensure that designated procedural safeguards are, in fact, followed. A particular problem which may need to be addressed is that, financial institutions can be penalized by banking regulators for being uncooperative with

---

[46]   See United States v. McNab, 324 F.3d 1266 (11th Cir. 2003).

[47]   See 16 U.S.C. § 3372 (2012).

FinCEN. Financial institutions are increasingly dropping customers on the merest suspicion of illegal activity out of fear of FinCEN requests for records.

In the meantime, various agencies continue to explore the scope and test the limitations of the Patriot Act. Many actions are the first of their kind and, as a result, are new to all involved parties. The Securities and Exchange Commission (SEC), for example, did not bring its first case against a brokerage firm for failure to report suspicious transactions until 2007. In that case, the SEC accused Park Financial and its principal of executing numerous trades in Spear & Jackson securities, despite obvious red flags, and of failing to file SARs. Spear & Jackson's former CEO allegedly used brokerage accounts, opened in the name of a series of British Virgin Island-based companies he controlled, to illegally trade Spear & Jackson stock. The brokerage accounts were opened at Park Financial, which, given the nature of the transactions and foreign base of the accounts, the SEC argued, represented the type of conduct Park Financial knew fell under SAR.

The SEC action highlights the rigor with which any financial institution is expected to use in alerting FinCEN. In turn, the action highlights the extent to which financial transactions are monitored, and the related information shared. The Patriot Act is left, then, as both the current and most questioned financial privacy related law. Congress is wrestling, as has been the case since the

BSA of 1970, with the proper balance between the right to financial privacy and the real need for disclosure of nonpublic personal information for the benefit of law enforcement.

B. MEDICAL PRIVACY

1. Introduction

Many people characterize their medical records as being among the information they most want kept out of the public eye. Medical records, however, have historically not been subject to systematic privacy regulations. Instead, the health care industry relied mainly on principles of medical ethics and tort law to protect the privacy of such records. Increasing concern over the use and distribution of individuals' medical records though, has led to a more formalized regulatory regime.

2. Health Insurance Portability and Accountability Act

At the Federal level the privacy of medical records is primarily governed by the Health Insurance Portability and Accountability Act of 1996 (HIPAA).[48] The Federal Privacy Rule, which officially implements HIPAA, became effective in April 2003.[49] HIPAA was enacted to prevent fraud and unauthorized access, use, and disclosure of "individually identifiable health information." It

---

[48]   Health Insurance Portability and Accountability Act (HIPAA) of 1996, Pub. L. No. 104–191,110 Stat. 1936 (1996).

[49]   45 C.F.R. § 164.534 (2012).

also is intended to reduce the costs of administrative operations in the healthcare industry by simplifying the exchange of electronically stored medical information and preventing fraud or unauthorized access, use, and disclosure of health information.

a. Protected Health Information

HIPAA regulates protected health information as it is used and disclosed by covered entities.[50] The health information protected under HIPAA includes any information relating to treatment or payment of healthcare. Health information is defined as any information that "relates to the past, present, or future physical or mental health or condition of an individual, the provision of health care to an individual, or the past, present, or future payment for the provision of health care to an individual."[51]

In addition, HIPAA seeks to protect elements of health information that could identify the patient. The statute defines individually identifiable health information as any information collected from an individual that relates to the past, present, or future physical or mental health or condition of an individual. It also includes in the definition the provision of health care to an individual, or the past, present, or future payment for the provision of health care to an individual, which identifies the individual, or which creates a reasonable basis to

---

[50]   45 C.F.R. § 164.502(a).

[51]   42 U.S.C. § 1320d(4)(B) (2000).

believe that the information can be used to identify the individual.[52]

The United States Department of Health and Human Services (HHS) lists some of the identifiers, which include name, social security number, address, zip code, phone number, photograph, employer, treatment date, and names of spouse and children.[53] If there is other healthcare information that has the potential to identify the patient, this information is also protected.

b. Covered Entities

HIPAA applies to "covered entities," which consist of three particular categories of persons. Those three categories are: (1) a health plan; (2) a health care clearinghouse; and (3) a health care provider who transmits any health information in electronic form.[54] A "health plan" is defined quite broadly, and includes individual and group plans providing or paying the cost of medical care, as well as most employer health benefit plans established pursuant to the Employee Retirement Income Security Act of 1974 (ERISA), Medicaid, Medicare, HMOs, other state and federal healthcare programs, and insurance companies that issue healthcare policies. The statute exempts small plans, meaning those with fewer than 50 participants and purely employer managed plans.

---

[52]   42 U.S.C. § 1320d(5)(M).

[53]   45 C.F.R. § 164.514(b).

[54]   42 U.S.C. § 1320d(2), (3), (5).

A "health care clearing house" is an "entity that processes or facilitates the processing of nonstandard data elements of health information into standard data elements."[55] A health plan or provider may contract with a healthcare clearinghouse to handle the transmitting or receiving of any of the HIPAA standard electronic transactions, which converts both the provider and the clearinghouse into a covered entity subject to HIPAA.[56]

A "health care provider" is defined as "a provider of medical or health services . . . and any other person or organization who furnishes, bills, or is paid for health care."[57] Once again, coverage under this definition is rather wide as it includes all types of medical doctors and other licensed professionals who provide treatment and/or diagnostic testing to patients. It also includes any healthcare professional who provides medical drugs or devices to patients.

Providers excluded under HIPAA are those who do not conduct any of the HIPAA-regulated electronic transactions. HIPAA only applies to those health care providers that transmit "health information in electronic form in connection with a transaction."[58] There are nine electronic transactions regulated by HIPAA, which include: claims, claim status, benefit eligibility inquiries,

---

[55] 42 U.S.C. § 1320d(2).

[56] 42 U.S.C. § 1320d-4(a)(2)(B).

[57] 45 C.F.R. § 160.103 (2012).

[58] 42 U.S.C. § 1320d-1(a)(3).

enrollment and disenrollment, healthcare payments, premium payments, referral authorization requests, coordination of benefits, and claims attachments. If a health care provider does not conduct any of the foregoing transactions electronically with any covered entity, the provider is not regulated by HIPAA.

Determining whether an entity is indeed a covered entity under HIPAA is not an easy task due to the complex language of the statute. An online resource made available by the Centers for Medicare and Medicaid Services, divisions of HHS, gives guidance and provides a helpful chart for navigating through the complexities.[59]

Health plans include ERISA group health plans that have 50 or more participants, or that are administered by a third party other than the plan sponsor.[60] If an organization does have a group health plan with 50 or more participants or has a plan administered or insured by someone other than the plan sponsor, then a plan is required to comply with the HIPAA privacy and security rules. Conversely, if no group health plan exists, or if the plan is self-administered, self-insured and contains fewer than 50 participants, the HIPAA rules do not apply. HIPAA still applies to the employer even if it would otherwise appear to be exempt, albeit indirectly. If the employer is performing functions

---

[59]   The resource is entitled "Covered Entity Charts" and is *available at* http://www.cms.hhs.gov/HIPAAGenInfo/06_AreYoua CoveredEntity.asp.

[60]   45 C.F.R. § 160.103.

for the group health plan, including processing claims, conducting audits, obtaining payment for denied claims, or administering flex account spending, HIPAA applies.

Compliance with the HIPAA provisions is required for all covered entities whenever protected health information is used or disclosed. Disclosure is mandated in only two circumstances. First, when the patient requests access to his or her healthcare information and, second, when the Secretary of HHS requests access to the information as part of an investigation or enforcement action concerning a covered entity's compliance with HIPAA.[61] In addition to these two mandatory disclosures, there exist six categories under HIPAA that permit or otherwise excuse limited use and disclosure of healthcare information: (1) To the individual, who is the subject of the information; (2) Treatment, Payment, or Healthcare Operations; (3) Inadvertent Disclosures; (4) When Authorized in Writing; (5) Agreed to Disclosures; and (6) Public Interest Disclosures.

c. Individual Rights

Since HIPAA is designed to protect an individual's healthcare privacy, there are eight fundamental rights afforded to individuals:

1. The right to access, inspect, and obtain a copy of protected health information about him or herself;

---

[61]   45 C.F.R. § 164.502(a)(2)(ii).

2. The right to have the covered entity correct the individual's protected health information;

3. The right to receive an accounting of disclosures made by a covered entity;

4. The right to request that a covered entity restrict the uses or disclosures of the individual's protected health information related to treatment, payment, or health care operations, although the covered entity is not required to agree to such a restriction;

5. The right to request confidential communications from providers of protected health information;

6. The right to object or agree before covered entities make certain disclosures, such as listing the individual's name in a facility directory;

7. The right to authorize disclosures to third parties pursuant to an authorization;

8. The right to receive adequate notice of the uses and disclosures that may be made by the covered entity.

d. Administrative Simplification

The "Administrative Simplification" provisions were designed to give the HHS power to create and publish rules to improve the electronic exchange of health information. Since patient privacy is vital, and electronic storage and transmission of records can pose serious threats of such privacy being compromised on a vast scale, Congress granted the

HHS authority to adopt rules to protect the confidentiality of individually identifiable health information. The most significant rule promulgated pursuant to the Administrative Simplification provisions is the Privacy Rule discussed above.

Civil enforcement of the Privacy Rule is principally done through the Office for Civil Rights (OCR), which is a division of HHS, but the Privacy Rule may also be enforced by a state attorney general where the attorney general has reason to believe that one or more of the residents of his or her State has been adversely affected by a violation of the rule. The OCR or state attorney general may obtain injunctive relief against further misconduct and also recover significant monetary penalties.[62] However, civil penalties cannot be imposed if any of three criteria are met. First, criminal enforcement overrides civil enforcement, thus, where there is an overlap of jurisdiction between the OCR and the U.S. Department of Justice, which prosecutes criminal violations of HIPAA, the OCR must accede to DOJ's control of the investigation. Second, the HHS Secretary may waive penalties if it is established that the person or entity responsible for the violation "did not know, and by exercising reasonable diligence would not have known," that a violation had been committed. Third, the Secretary can also excuse the violation if it is determined that "the failure to comply was due to reasonable cause

---

[62] The civil penalties for HIPAA violations were drastically revised in 2009 as part of the HITECH Act. The current penalty structure is discussed in Chapter 3, Part II.B.2.k.(ii).

and not to willful neglect; and the failure to comply is corrected." Finally, even if none of the criteria are met, the Secretary has the discretion to waive the penalty to the extent that "payment of such penalty would be excessive relative to the compliance failure involved."

Criminal violations can bring a fine of up to $50,000 or imprisonment, or both, for not more than one year. If the crime was perpetrated using false pretenses, then the fine can increase to $100,000 or not more than five years in prison, or both. Furthermore, if the offender commits the crime for personal gain, or to inflict malicious harm, the penalty can be up to $250,000 or imprisonment for up to ten years, or both.[63]

e. HIPAA Enforcement Rule

On March 16, 2006, the Enforcement Rule took effect in an effort to create a unified and comprehensive approach to enforcing all the HIPAA Administrative Simplification rules, which includes, in addition to the Privacy Rule, the Security Rule, the Electronic Transaction and Code Set Rule, and the Identifier Standards.[64] The new Enforcement Rule follows some of the same principles of previous individualized rules, including the Privacy rule, by encouraging voluntary compliance. The Secretary of

---

[63]   42 U.S.C. § 1320d-6 (2012).

[64]   HIPAA Administrative Simplification: Enforcement, 71 Fed. Reg. 8390, 8391 (Feb. 16, 2006).

HHS may also provide technical assistance to covered entities to enhance voluntary compliance.[65]

The Enforcement Rule stresses the use of self-regulatory means to ensure compliance. Self-regulatory includes "demonstrated compliance, or a completed corrective action plan or other agreement."[66] The Secretary has broad discretion to settle any matter of noncompliance and to encourage covered entities to comply voluntarily. If a covered entity does not comply via informal means, then HHS must give notice to the entity and provide an opportunity "to submit written evidence of any mitigating factors or affirmative defenses for consideration."[67]

The Secretary of HHS is to consider six factors in determining civil monetary penalties. First, the nature of the violation, in light of the purpose of the rule violated. Second, the circumstances and consequences of the violation, including but not limited to: (a) the time period during which the violation occurred, (b) whether physical harm was caused by the violation, (c) whether the violation facilitated or hindered an individual's ability to obtain health care, and (d) whether financial harm resulted from the violation. Third, the degree of culpability of the covered entity, which includes but is not limited to: (a) whether the violation was intentional, and (b) whether the violation was

---

[65]   45 C.F.R. § 160.304(b) (2012).

[66]   *Id.* at § 160.312(a)(1).

[67]   *Id.* at § 160.312(a)(3)(i).

beyond the direct control of the covered entity. Fourth, whether the company had a history of prior compliance with the administrative simplification provision. Fifth, the financial condition of the covered entity. And finally, whether there are any other matters as justice may require.[68]

There have been a number of civil and criminal penalties imposed under HIPAA. The first of these was a criminal matter, *United States v. Gibson*, No. CR04–0374RSM, 2004 WL 2188280 (W.D. Wash. 2004). Gibson was a phlebotomist who used a cancer patient's name, date of birth, and Social Security number to obtain four credit cards in the patient's name. This information, which is protected health information under HIPAA, was collected by Gibson's employer for payment of health care services. After obtaining the credit cards, Gibson charged more than $9,000 on the cards for various items. When Gibson's employer discovered what he had done, he was terminated. The Department of Justice filed criminal charges against Gibson and, under a plea agreement, he was sentenced to sixteen months in prison and ordered to pay $15,000 in restitution.

Interestingly, Gibson was prosecuted despite not meeting the definition of a "covered entity." HIPAA states that it only applies to "covered entities," as defined above, and HHS has repeatedly stated that the imposition of privacy standards do not extend beyond these entities. The DOJ's decision to prosecute Gibson under HIPAA was specifically

---

[68]   *Id.* at § 160.408.

influenced by the fact that Gibson unlawfully obtained the health information while carrying out his employment duties as a health care technician.

Within a year after the *Gibson* case, the DOJ issued a memorandum that spoke to the issues present in the action, namely that he was not a covered entity within the scope of HIPAA. The opinion stated that only "covered entities" and "those persons rendered accountable by general principles of corporate criminal liability" may be prosecuted for violations under 42 U.S.C. § 1302d-6.[69] Despite this reserved language, the DOJ's determination that HIPAA could be extended to directors, officers, and employees of covered entities radically increased the reach of privacy protection under the statute.

f. Emergency Exception

In response to Hurricane Katrina in 2005, the OCR issued two separate Special Bulletins to give guidance to covered entities in emergencies. The first bulletin stated that the HIPAA Privacy Rule allows the sharing of health information to assist disaster relief efforts. The second bulletin expanded on the first. It allowed that "business associates that are managing such information on behalf of covered entities may make these disclosures to the extent permitted by their business associate agreement

---

[69] Memorandum from Steven G. Bradbury, Principal Deputy Assistant Attorney Gen., Office of Legal Counsel, to Gen. Counsel, Dep't of Health & Human Servs. (June 1, 2005), *available at* http://www.justice.gov/olc/hipaa_final.htm.

with the covered entities, as provided in the Privacy Rule."[70] It also emphasized that HIPAA permits HHS to take into consideration the circumstances surrounding violations of the Privacy Rule, proper allowance would be made for the complications created by the hurricane in any investigation. The bulletin cautioned that, even in emergency situations, proper safeguards still need to be in place for exchange of the information.

g. HIPAA Requirements

As has been previously discussed, health information of an individual, which also includes information about the payment for the individual's health care, is protected under HIPAA. HIPAA does allow, however, health plans to disclose some protected health information as necessary to carry out internal operations and to provide payment for a participant's treatment.[71]

HIPAA requires a "firewall" between the plan and the employer to prevent the plan from disclosing health information to the employer for purposes of employment-related actions. Otherwise, a plan participant must give written authorization for any other disclosures, barring certain exceptions. Furthermore, HIPAA requires the plan to enter

---

[70]   Bulletin from Office for Civil Rights, Dep't of Health & Human Servs., Hurricane Katrina Bulletin #2: HIPAA Privacy Rule Compliance Guidance and Enforcement Statement for Activities in Response to Hurricane Katrina (Sept. 9, 2005), *available at* http://www.hhs.gov/ocr/privacy/hipaa/understanding/special/emergency/enforcementstatement.pdf.

[71]   45 C.F.R § 164.506.

"business associate contracts." The contracts are with third-party administrators who handle protected health information on behalf of the plan and require the business associate to follow the basic HIPAA confidentiality and security rules. Examples of third-party administrators include lawyers, accountants, IT personnel, and benefits consultants.

h. Rights of Plan Participants

Participants are allowed to access and amend their health information from group health plans. The participants must also be allowed to obtain an accounting of when their health information for certain disclosures was made.[72]

i. HIPAA Preemption Rules

Although many states may have their own laws which create a privilege for medical records and contain rules about the disclosure of such information, HIPAA's general preemption rule is that any conflicting state law is superseded by HIPAA.[73] Any preemption by HIPAA will not be triggered unless the state law is contrary to the HIPAA provisions.[74] To give guidance, HIPAA defines "contrary" in two ways. First, the statutory schemes are considered contrary where a covered entity would find it impossible to comply with both the state and federal requirements. If a covered

---

[72]   *Id.* at §§ 164.524–164.528.

[73]   *Id.* at § 160.203.

[74]   *Id.* at § 160.203.

entity were required by state law to take some type of action that would violate HIPAA, then HIPAA prevails. The second definition of contrary recites that a state law is contrary to HIPAA when it "stands as an obstacle to the accomplishment and execution of the full purposes and objectives" of HIPAA.[75]

The Secretary of HHS can determine that a contrary state law will not be preempted if the law is necessary for regulating the state's healthcare and insurance.[76] For example, the Secretary may determine that a state law is designed to prevent healthcare fraud and abuse or that it concerns efforts to regulate the manufacture or distribution of controlled substances. Furthermore, HIPAA's preemption provision serves as a "floor," rather than a "ceiling," in that it expressly does not preempt contrary state laws to the extent such laws provide more stringent protection for individually identifiable health information than HIPAA.

j. Genetic Information

The HIPAA Privacy Rule includes "genetic information" as a possible form of "protected health information."[77] The term genetic information encompasses information about genes, gene

---

[75]   *Id.* at § 160.202(2).

[76]   *Id.* at § 160.203(a).

[77]   *Does the HIPAA Privacy Rule Protect Genetic Information?*, DEP'T OF HEALTH & HUMAN SERVS., http://www.hhs.gov/ocr/privacy/hipaa/faq/protected_health_infor mation/354.html (last updated Mar. 14, 2006).

products, and inherited characteristics that may derive from the individual or a family member, whether collected through direct testing or through the assembly of family medical histories. Genetic information gains protection under HIPAA as long as it relates to medical records and other personal health information maintained by covered entities. Any genetic information that is individually identifiable, in the sense of being associated with a personal identifier, cannot be disclosed or used by any covered entities, except as permitted by the Privacy Rule. The key limitation here is that these restrictions on disclosures apply only to covered entities (and potentially their directors, officers, and employees under the DOJ's interpretation of the statute in *Gibson*), thus many educational institutions and private genetics labs are not subject to the Rule.

Pursuant to the HIPAA's allowance for more stringent health information privacy laws at the state level, many jurisdictions have enacted their own legislation governing genetic privacy. Before disclosing previously provided genetic information, informed consent is required in twenty-six states. Furthermore, criminal and/or civil penalties exist in eighteen states for violations of their respective genetic privacy laws.

k. HITECH Act of 2009

In 2009, HIPAA was extensively amended by the Health Information Technology for Economic and

Clinical Health Act (HITECH Act).[78] Among the amendments were several with significant implications for patient privacy.

(i) Breach Notification

The HITECH Act imposed detailed breach notification requirements on all covered entities, as well as their business associates, in the event that "unsecured protected health information" is improperly accessed or otherwise disclosed.[79] Unsecured protected health information is protected health information that is not secured through "the use of a technology or methodology" prescribed by HHS.[80]

If a covered entity learns, or has a basis to reasonably believe, that "unsecured protected health information" held by itself, or a business associate performing services on its behalf,[81] has been improperly disclosed, the covered entity generally must notify each individual whose information has been, or is reasonably believed to have been,

---

[78]   Pub. L. No. 111–5, § 13001, 123 Stat. 226 (2009).

[79]   42 U.S.C. § 17932 (2012).

[80]   HHS's regulations concerning specific technologies and methodologies for securing protected health information are codified at 45 C.F.R. § 164.302, et seq.

[81]   While a business associate is required by the HITECH Act to notify the responsible covered entity about a breach that takes place while the unsecured protected health information is in the business associate's possession, it is still the responsibility of the covered entity to notify affected individuals. 42 U.S.C. § 17932(b) (2012).

disclosed.[82] The statute imposes a timeliness requirement for such notice, generally requiring a covered entity to notify the affected individuals within 60 calendar days of discovering the breach. The specific form and content of such notifications is also prescribed.[83] Of particular significance is that, in addition to direct notices to affected individuals, a covered entity must provide immediate notice of the breach to the Secretary of HHS and also timely notice to "prominent media outlets serving a State or jurisdiction" if the unsecured protected health information of more than 500 residents of that State or jurisdiction is, or is reasonably believed to have been, improperly disclosed.[84]

(ii) Increased civil penalties and broader enforcement authority

Originally, enforcement of HIPAA's Privacy Rule was left entirely to OCR and penalties were limited to $100 per violation, up to a maximum of $25,000 per type of violation per year. As a result, many covered entities were willing to treat potential civil

---

[82]   HHS has set forth a handful of exceptions to the notice requirement. These principally concern situations where protected health information is inadvertently disclosed internally at a covered entity or business associate and there is no reason to believe the information was disclosed outside the institution or is otherwise at risk of misuse. 74 Fed. Reg. 42,740, 42,746–47 (Aug. 24, 2009).

[83]   42 U.S.C. § 17932(d)–(f).

[84]   42 U.S.C. § 17932(e)(2) & (3). Covered entities are also required to report breaches involving fewer than 500 individuals to the Secretary, but only as an annual compilation. No media notice is required for such smaller breaches.

penalties as a mere "cost of doing business" given that rigorous compliance would have been more expensive than risking an occasional penalty. The HITECH Act changed this dynamic considerably.[85] Most immediately, the Act introduced a new tiered penalty structure with substantially greater monetary penalties depending on the violator's degree of culpability. Penalties remained $100 per violation, up to a maximum of $25,000 per type of violation per year for violators that did not know (and by exercising reasonable diligence could not have known) that their actions violated the Privacy Rule, but a violator could be held liable for as much as $50,000 per violation and up to a maximum of $1.5 million per type of violation per year if it was determined that the violation was the result of "willful neglect" or if the violation resulted from a failure to correct a previous violation.

In response concerns that OCR was insufficiently interested in bringing enforcement actions, the HITECH Act amended HIPAA to grant state attorney generals independent authority to bring enforcement actions relating to violations of the Privacy Rule that impacted residents of their states. To further enhance the likelihood of enforcement actions being taken, the HITECH Act also directed the Secretary of HHS, in cooperation with the Government Accountability Office, to develop a methodology for awarding part of any monetary penalties collected to individuals harmed by the violation. The rationale was that such a quasi-

---

[85]   42 U.S.C. § 1320–d(a) (2012).

compensatory approach would incentivize reporting of HIPAA violations. As of December 2013, however, HHS has not promulgated a rule for such awards.

(iii) Extending   privacy   and   security requirements to business associates

Originally, HIPAA's Privacy Rule and Security Rule applied to business associates only indirectly through covered entities' business associate agreements. While business associates still must comply with the obligations set for them by covered entities through business associate agreements, the HITECH Act also directly imposed a duty to comply with the Privacy Rule and Security Rule in the same manner as covered entities.[86] Furthermore, business associates were also made subject to the same new tiered penalties and expanded enforcement regime that covered entities are subject to under the Enforcement Rule.

3. Genetic Privacy

The Genetic Information Nondiscrimination Act of 2008 (GINA)[87] was principally introduced to prohibit discrimination on the basis of genetic information with respect to health insurance and employment. GINA, however, also contains two specific privacy components.

---

[86]   42 U.S.C. §§ 17931 & 17934 (2012).

[87]   Pub.L. 110–233, 122 Stat. 881 (2008) (codified in scattered sections of titles 26, 29, and 42 U.S.C.).

First, GINA expressly makes genetic information (defined as information about an individual's genetic tests and the tests of that individual's family members, as well as information about any genetic disease, disorder, or condition of an individual's family members) a form of protected health information subject to HIPAA. Second, GINA makes it unlawful in most instances for employers to request employees or job applicants to provide genetic information or to otherwise require that such information be made available as a condition of employment. Violations of GINA's privacy provisions are dealt with via the same enforcement mechanism as a HIPAA violation or via a Title VII employment discrimination claim, depending on the nature of the violation.

C. OTHER PRIVACY LEGISLATION

The following are some of the more notable Federal statutes that address the many privacy concerns that exist today.

1. Privacy Act of 1974

Congress passed the Privacy Act of 1974[88] to protect federal records containing personally identifiable information by prohibiting agencies from disclosing such information without consent, and to address the dangers posed by the widespread use of Social Security numbers as personal identifiers. Under the Privacy Act, a governmental

---

[88]   Pub. L. No. 93–579, 88 Stat. 1896 (1974) (codified at 5 U.S.C. § 552).

agency cannot deny a right, benefit, or privilege simply because the individual refused to disclose his or her Social Security number. The Act also gives individuals access to consumer records collected by federal agencies, including the right to correct or delete the records. When an agency requests an individual's Social Security number, it must inform the individual whether the disclosure is voluntary or mandatory, to what purposes the number will be used, and by what statutory authority the number is solicited. Social Security numbers may be collected under the Privacy Act if it is in conformity with other federal laws, including collection of tax and immigration information.

The Privacy Act does not protect the privacy of non-governmental records, such as bank statements, credit reports, and medical records (although these may be protected by state laws or other federal laws), and thus does not apply in disputes arising between private institutions, including credit card issuers and banks, and identity theft victims.

2. Driver's Privacy Protection Act

The Drivers Privacy Protection Act of 1994 (DPPA)[89] allows criminal and civil liability to be imposed upon any person who knowingly obtains, discloses, or otherwise uses personal information from motor vehicle records. The DPPA allows for a private cause of action to remedy violations. The

---

[89]   Pub. L. No. 103–322, 108 Stat. 2099 (1994) (codified as amended at 18 U.S.C. § 2721 *et seq.*).

plaintiff can recover actual damages, reasonable attorney fees, other litigation costs reasonably incurred, and other preliminary and equitable relief the court deems to be appropriate. The plaintiff can recover punitive damages upon showing proof of reckless or willful disregard of the law. A plaintiff can recover liquidated damages under the DPPA without having to prove actual damages, leaving the finding of an appropriate award to the court's discretion given the circumstances. Although Congress' express legislative intent was not to combat identity theft in passing the DPPA, some courts have allowed identity theft claims to proceed under that law.

A potential plaintiff under the DPPA is any individual whose personal information has been improperly obtained from a motor vehicle record. In *Margan v. Niles*, 250 F. Supp. 2d 63 (N.D.N.Y. 2003), a workers' compensation claimant learned he was being followed by private investigators. The subject obtained the license plate numbers of the investigators' cars. Then he asked a police officer, who happened to be his friend, to use a police database to gather information about the investigators, including their identities, addresses, and other identifying information. Upon receiving such information, the claimant began to harass the investigators and their families. The investigators and their family members were allowed to bring claims under the DPPA since their information had been obtained through the use of a police database.

3. Electronic Communications Privacy Act

The Electronic Communications Privacy Act of 1986 ("ECPA")[90] was enacted to regulate how the government and individuals obtain access to electronic communications and how these communications are kept and maintained by "electronic communications services" or by "remote computing services." The definition of electronic communications service under the ECPA includes any service that provides users "the ability to send and receive wire or electronic communications."[91] The entities regulated by the ECPA include internet service providers, banks, and telephone companies. The ECPA protects information stored by communication services by requiring the service provider to restrict access to only authorized individuals. If the information is in electronic storage, it is illegal for any person to read or alter the information unless one of the limited exemptions provided for under the statute applies.

There are three categories of information covered by the ECPA as stored electronic communication services: (1) subscriber information, (2) transaction records, and (3) actual content of communications. "Subscriber information" includes the subscriber's name, physical address, IP address, type of service, and method of payment. Subscriber information can be obtained via a subpoena without having to notify the account holder. The transaction records can be

---

[90]   Pub. L. No. 95–351, 82 Stat. 212 (1986) (codified at 18 U.S.C. § 2701 *et seq.*).

[91]   18 U.S.C. § 2510(15) (2012).

obtained through a court order. These records contain information pertaining to particular communications, but such records do not include the actual communications content. In order for the government to access transaction records, it must show reasonable grounds that the information sought is relevant to an ongoing criminal investigation.

The actual content of the communication may also be obtained, but stricter requirements must be met before access is granted. If the information has been in electronic storage for less than 180 days and is unopened, then the government must have a search warrant to access the information. The issuance of a search warrant requires the government to show probable cause that a crime has been committed and that evidence of the crime is contained in the contents of the information. The subscriber must be notified that the information is sought after, but a prosecutor can delay notification if permission is granted from the court. If the government seeks to delay the notification to the subscriber, it must show that the notification would endanger an individual's life, bring about the tampering or destruction of evidence, seriously jeopardize an investigation, or lead to the intimidation of witnesses. In a situation where the communication is older than 180 days and unopened, the government may access the information via a subpoena or court order, or by search warrant as well.

The ECPA's protections of privacy in the workplace are narrow. The ECPA has categorized communications in two ways: (1) stored communications, and (2) live communications. Electronic storage is defined as "any temporary or intermediate storage of wire or electronic communication incidental to the electronic transmission thereof."[92] While electronic communication is defined as "any transfer of signs, signals, writing, images, sounds, data, or intelligence of any nature, transported in whole or in part by wire, radio, electromagnetic, photoelectric, or photo-optical system."[93] An employer is not restricted from accessing stored communications. A number of courts have held that, even though an employer may not intercept an e-mail during its transmission, an employer may nevertheless access stored copies as it pleases.[94] This necessarily creates an exception that swallows the rule in numerous instances, as electronic communications are often automatically stored on a computer hard drive or server as part of the sending and receiving process.

An exception to the ECPA for monitoring of live communications exists if employees give consent to interception, and even if an employer does not seek their permission, such monitoring may still fall

---

[92]   18 U.S.C. § 2510(17).

[93]   18 U.S.C. § 2510(12).

[94]   *See*, *e.g.*, Wesley College v. Pitts, 974 F. Supp. 375, 377 (D. Del. 1997); United States v. Reyes, 922 F. Supp. 818, 836 (S.D.N.Y. 1996); Bohach v. Reno, 932 F. Supp. 1232, 1236–37 (D. Nev. 1996).

under an exception if the violation occurs during the ordinary course of business. Although an employee does retain a reasonable expectation of privacy in the workplace, the employer's interests in preventing illegal, disruptive, or inappropriate communications is typically considered to outweigh the employee's workplace privacy interests.

4. Children's Online Privacy Protection Act

The Children's Online Privacy Protection Act of 1998 (COPPA) was designed to protect children from unfair and deceptive acts in connection with the collection and use of personal information from and about children on the Internet by prohibiting the unauthorized online collection of personal information from children under age 13.[95] The FTC's final regulations implementing COPPA became effective on April 21, 2000.[96] COPPA's primary goals are to give parents control over what information is collected from their children online and how the information may be used.

COPPA applies to operators of: (1) commercial websites and online services directed at children under 13 that collect personal information from them; (2) general audience sites that knowingly collect personal information from children under 13 and; and (3) general audience sites that have a separate children's area and which collect personal

---

[95]   Pub. L. No. 105–277, 112 Stat. 2681 (1998) (codified at 15 U.S.C. § 6501 *et seq.*).

[96]   16 C.F.R. § 312 *et seq.* (2012).

information from children under 13.[97] In determining if a site is "directed at children" the FTC looks at the site based on subject matter, visual or audio content, age of models on the site, language, and if the site uses animated characters or other child-oriented features.

If a site qualifies as "directed at children" the act places numerous requirements on the site operator. First, it must post a privacy policy on the front page of the website and link to the privacy policy on every page where personal information is collected. The policy must describe the information collected. Second, the operator must provide notice about the site's information collection practices to parents and obtain verifiable parental consent before collecting personal information from children. Third, parents must be given a choice as to whether their child's personal information will be disclosed to third parties. Fourth, parents are to be given access to their child's personal information and the opportunity to delete that information and opt-out of future collection or use of the information. Fifth, the operator cannot condition a child's participation in a game, contest or other activity on the child's disclosure of more personal information than is reasonably necessary to participate in the activity. Finally, the operator must maintain the confidentiality, security, and integrity of personal information collected from children.[98] This can be a significant burden on operators because if they give

---

[97]   *Id.* at § 312.4(b).

[98]   *Id.* at § 312.3.

a child's personal information to a third party, they must have a procedure for recovering and deleting all such information, notwithstanding that it is no longer in their possession.

In order to encourage active industry self-regulation, COPPA also includes a safe harbor provision, which allows industry groups and others to request FTC approval of self-regulatory guidelines to govern the participating websites' compliance with the COPPA rules. If an operator can demonstrate full compliance with approved guidelines, that operator will be deemed to be in compliance with the regulations. Self-regulatory guidelines are those issued by representatives of the marketing or online industries or by others, who after notice and comment, are approved by the FTC. The regulations also detail the step-by-step procedure and criteria for approval of the guidelines.

5. Family Education Rights and Privacy Act

As the name suggests, the Family Education Rights and Privacy Act of 1974 (FERPA)[99] protects the privacy of student educational records. It applies to all schools that receive funds under applicable programs of the U.S. Department of Education, and these schools must comply to enjoy continued eligibility for funding. The rights under FERPA extend to parents until the student reaches the age of 18, whereupon the rights transfer to the student.

---

[99]   Pub. L. No. 93–380, 88 Stat. 484 (1974) (codified as amended at 20 U.S.C. § 1232g).

FERPA also governs how state agencies must transmit testing data to federal agencies.

FERPA allows parents to inspect their minor children's educational records. A student or parent may request that a school correct records they believe to be inaccurate or misleading. If the school refuses, the school must provide a formal hearing. If after the hearing, the student or parent is not satisfied, they have the right to put a dissenting statement into the student's record.

Under FERPA, schools must get written permission in order to release any information from a student's education record unless it is for:

1. School officials with a legitimate education interest;

2. Other schools to which a student is transferring;

3. Appropriate parties in connection with financial aid to a student;

4. Organizations conducting studies for or on behalf of the school;

5. Accrediting organizations;

6. By order of law;

7. Appropriate officials in cases of health and safety emergencies.

Schools can also give out "directory" information (name, address phone number, date of birth, and dates of attendance). Schools must give notice and afford the student or parent an opportunity to deny the release of such information. In addition, FERPA allows student records to be released to qualified persons, including school officials who have a reason to know the information, research organizations, federal and state education officials, and individuals with a lawful subpoena.[100]

6. E-Government Act

To ensure agency compliance with privacy laws and regulations, the E-Government Act was passed in 2002 requiring agencies to publish Privacy Impact Assessments (PIA).[101] Agencies are required to submit PIAs any time personal information is collected on ten or more people. Assessments must include what information is collected and why, how the information is used and secured, and with whom the information is shared.

D. SIGNIFICANT LEGISLATION WITH INCIDENTAL PRIVACY IMPACTS

In addition to statutory schemes expressly enacted, in whole or in part, for purposes of protecting personal privacy, numerous other Federal statutes impact individuals' privacy interests. The legislation discussed below is by no means a comprehensive list as the complexity of different statutory and regulatory schemes can have interactions with other statutes and regulations

---

[100]   20 U.S.C. § 1232g(b)(1) (2012).

[101]   Pub. L. No. 107–347, 116 Stat. 2899 (2002) (codified as amended in scattered sections of 5, 10, 13, 15, 18, 28, 31, 40, 41, and 44 U.S.C.).

that were not contemplated even by the legislators voting on the bills.

1. Freedom of Information Act

The Freedom of Information Act of 1966 (FOIA)[102] was passed to give the public access to information collected by federal government agencies. Under FOIA, an individual may request public information from an executive branch government agency and that agency is required to make a full disclosure, barring any applicable exemptions.

FOIA has nine exemptions, one of which protects privacy interests of individuals regarding their own sensitive personal information.[103] Information contained in medical, personal, or similar types of files is covered, for example. To determine if the personal identifying information exemption applies, the standard is whether the requested information includes information applicable to a particular individual. This is preliminarily determined by the agency that has been served the request. A court thereafter must determine if the release of the information would constitute a clearly unwarranted invasion of privacy, which turns on a balancing test weighing the individual's right to privacy against the basic policy of disclosing information under public request and scrutiny.

---

[102] Pub. L. No. 89–554, 80 Stat. 383 (1966) (codified as amended at 5 U.S.C. § 552).

[103] 5 U.S.C. § 552(b)(6) (2012).

2. Economic Espionage Act

The Economic Espionage Act of 1996 (EEA),[104] makes the theft or misappropriation of a trade secret a federal crime. It was passed to fill the void between existing federal and state laws, and as a general American economic protection initiative. The Department of Justice is responsible for regulating and enforcing the EEA. While "trade secrets" are usually thought of as chemical formulas or other scientific data, customer lists and personal information concerning customers are potentially protectable as a trade secret under the Act, although the power to enforce protection of that information is actually vested in the commercial entity that originally collected the information, rather in the individual customers themselves.

The EEA has two provisions that criminalize two types of activities. First, 18 U.S.C. § 1831 criminalizes the theft of trade secrets to benefit foreign powers. Second, 18 U.S.C. § 1832 criminalizes the theft of trade secrets for commercial or economic purposes. The two provisions differ in their target, and in the severity of the punishment. Section 1831 applies to someone who intends, or knows, that a violation will benefit any foreign government or agent. Under Section 1831, an individual can be fined up to $500,000 and imprisoned for up to 15 years, and businesses can be fined up to 10 million dollars. Section 1832 targets theft more generally, without specifying a foreign

---

[104] Pub. L. No. 194–294, 110 Stat. 3488 (1996) (codified at 18 U.S.C. § 1831 *et seq.*).

beneficiary. Under Section 1832, individuals can be fined up to $500,000 and imprisoned up to 10 years, and businesses can be fined $5 million.

The EEA has a very broad definition of a trade secret. Encompassed are thoughts and ideas in someone's head and purely oral communications; there is no requirement that the information be stored electronically or have been stolen in hardcopy form. This broad definition has serious implications for businesses that hire workers from competitors. The act punishes anyone who knowingly:

(1) steals, or without authorization appropriates takes, carries away, or conceals, or by fraud, artifice, or deception obtains a trade secret;

(2) without authorization copies, duplicates, sketches, draws, photographs, downloads, uploads, alters, destroys, photocopies, replicates, transmits, delivers, sends, mails, communicates, or conveys a trade secret; or

(3) receives, buys, or possesses a trade secret, knowing the same to have been stolen or appropriated, obtained, or converted without authorization.[105]

3. USA PATRIOT Act

Although the USA PATRIOT Act[106] was discussed above in regard to its impact on financial privacy,

---

[105]   18 U.S.C. § 1831 (2012).

[106]   Pub. L. No. 107–56, 115 Stat. 272 (2001) (codified as amended at scattered sections of 12, 15, 18, and 31 U.S.C.).

the Act contains numerous other provisions that also affect individual privacy. A complete examination of the Act's provisions is beyond this book's scope, but certain key sections with privacy implications include:

Section 105: Creates a "national network of electronic crimes task forces" to be set up by the Secret Service throughout the country to prevent, detect, and investigate various electronic crimes "including potential terrorist attacks against critical infrastructures and financial payment systems"—which encompasses a wide variety of computer crimes.

Section 203: Requires information sharing, including previously secret grand jury testimony, between any number of federal agencies, so long as the information involves "foreign intelligence." The broad definition of that term found in the Foreign Intelligence Surveillance Act (FISA) includes the following: "information, whether or not concerning a United States person, with respect to a foreign power or foreign territory that relates to the national defense or the security of the United States or the conduct of the foreign affairs of the United States." This information, which is in the possession of any federal investigative or law enforcement officer or attorney can be shared, without any court review or involvement, with any other federal "law enforcement, intelligence, protective, immigration, national defense, or national security official."

Section 212: Provides for voluntary and required disclosures to federal investigators by firms such as Internet service providers.

Section 218: Changes the scope of warrants under FISA from foreign intelligence being "a significant purpose" to "a purpose" of the investigation and so lowers the standard for obtaining a FISA warrant. Note that an investigation under FISA even though it usually involves foreign nationals or aliens does not have to be so restricted, and can include United States citizens under the broad definition of "foreign intelligence."

Section 403: Mandates a dramatic new information system to allow State Department access to certain criminal files kept by the FBI, such as National Crime Information Center (NCIC) files. NCIC is a computerized index of criminal justice information. It provides authorized agencies with information such as criminal record histories, fugitives, stolen properties, and missing persons.

Sections 507 and 508: Allow government investigators access to educational records, without a court order.

4. Federal Information Security Management Act

The Federal Information Security Management Act of 2002 (FISMA) was designed to protect the information systems of the federal government.[107] Government agencies and contractors must establish a security program to improve and protect the information systems. These security programs must include the creation of security procedures and policies, annual reporting to Congress, security safeguard implementation, and continuous evaluations. While not specifically directed at the protection of individuals' privacy, the fact that government agencies maintain databases replete with personal information and which are frequently the target of identity thieves or other criminals, means that the benefits of increased security for these databases will accrue at least in part to the individuals whose personal information is stored therein.

E.   FEDERAL AGENCIES

Numerous federal agencies are tasked with policing the statutory schemes discussed above, both externally and internally. A complete review of these agencies and their respective privacy law enforcement duties is beyond the scope of this Nutshell. Instead, in this section we will examine two agencies, which in many ways represent the outer limits of external and internal privacy regulation: the Federal Trade Commission (FTC), which is the primary enforcer of many federal privacy laws, and the Department of Homeland Security (DHS), which must work to balance its

---

[107]   Pub. L. No. 107–347, 116 Stat. 2899 (2002) (codified as amended in scattered sections of 15, 40, and 44 U.S.C.).

mission of collecting information essential for national security with traditional American concerns regarding concentration of surveillance powers.

1. The Federal Trade Commission

Privacy is a key element of the FTC's consumer protection mission. Advances in computer technology have made it possible for detailed information about individuals to be compiled and shared more easily than ever. These advances have resulted in many benefits for both society as a whole and individual consumers. Yet, as personal information is more frequently transmitted and becomes more accessible, steps to prevent and protect against the misuse of this information become more important at every stage of a transaction.

Congress established the FTC as the primary agency responsible for protecting consumers and preserving competition between businesses, while curbing the worst abuses of the free market.[108] To these ends, the FTC investigates reports of unfair competition and deceptive trade practices. The main tool provided to the FTC for this purpose is Section 5 of the Federal Trade Commission Act ("FTCA," codified as 15 U.S.C. § 45), but the FTC also has the power to promulgate quasi-legislative regulations and quasi-judicial orders addressing more specific issues within the scope of its Section 5 authority.

---

[108]   Federal Trade Commission Act, Pub. L. No. 63–203, 38 Stat. 717 (1914) (codified as amended at 15 U.S.C. §§ 41 to 58).

Additionally, due to its status as the Federal government's primary defender of consumers' interests, Congress has also vested it with authority to enforce many specific pieces of privacy legislation enacted in recent years.

a. Section 5 of the FTCA

Section 5 of the FTCA was intended to permit a flexible approach to regulating business practices.[109] As a result, Section 5 avoids the approach of some consumer protection legislative schemes which attempt to exhaustively list what constitutes a "deceptive" or "unfair" trade practice in favor of the simple statement, "Unfair methods of competition in or affecting commerce, and unfair or deceptive acts or practices in or affecting commerce, are hereby declared unlawful."[110] The FTC is therefore "empowered and directed to prevent persons, partnerships, or corporations . . . from using unfair methods of competition in or affecting commerce and unfair or deceptive acts or practices in or affecting commerce," except for certain types of businesses which are separately regulated by other Federal agencies, such as financial institutions.[111] Section 5 does not, however, extend to export trade with foreign nations unless the unfair methods of competition employed against foreign competitors or consumers also injure U.S. consumers or businesses

---

[109] *See* FTC v. Sperry & Hutchinson Co., 405 U.S. 233, 239–40 (1972).

[110] 15 U.S.C. § 45(a)(1) (2012).

[111] *Id.* at § 45(a)(2).

or "involve material conduct occurring within the United States."[112]

The FTC was also authorized to provide a wide range of remedies for Section 5 violations. The most typical remedy is a cease-and-desist order, which enjoins the illegal conduct and prohibits future violations. Other remedies include "fencing-in," which involves the FTC not only entering a cease-and-desist order regarding a specific practice or product, but also covering related practices or products so as to prevent the sanctioned party from circumventing the FTC's action. Corrective advertising to rectify misleading impressions created by earlier false advertising, redress to injured consumers, and civil penalties may also be assessed.

In extreme circumstances, the FTC may order a "sweep" of an entire industry based on pervasive unfair trade practices. The FTC's 2008 "Operation Clean Sweep," for example, was aimed at credit repair organizations that deceptively claimed they could remove negative information from consumers' credit reports for a fee even if that information was accurate and timely. That sweep resulted in thirty six separate legal actions filed in twenty two different states.[113]

---

[112]   *Id.* at § 45(a)(3), (4).

[113]   Press Release, FTC, 'Operation Clean Sweep': FTC and State Agencies Target 36 'Credit Repair' Operations (Oct. 23, 2008), *available at* http://www.ftc.gov/opa/2008/10/opcleansweep. shtm.

b. The Evolution of the Unfairness Doctrine

Congress left it to the FTC and courts to determine how to define "unfair" in the context of Section 5. This has led to a gradual expansion of the definition of what constitutes unfair competition. Originally, Section 5 only specifically proscribed "unfair methods of competition," and thus it was understood that the FTC's main concern was protecting competitors and preventing the formation or abuse of monopoly power. Yet it did not take long before the FTC began to interpret the language of the FTCA to permit an emphasis on consumer protection. As early as 1916, in the *Circle Cilk Co.* decision, 1 F.T.C. 13 (1916), the FTC entered a cease-and-desist order based on practices found to have "deceived some of the consuming public." *Id.* at 15. Originally, the FTC indicated that a finding of actual deception was necessary,[114] but by 1919, the FTC expanded the scope of unfair competition to include a mere "tendency" to deceive.[115]

The courts, however, acted to limit the FTC's efforts to expand the range of conduct it could punish. In *FTC v. Gratz*, 253 U.S. 421 (1920), the first U.S. Supreme Court decision to address the scope of the FTC's authority under Section 5, the Court found that the term "unfair methods of competition" did not reach "practices never heretofore regarded as opposed to good morals

---

[114]   Circle Cilk Co., 1 F.T.C. 13, 19 (1916); *see also* Geographical Publ'g Co., 1 F.T.C. 235, 239 (1918) (finding intentional deception).

[115]   Gordon Van Tine Co., 1 F.T.C. 316 (1919).

because characterized by deception, bad faith, fraud or oppression, or as against public policy because of their dangerous tendency unduly to hinder competition or create monopoly." *Id.* at 427. Eleven years later, in *FTC v. Raladam Co.*, the Supreme Court held that for conduct to be punishable under Section 5 the conduct must have injured, or have the tendency to injure, an actual or potential competitor or competition generally and that consumer injury alone was insufficient.[116] The Court noted that public interest is only one part of the analysis the FTC must consider before issuing a cease-and-desist order.

Congress responded to the *Raladam* decision by passing the Wheeler-Lea Act amending Section 5(a)(1) to apply to both unfair competition and deceptive acts or practices.[117] This clarified that the FTC's jurisdiction extended to the protection of consumers without needing to consider whether the conduct could also be considered anticompetitive. The FTC broadly defined the term "deceptive" as any act or practice that has the tendency to mislead a substantial amount of the consuming public in a material way. As the Second Circuit Court of Appeals explained in affirming an FTC order against a skin cream manufacturer, the "fact that a false statement may be obviously false to those who are trained and experienced does not change its character, nor take away its power to deceive others

---

[116]   FTC v. Raladam Co., 283 U.S. 643, 652–654 (1931).

[117]   Wheeler-Lea Act of 1938, Pub L. No. 75–447, 52 Stat. 111 (1938) (codified as amended at 15 U.S.C. §§ 45 to 57).

less experienced. The important criterion is the net impression which the advertisement is likely to make upon the general populace."[118] The FTC also found favor with the courts on the question of whether representations with the capacity or tendency to deceive are sufficient to find a Section 5 violation.[119] As one court explained, "since the purpose of the statute is not to punish the wrongdoer but to protect the public, the cardinal factor is the probable effect which the advertiser's handiwork will have upon the eye and mind of the reader."[120] This was drawn from the conclusion that the main purpose of the Wheeler-Lea Act's amendment to Section 5 of the FTCA was to give "to the consumer the right to rely upon representations of facts as the truth."[121]

During the 1960s, the FTC continued its jurisdictional expansion. In 1964, it issued the "Cigarette Rule," which became the first of several policy statements to provide a better understanding of what constituted an unfair act or practice.[122] The

---

[118] Charles of the Ritz Distribs. Corp. v. FTC, 143 F.2d 676, 679–80 (2d Cir. 1944) (internal quotation marks and citations omitted).

[119] See FTC v. Sterling Drug, Inc., 317 F.2d 669 (2d Cir. 1963).

[120] Id. at 674.

[121] See In re Pfizer, Inc., 81 F.T.C. 23 (1972).

[122] Statement of Basis and Purpose of Trade Regulation Rule 408, Unfair or Deceptive Advertising and Labeling of Cigarettes in Relation to the Health Hazards of Smoking, 29 Fed. Reg. 8325, 8355 (July 2, 1964). The regulation was preempted by the Federal Cigarette Labeling and Advertising Act, Pub. L. No. 89–92, 79 Stat. 283 (1965) (codified as amended at 15 U.S.C. §§ 1331–1340).

FTC gave three criteria to consider when investigating possible unfair acts or practices: (1) whether the practice offends established public policy concepts of unfairness; (2) whether it is immoral, unethical, oppressive, or unscrupulous; and (3) whether it causes substantial injury to consumers or competitors. All three elements did not have to be satisfied and a practice could be determined to be unfair based on a sufficiently severe infraction of one of the elements. The U.S. Supreme Court affirmed this approach in *FTC v. Sperry & Hutchinson Co.*, 405 U.S. 233, 244 (1972), holding that Section 5 empowered the FTC to proscribe practices as unfair or deceptive regardless of their effect on competition because Section 5 "considers public values beyond simply those enshrined in the letter or encompassed in the spirit of the antitrust laws."

c. The 1980s: The Halt of FTCA Section 5 Jurisdictional Expansion

By the late 1970s and early 1980s, public policy began placing increased emphasis on free markets as efficient and self-correcting means of regulating business behavior, while mergers were viewed as expanding business and creating growth benefiting the overall economy. Courts, following influential scholarship from a variety of sources that hybridized traditional legal and economic principles, also increasingly agreed that antitrust and other forms of market regulation imposed substantial costs on the American economy. Meanwhile, Congress was expressing growing apprehension over the FTC's aggressive pursuit of alleged Section 5 violators, and began to take steps to pass legislation that would have sharply reduced the FTC's discretion in defining unfair and deceptive practices. To respond to these pressures and head off congressional action, the FTC introduced two key policy statements in the early 1980s that were designed as a form of self-restraint and which led to a significant decrease in FTC Section 5 actions.

(i) The Unfairness Policy Statement, 1980

In the 1980 "Unfairness" Policy Statement (Unfairness Statement), the FTC changed its approach to the unfairness doctrine from the moral and ethical concepts emphasized by the "Cigarette Rule" and the *Sperry & Hutchinson* decision to one based on a cost-benefit analysis. The Unfairness Statement set forth that a practice is unfair if: (1) it causes substantial consumer injury as monetary harm; (2) the injury is not outweighed by benefits to the consumer or to competition; and (3) the injury caused by practice could not be reasonably avoided by the consumer. The Statement narrowed the effective scope of Section 5 by adding the need for "substantial" consumer injury; adopting a cost-benefit analysis which included weighing the harm against competitive benefits; and by limiting public policy to only "clear and well-established" statements.[123]

---

[123] Letter from Michael Pertschuk, FTC Chairman, to Sens. Wendell H. Ford & John C. Danforth (Dec. 17, 1980). Congress codified the Unfairness Statement in 1994. *See* Pub. L. No. 103–

(ii) The Deception Policy Statement, 1983

In 1983, the FTC issued another policy statement (the "Deception Statement"); this time limiting what constitutes "deceptive" conduct by defining it as a material representation, omission, or practice that is likely to mislead a reasonable consumer to that consumer's detriment.[124] The FTC defined an act or practice as material if it is "likely to affect a consumer's conduct or decision with regard to a product or service." A "reasonable consumer" is defined by the circumstances of each case, but in any event, it does not automatically equate to a majority of consumers, because a practice may still be deceptive if it "misleads a significant minority of reasonable consumers." The deception must be material, although there is no requirement that the manufacturer intended any deception or that anyone was actually deceived or injured.

d. Unfair Competition in the Internet Age: Protecting Privacy

Although the FTC still operates under the constraints of the Unfair and Deception Statements, it began to find new vigor during the Internet boom of the late 1990s. The growth of online commerce, which often involves consumers engaging in transactions with parties that they have little or no prior business relationship with, stimulated both a

---

312, § 9, 108 Stat 1691, 1695 (1994) (codified as 15 U.S.C. § 45(n)).

[124]   Letter from James C. Miller, III, FTC Chairman, to Rep. John D. Dingell (Oct. 14, 1983).

quantitative and qualitative change in the types of unfair and deceptive practices unscrupulous individuals could engage in. As consumer deception online typically features victims and perpetrators located in different states or even different nations, the FTC naturally found itself obliged to play a greater role in such investigations. The Commission has shown major concern over a few areas of the internet including misrepresentations of how information is collected and used including violations of company privacy policies, consumer fraud including deceptive advertising and marketing, inadequate security measures to avoid security breaches, and COPPA violations.

The FTC generally supported industry self-regulation as the primary means of addressing online privacy concerns. As the FTC itself explained in a report to Congress, "Self-regulation is the least intrusive way and most efficient to ensure fair information practices, given the rapidly evolving nature of the Internet and computer technology."[125] Self-regulation avoids the heavy burdens of cost and inflexibility of government regulations, and the FTC has expressed concern that overly formalizing privacy standards through the bureaucratic process could stunt technological growth and market development. To this end, the FTC mostly relied on industry organizations to adopt their own codes of conduct or best practices for the first several years of the Internet's growth. With the growth of e-

---

[125] *See Self-Regulation and Privacy Online: A Report to Congress*, FTC 6 (July 1, 1999).

commerce and corresponding fears about the security of consumers' personal data, however, in recent years the FTC has begun to more actively use its authority to protect consumers under Section 5.

Early enforcement actions concerning privacy or personal data on the internet stemmed principally from consumer deception. The first major case the FTC brought concerning Internet privacy was in 1998 against the operators of the GeoCities online community.[126] Although GeoCities had a posted privacy policy which stated that it distributed users' personal information to third parties on only an opt-in basis, evidence suggested that GeoCities was in fact selling or otherwise disseminating its users' personal information without their knowledge. Furthermore, to be able to access certain parts of the website, users were required to provide personal information through forms that suggested GeoCities was handling the information, when in fact the users' information was being directly collected by third parties, which had partnered with GeoCities. The following year, GeoCities settled with the FTC, and agreed to the entry of a consent order prohibiting GeoCities from making further misrepresentations and required the company to post notice of their informational practices. GeoCities was further ordered to revise its privacy policy to accurately reflect how it uses data collected through the website and also ordered it to contact

---

[126] *See Analysis of Proposed Consent Order to Aid Public Comment*, FTC (Aug. 1998), http://www.ftc.gov/os/1998/08/9823015.ana.htm.

all individuals it had collected personal information from to give them the option to have their collected data deleted.[127]

In response to the concerns raised by the *GeoCities* case, the FTC began to demonstrate increased skepticism toward self-regulation. Whereas only two years earlier the FTC had praised self-regulation, in 2000 the Commission stated that due to the fact that "self-regulatory initiatives to date fall far short of broad-based implementation of effective self-regulatory programs, the Commission has concluded that such efforts alone cannot ensure that the online marketplace as a whole will emulate the standards adopted by industry leaders."[128] The FTC reasoned that a company's privacy policy should be easily accessible and understandable so that the consumer is aware of what information is being collected and how the information is used. The FTC also stressed that companies take appropriate steps to ensure the security and integrity of the collected information. The FTC concluded that most consumers do not realize that companies were collecting and using their personal information. To rectify this situation while awaiting specific legislation from Congress, the FTC began to place greater emphasis on what it termed the "Fair Information Practice Principles" to provide guidance to companies that were collecting personal

---

[127]   *See In re* Geocities, 127 F.T.C. 94 (Feb. 5, 1999).

[128]   *Privacy Online: Fair Information Practices in Electronic Marketplace*, FTC ii–iii (May 2000), http://www.ftc.gov/reports/privacy2000/privacy2000.pdf.

information.[129] The "Fair Information Practice Principles" were first articulated by the FTC in 1998 and were modeled on the OECD's privacy guidelines. In 2000, the FTC included four core principles: Notice, Choice, Access, and Security. The Principles were updated in 2012 to add a fifth principle-Enforcement. The Principles are defined by the FTC as:

1. Notice: those collecting data must disclose their information practices before collecting it from consumers;

2. Choice: consumers must be given options if and how their personal info may be used for other purposes;

3. Access: consumers should be able to access and correct data collected about them;

4. Security: data collectors must take reasonable steps to assure info collected from consumers is secure from public use; and

5. Enforcement: the core principles of privacy protection can only be effective through enforcement mechanisms including: industry self-regulation, the creation of private rights of action, and government enforcement through civil and criminal penalties.[130]

In addition to the Principles, in March 2012, the FTC issued a final report on the best practices for

---

[129]   *Id.*

[130]   *Fair Information Practice Principles*, FTC (Nov. 23, 2012).

businesses in order to protect consumer privacy.[131] The recommendations in the current report are an expansion of a December 2010 staff report. The 2012 report provides three specific recommendations for companies that use consumer data to include:

1. Privacy by Design: companies should incorporate privacy protections for consumers at each stage of product development;

2. Simplified Consumer Choice: companies should provide consumers with the option to decide what information is shared about them, and with whom; and

3. Transparency: companies should disclose details about the collection and use of consumers' information, as well as providing access to that data.[132]

In 2001, the FTC further committed itself to greater use of its Section 5 powers to attack practices that compromise consumers' privacy online by using both its deception and unfairness standards. Under this more aggressive standard, a company's violation of its own privacy policy is considered by the FTC to be an unfair and deceptive practice. Likewise, the FTC has increasingly

---

[131] Protecting Consumer Privacy in an Era of Rapid Change, FTC (Mar. 2012), http://www.ftc.gov/os/2012/03/120326 privacyreport.pdf.

[132] Press Release, FTC, FTC Issues Final Commission Report on Protecting Consumer Privacy (Mar. 26, 2012), *available at* http://www.ftc.gov/opa/2012/03/privacyframework. shtm.

pursued Section 5 violations pertaining to privacy when a company makes affirmative misrepresentations in collecting information, and particularly when such information is collected from children. As part of this effort, the FTC uses the Fair Information Practice Principles as its guide.

The FTC's pursuit of an action against Gateway Learning Corp.[133] is an example of this stepped up enforcement. Gateway was a seller of popular educational materials and products for children. Its privacy policy represented that it did not sell, rent, loan, or otherwise disclose personal information that it collected from its customers. Notwithstanding this policy, Gateway leased information to third parties without disclosing to its customers that it was doing so. Gateway then altered its privacy policy on a retroactive basis to state that it was entitled to disclose personal information to third parties, but again failed to notify its existing customers of the change despite the fact that its posted privacy policy stated that Gateway would provide notice of any material changes in the terms of the policy.[134]

The FTC commenced an enforcement action on the grounds that this behavior constituted both deceptive and unfair trade practices. As set forth in the FTC's complaint, the dissemination of personal

---

[133] *In re* Gateway Learning Corp., No. C–4120, 2004 WL 2618647 (Sept. 10, 2004), *available at* http://www.ftc.gov/os/caselist/0423047/040917do0423047.pdf.

[134] *Analysis of Proposed Consent Order to Aid Public Comment*, FTC (Jul. 7, 2004), http://www.ftc.gov/os/caselist/0423047/040707anl0423047.pdf.

information to third parties in violation of the published privacy policy constituted a form of deceptive trade practice, while the retroactive amendment of the policy was an unfair practice.[135] The FTC and Gateway ultimately settled the action with Gateway being required to disgorge the profits it had earned from improperly sharing its customers' information and to agree not to disclose previously collected customer information, or to alter its privacy policy retroactively, without express affirmative consent from the customers.

The FTC has further expanded its Section 5 powers to tackle unfair and deceptive trade practices in social networking. The FTC's pursuit of an action against Google Inc. is an example of the FTC's attempt to keep pace with advancing technology. Google Inc. is a leading internet search engine and web-based email provider, and in 2010, launched its own social network, Google Buzz through its Gmail web-based email product.[136] Social networking is comprised of online communities of people who use dedicated websites to communicate with other site members by: posting messages, videos, and photographs on user-created personalized pages. Google led Gmail users to believe that users could choose to accept or decline membership in the social network. However, some

---

[135] Complaint at 5, *In re* Gateway Learning Co., No. C–4120, 2004   WL   2618647   (Sept.   10,   2004),   *available   at* http://www.ftc.gov/os/caselist/0423047/040707cmp0423047.pdf.

[136] Press Release, FTC, FTC Charges Deceptive Privacy Practices in Google's Rollout of Its Buzz Social Network (Mar. 30, 2011), *available at* http://www.ftc.gov/opa/2011/03/google.shtm.

of the users who declined were partially enrolled. The FTC alleged that those who voluntarily joined were inadequately informed about the potential of personal information disclosures. Google received thousands of complaints from users and consumers who were concerned about public disclosure of their email contacts.

The FTC charged Google with using deceptive tactics, and violating its own privacy promises to consumers. As part of its settlement agreement with the FTC, Google agreed to obtain users' consent before sharing user information with third parties, it would undergo audits every two years over a period of twenty years to assess its privacy and data protection practices, and implement a comprehensive privacy program to protect the privacy of consumers' information.[137] This was the first time an FTC settlement order required a company to implement a comprehensive privacy program for consumer protection.

(i) Misrepresentations in collecting personal information

Although this discussion has mainly focused on the FTC's activities concerning privacy issues online, it bears mention that even before the Internet, the FTC found that a company had acted both deceptively and unfairly in collecting consumers' personal privacy. In the case of *In re Metromedia, Inc.*, 78 F.T.C. 331 (1971), a company

---

[137]   *Id.*

sent consumers a form letter with a questionnaire that could be returned in exchange for the opportunity to be eligible for prizes. The company claimed the letter was sent to find out people's habits and characteristics and assured them that no salesperson would call and that there was nothing to buy. The FTC found that the company violated Section 5 by failing to disclose that the real purpose for collecting the information was to compile and sell mailing lists to third parties.[138] The FTC stressed the importance of the consumers' interest in privacy, noting that most consumers prefer that their names not be placed on mailing lists because they feel it is an invasion of personal privacy being subject to advertisers.

(ii) Protecting children

As discussed above in Chapter 3, Part II.C.4, Congress enacted the Children's Online Privacy Protection Act (COPPA) in 2000 to protect the personal information of children under the age of 13.[139] Under COPPA, both the state attorneys general and the FTC can bring enforcement actions.[140] The FTC has the right to intervene in any action brought under the statute by a state attorney general.[141] To implement its enforcement regime for COPPA, the FTC promulgated the

---

[138]   *In re* Metromedia, Inc., 78 F.T.C. 331, 337 (1971).

[139]   15 U.S.C. § 6501–06 (2012).

[140]   *Id.* at §§ 6502(c), 6504(a)(1).

[141]   *Id.* at § 6504(b)(1).

Children's Online Privacy Protection Rule (COPPR), also discussed above.[142]

Although some critics have suggested that COPPA has not been effective because of surveys that suggest most businesses which would be subject to the statute are not in compliance, there is little doubt that the FTC has sought sizeable penalties in those instances where it has brought enforcement actions under the statute. In 2006, the FTC settled a COPPA enforcement action against the social networking website Xanga.com for $1 million dollars.[143] The FTC had alleged that Xanga.com knowingly allowed minors to sign up for services on the site without parental consent. Although Xanga.com had a stated policy that children under the age of 13 were not allowed to join the site, all children had to do to join was to check a box confirming they were over 13 even if they had entered a birth date showing otherwise.

In 2011, the FTC settled the largest civil penalty for a COPPA enforcement action against Playdom Inc., a developer and operator of online multi-player games, for $3 million dollars.[144] Playdom acquired online websites specifically directed to children as

---

[142]   16 C.F.R. § 312 (2012).

[143]   United States v. Xanga.com, Inc., No. 06–CIV–6853(SHS) (S.D.N.Y. filed Sept. 7, 2006), *available at* http://www.ftc.gov/os/caselist/0623073/xangaconsentdecree.pdf.

[144]   Press Release, FTC, Operators of Online "Virtual Worlds" to Pay $3 Million to Settle FTC Charges That They Illegally Collected and Disclosed Children's Personal Information (May 12, 2011), *available at* http://www.ftc.gov/opa/2011/05/playdom.shtm.

well as general websites that attracted large numbers of children. However, the acquired websites did not comply with COPPA regulations. The FTC alleged that Playdom illegally collected and disclosed personal information from hundreds of thousands of children under age thirteen without their parents' prior consent, in violation of COPPA. Additionally, Playdom's privacy policy misrepresented that the company would prohibit children under age thirteen from posting personal information online. The large monetary sanction against Playdom represents the FTC's commitment to deterring COPPA violations while at the same time safeguarding children's personal information.

(iii) Spyware

So-called "spyware," and its associated privacy implications, have been an increasing concern for the FTC. The FTC defines spyware as "software that aids in gathering information about a person or organization without their knowledge and which may send such information to another entity without the consumer's consent, or that asserts control over a computer without the consumer's knowledge."[145]

The FTC has successfully pursued a number of Section 5 enforcement actions related to spyware in recent years. In 2006, for example, the FTC settled

---

[145]   Federal Trade Commission, Public Workshop: Monitoring Software on Your PC: Spyware, Adware, and Other Software, 69 Fed. Reg. 8538 (Feb. 24, 2004).

two spyware cases,[146] for a combined judgment of $3.61 million. In both cases, the FTC had alleged that companies covertly placed software on web users' computers by exploiting security defects in their Internet browsers. The primary manifestation of the spyware in both instances were "pop-ups," advertisements that appear in new browser windows over the user's original screen, and redirection of users to commercial websites. The software also collected personal information from the users' machines, including web surfing habits and passwords entered online.

In 2010, the FTC settled a case against CyberSpy Software, LLC., a spyware company, which advertised and sold a keylogging software program.[147] According to the FTC, the software tracked and "recorded every keystroke typed on an infected computer; captured images of the computer screen; obtained passwords, and recorded Web sites visited." The FTC complaint alleged that the spyware program was advertised and sold as being "100% undetectable" in that the program could be disguised in an ordinary email or file attachment and once opened, the program would download and install onto the users' computer without the users' knowledge or consent. The final order required the company to cease advertising that their software could be concealed and installed onto a third party's

---

[146] FTC v. Odysseus Mktg., Inc., No. 05–CV–00330–SM (D.N.H. Oct. 24, 2006); FTC v. Seismic Entertainment Prods., Inc., No. 04–CV–00377–JD (D.N.H. Mar. 22, 2006).

computer without that operator's knowledge. Additionally, the company was required to inform purchasers of the legal ramifications of improper use of the software and remove remaining versions of the software from previously installed computers.

(iv) Malware

In addition to spyware, malicious software or "malware" has become an increasing concern for the FTC. Such software damages a computer or network of computers through the use of: viruses, spyware, and worms that have the ability to pilfer personal information, send spam, and commit fraudulent transactions without the consumer's knowledge or consent. The FTC has successfully used its Section 5 enforcement powers against malware distributors over the past few years.

In 2010, the FTC used its section 5 powers to permanently shut down internet service provider 3FN.[148] The FTC charged 3FN with actively recruiting and colluding with criminals to distribute illegal, harmful, spyware and malware programs that compromised thousands of computers. The FTC complaint further alleged that the company protected its clientele by "either ignoring take-down requests issued by the online security community, or shifting its criminal elements to other Internet protocol addresses it controlled to evade detection." The FTC determined that 3FN's actions harmed

---

[148] Press Release, FTC, FTC Permanently Shuts Down Notorious Rogue Internet Service Provider (May 19, 2010), *available at* http://www.ftc.gov/opa/2010/05/perm.shtm.

consumers, was an unfair trade practice, and its operation violated federal law. In addition to ceasing operations, the company was required to turn over to the FTC $1.08 million dollars in ill-gotten profits.[149]

Thieves, preying on consumers' fears about malware, have created financially-lucrative schemes to fraudulently induce customers into purchasing, "scareware," unnecessary software to remove non-existent malware. Notably, in 2012, the FTC pursued an enforcement action against a syndicate that used computer scareware pop-ups and online advertisements to scam consumers into believing that their computers were infected with malware and then sold them software for $40 to $60 to remedy the fictional problem.[150] This ruse conned more than one million consumers into purchasing unnecessary software. At the request of the FTC, the U.S. District Court for the District of Maryland imposed a judgment of more than $163 million on the final defendant in the case. As part of the settlement, the defendant was permanently barred from selling computer security software, and forbidden from taking part in any form of deceptive marketing.

---

[149] FTC v. Pricewert LLC., No. C-09- 2407 RMW, 2010 WL 2105670 (N.D. Cal. Apr. 8, 2010), *available at* http://www.ftc.gov/os/caselist/0923148/100408pricewertorder-det.pdf.

[150] Press Release, FTC, FTC Case Results in $163 Million Judgment Against "Scareware" Marketer (Oct. 2, 2012), *available at* http://www.ftc.gov/news-events/press-releases/2012/10/ftc-case-results-163-million-judgment-against-scareware-marketer.

(v) Inadequate security: expanding FTC jurisdiction

The FTC has used deception standards to bring enforcement actions against companies for failing to provide information security consistent with the companies' public representations regarding security, or for not following their own privacy policies. But after several major breaches of computer databases in 2005, the FTC began bringing enforcement actions pursuant to its ability to prosecute unfair trade practices against companies that were failing to provide reasonable and adequate security, even without having made false representations to their customers or other parties.[151]

In early 2006, the FTC settled with ChoicePoint, a data mining company, for a $10 million penalty and $5 million for compensation to injured customers after the company sold personal information on over 150,000 individuals to people with ties to identity theft rings.[152] The FTC concluded that ChoicePoint did not have reasonable procedures for ascertaining what purpose its

---

[151] Thomas J. Smedinghoff, *The Challenge of Electronic Data: Corporate Legal Obligations to Provide Information Security*, 10 NO. 3 WALLSTREETLAWYER.COM: SEC. ELEC. AGE 1 (2006).

[152] Jason Krause, *Stolen Lives*, 92 MAR A.B.A. J. 36, 38 (2006); Evan Perez & Rich Brooks, *File Sharing: For Big Vendor of Personal Data, A Theft Lays Bare the Downside*, WALL ST. J., May 3, 2005, at A1. *See also* Bob Sullivan, *Database Giant Gives Access to Fake Firms*, NBC (Feb. 14, 2005, 6:38 PM), http://msnbc.msn.com/id/6969799.

customers intended to use the personal information for. The FTC was able to identify over 1,400 consumers who had experienced an out-of-pocket loss due to ChoicePoint's inadequate security measures.[153] The settlement bars ChoicePoint from selling personal information without taking reasonable precautions to ensure that the information is only provided to customers with lawful purposes in mind.

Several other companies experienced security breaches around this same time, causing heightened concern for consumer privacy and leading to yet further FTC scrutiny.[154] CardSystems Solutions, Inc. settled with the FTC in 2006 on charges for failure to use appropriate security measures to protect sensitive information of millions of consumers.[155] The FTC found the breach of CardSystems' database resulted in millions of dollars of fraudulent charges. FTC determined that the company did not adequately manage its security practices and failed to prevent unauthorized access to its database. CardSystems was required to implement a formal security program that met certain minimum guarantees and agree to third-

---

[153]   United States v. ChoicePoint, Inc., No. 1:06-cv-00198-JTC (N.D. Ga. Feb. 15, 2006), *available at* http://www.ftc.gov/os/caselist/choicepoint/stipfinaljudgement.pdf.

[154]   *See Chronology of Data Breaches: Security Breaches 2005–Present*, PRIVACY RIGHTS CLEARINGHOUSE, http://www.privacyrights.org/data-breach (last updated Nov. 12, 2013).

[155]   *CardSystems Solutions Settles FTC Charges*, FTC (Feb. 23, 2006), http://www.ftc.gov/opa/2006/02/cardsystems_r.htm.

party audits of its privacy practices every other year for 20 years.

Also in 2006, the FTC ordered Qchex, an online checking company, to stop its business practice of e-mailing personal checks without first verifying the identity of the maker of each check.[156] The FTC commenced the investigation after receiving over 600 consumer complaints claiming Qchex had fraudulently withdrawn money from their accounts, as well as at least twenty fraudulent checks processed by Qchex that were drawn on the FTC and Federal Communications Commission's own accounts.[157] The FTC argued that by not requiring identity authentication before sending the checks, the company committed an unfair trade practice in violation of Section 5 of the FTCA.[158] The checks did not have to be signed and were instead stamped "signature not required" which allowed users to write fraudulent checks.

Guidance Software, Inc. also settled with the FTC in late 2006 for failing to use reasonable security measures to protect consumer data and for not

---

[156]   Press Release, FTC, Court Halts Illegal Operations of Online Check Processing Firm (Oct. 2, 2006), *available at* http:// www.ftc.gov/news-events/press-releases/2006/10/court-halts-illegal-operations-online-check-processing-firm.

[157]   Bob Sullivan, *Targeted in Online Check Scam, FTC Sues*, NBC (Sept. 25, 2006, 5:43 PM), http://www.msnbc.msn.com/id/ 14995196/.

[158]   Complaint, FTC v. Neovi, Inc., No. 3:06–cv–01952–WQH-JMA (S.D. Cal. filed Sept. 19, 2006), *available at* http://www. ftc.gov/os/caselist/0523155/060919neovicmplt.pdf.

following its own privacy policy.[159] Guidance's inadequate security measures allowed hackers to obtain credit card information from thousands of customers. The settlement requires Guidance to implement a security program and to be subject to biannual third-party audits. This was the FTC's fourteenth challenge against companies for unreasonable data security measures in handling sensitive consumer data.

The FTC is active in data security breach cases where consumer information is compromised. In June 2012, the FTC filed a complaint against Wyndham Worldwide Corporation for failing to protect consumers' information, resulting in three separate data breaches in less than two years.[160] The FTC complaint alleges that Wyndham failed to take adequate security measures including: a failure to use complex user IDs and passwords, firewalls, and permitting improper software configurations resulting in the storage of unencrypted credit card information. These lapses in security protocols allowed intruders to access the company's corporate network and led to the compromise of more than 500,000 payment card accounts. Following this initial breach, Wyndham failed to remedy its

---

[159] Press Release, FTC, Guidance Software Inc. Settles FTC Charges (Nov. 16, 2006), *available at* http://www.ftc.gov/news-events/press-releases/2006/11/guidance-software-inc-settles-ftc-charges.

[160] Complaint, FTC v. Wyndham Worldwide Corp., No. 2:12-cv-01365-SPL (D. Ariz. filed June 26, 2012), *available at* http://www.ftc.gov/os/caselist/1023142/120626wyndamhotelscmpt.pdf.

security measures and intruders breached the Wyndham network two additional times. According to the FTC, the three data breaches have contributed to "fraudulent charges on consumers' accounts, millions of dollars in fraud loss, and the export of hundreds of thousands of consumers' payment card account information to an Internet domain address registered in Russia."

In January 2013, the FTC settled with Cbr Systems, Inc., a leading umbilical cord blood and tissue bank, for exposing nearly 300,000 customers' personal information to a data breach as a result of inadequate security practices.[161] According to the FTC, Cbr did not have reasonable policies and procedures to protect sensitive consumer information which contributed to a December 2010 security breach. The breach occurred when assorted digital storage devices containing consumers' names, Social Security numbers, and credit and debit card numbers were left unattended in a Cbr employee's personal vehicle. The settlement required Cbr to establish and maintain a comprehensive security program and submit to security audits every other year for 20 years. As a result of Cbr's security policies, nearly 300,000 consumers whose information was improperly safeguarded by the company are now at greater risk for identity theft.

---

[161] Press Release, FTC, Cord Blood Bank Settles FTC Charges that it Failed to Protect Consumers' Sensitive Personal Information (Jan. 28, 2013), *available at* http://ftc.gov/opa/2013/01/cbr.shtm.

Despite the success of these enforcement efforts, however, identity theft will remain a major challenge for the FTC into the foreseeable future. In 2012, 18% of almost 369,000 complaints concerned identity theft; this represents the thirteenth year in a row where identity theft topped the list of complaints.[162]

Consumers are spending more time on social networking websites and providing those websites with access to the consumers' personal information. The amount of data collected by these websites highlights the importance of implementing comprehensive data security measures. One prominent example of the FTC's enforcement of social networking websites is the 2011 Twitter settlement.[163] Twitter's privacy policy led users to believe that information conveyed to Twitter would be safeguarded, remain confidential, and that the company would employ sophisticated measures to protect unauthorized access. However, lapses in Twitter's security measures allowed hackers to obtain administrative control over the website on two occasions between January and May of 2009.[164] Hackers had access to non-public user information,

---

[162]   Press Release, FTC, FTC Releases Top 10 Complaint Categories for 2012 (Feb. 26, 2013), *available at* http://ftc.gov/opa/2013/02/sentineltop.shtm.

[163]   Twitter, Inc., No. 092-3093, 2011 WL 914034 (F.T.C. Mar. 2, 2011), *available at* http://www.ftc.gov/os/caselist/0923093/110311twitterdo.pdf.

[164]   Press Release, FTC, FTC Accepts Final Settlement with Twitter for Failure to Safeguard Personal Information (Mar. 11, 2011), *available at* http://www.ftc.gov/opa/2011/03/twitter.shtm.

private communications, and the ability to send out unauthorized messages. The settlement required Twitter to maintain a comprehensive information security program, and to agree to independent audits every other year for 10 years.

e. Recent Regulations: The Disposal Rule

The Disposal Rule became effective June 1, 2005, giving the FTC authority to require businesses to take appropriate measures in disposing of sensitive information from consumers' files.[165] The Disposal Rule applies to "consumer reports" or information derived from consumer reports. Consumer reports include information such as establishing an individual's credit, employment or insurance history, background checks, past checks, residential history, and medical history.[166] Any company that uses consumer reports must comply with the Disposal Rule including lenders, insurers, employers, landlords, government agencies, auto dealers, debt collectors, and credit reporters. Proper disposal is reasonable and appropriate if measures are taken to prevent unauthorized access or use of information derived from consumer reports. The company must use due diligence by hiring a document destruction company or otherwise following proper in-house document destruction procedures for both hardcopy and electronic data.

---

[165] Press Release, FTC, FACTA Disposal Rule Goes into Effect June 1 (June 1, 2005), *available at* http://www.ftc.gov/news-events/press-releases/2005/06/facta-disposal-rule-goes-effect-june-1.

[166] *Id.*

The rule emphasizes self-regulation, leaving it up to the regulated businesses and organizations to determine what measures are reasonable for disposal depending on the sensitivity of the information, the costs and benefits of disposal methods, and changes in technology.[167]

Violating the Disposal Rule through the improper disposal of consumer information can result in civil penalties and enhanced monitoring requirements. Even though the Disposal Rule went into effect in 2005, it was not until 2007 that the FTC first used the Disposal Rule in an enforcement action. In late 2007, the FTC settled with American United Mortgage Company, for a $50,000 penalty, after the company improperly discarded documents containing personal information about consumers in unsecured dumpsters.[168]

More recently, in November 2012, PLS Financial Services, a company that operates payday loan and check cashing stores, agreed to pay a $101,500 civil penalty for violating the Disposal Rule.[169] An FTC investigation found that PLS discarded fully intact documents containing personally identifying consumer information into publically-accessible

---

[167]   *Id.*

[168]   Press Release, FTC, Company Will Pay $50,000 Penalty for Tossing Consumers' Credit Report Information in Unsecured Dumpster (Dec. 18. 2007), *available at* http://www.ftc.gov/opa/2007/12/aumort.shtm.

[169]   Press Release, DOJ, Company to Pay $101,500 Civil Penalty for Dumping Sensitive Consumer Documents in Publically-Accessible Dumpsters (Nov. 1, 2012) *available at* http://www.justice.gov/opa/pr/2012/November/12-civ-1307.html.

dumpsters. Violations of the Disposal Rule can result in a civil penalty of up to $3,500 per violation. In addition to the monetary sanction, the company was required to implement and maintain a comprehensive information security program and obtain impartial third-party biennial assessments of their information security procedures for twenty years.

2. The Department of Homeland Security

The Department of Homeland Security (DHS) was established in 2002 by the Homeland Security Act.[170] DHS is a cabinet-level executive department tasked with preventing terrorist attacks within the United States, reducing vulnerability to terrorist attacks, and otherwise minimizing the damage of these attacks if they occur.[171] The Homeland Security Act brought over a dozen Federal agencies that had either been independent or under the supervision of different executive departments, including the Immigration and Naturalization Service, the Federal Emergency Management Agency, and the Secret Service, under the umbrella of DHS. The concentration of so many different agencies, many of which have reason to collect individuals' personal information under a variety of circumstances, under one supervising authority raised unparalleled concerns about the threat this newly created entity would pose to individual privacy.

---

[170]   6 U.S.C. § 111(a) (2012).

[171]   *Id.* at § 111(a), (b).

To address these concerns, the DHS has an intricate system to ensure adequate measures are taken to ensure privacy protection inside and outside of the agency. The DHS is the first federal agency to have a statutorily required chief privacy officer (CPO),[172] something that had become increasingly common in the business world over the preceding years. (Private sector CPOs are discussed in Chapter 3, Part V(E)). The CPO reports directly to the Secretary of Homeland Security and oversees the DHS Privacy Office.[173]

The mission of the DHS Privacy Office is to protect individuals' privacy rights, with particular emphasis on maintaining the security of their "personally identifiable information." The DHS Privacy Office defines "personally identifiable information" as information in a system or online collection that "directly or indirectly identifies an individual."[174] This can include information such as names, Social Security numbers, date and place of birth, and biometric records, among others. The Privacy Office establishes contracts and relationships with vendors and ensures that they have adequate protections to safeguard consumer privacy. Pursuant to the E-Government Act of 2002, discussed above, the Privacy Office also issues PIAs

---

[172]   *Id.* at § 142.

[173]   *Authorities and Responsibilities of the Chief Privacy Officer*,   DHS,   http://www.dhs.gov/chief-privacy-officers-authorities-and-responsibilities (last visited Nov. 14, 2013).

[174]   *Privacy Impact Assessments: Official Guidance*, DHS 8 (Mar. 2006), http://www.dhs.gov/xlibrary/assets/privacy/privacy_pia_guidance_march_v5.pdf.

concerning any new information technology or programs implemented by DHS's subsidiary agencies, such as the "Secure Flight" program, a passenger screening system developed by the Transportation Security Administration (TSA). These assessments address how long collected personal information is retained, with whom it is shared, and the rights of individuals to access and correct the information.[175] To determine whether individuals reasonably believed that their personal information would be kept private, DHS will look at the circumstances of how the data was collected, whether the consumer had notice, and the risk of harm to the consumer by using the data, such as medical or financial information.

The DHS also established the Data Privacy and Integrity Advisory Committee in 2004 to advise the CPO and Secretary on issues affecting individual privacy. The goal of the committee is to limit information disclosure to ensure that it is only used for authorized purposes, maximize security and confidentiality in the handling of information, protect the constitutional and statutory rights of individuals whose personal information has been collected, and improve both the integrity of data and increase personal privacy through timely destruction of information that has been collected. The committee advises DHS on length of data retention, limits, and methods of enhancing

---

[175] *Privacy Impact Assessment for the United States Visitor and Immigrant Status Indicator Technology (US–VISIT) Program*, DHS 3–4 (Dec. 22, 2005), http://www.dhs.gov/xlibrary/assets/privacy/privacy_pia_usvisit_update_12-22-2005.pdf.

security. The committee must have at least sixteen members appointed by the Secretary, with new members having terms not to exceed three years.[176]

Given its broad powers, the DHS has been under scrutiny by a number of organizations concerned with privacy issues. In July 2004, for example, the Electronic Privacy Information Center (EPIC), a non-profit group, challenged the release of data from the U.S. Census Bureau to the DHS, which had included municipal and zip code-level breakdowns on Arab American populations, including their countries of origin.[177] DHS explained that information was needed to determine which airports needed Arabic language signage.[178] In any event, setting aside truth or falsity of DHS's explanation, the release of information from the Census Bureau would not have triggered Privacy Office oversight because the data was "anonymized," *i.e.*, no specific individuals could be identified from it, thus it did not constitute "personally identifiable information."

III.   STATE CONSTITUTIONS

Privacy interests are a matter of great concern at the level of state government, particularly as a

---

[176]   *See Data Privacy and Integrity Advisory Committee Charter*, DHS (May 8, 2012) http://www.dhs.gov/xlibrary/assets/privacy/privacy_dpiac_charter_may2012.pdf.

[177]   Douglas J. Sylvester & Sharon Lohr, *Counting on Confidentiality: Legal and Statistical Approaches to Federal Privacy Law after the USA Patriot Act*, 2005 WIS. L. REV. 1033, 1043 (2005).

[178]   *See* Lynette Clemetson, *HS Given Data on Arab Americans*, NY TIMES, July 30, 2004, at A14.

number of state constitutional provisions provide better articulated and broader protection for individual privacy than the U.S. Constitution under the Fourth Amendment.

In 1905, the Georgia Supreme Court recognized privacy as an independent and distinct right under the Georgia Constitution. In *Pavesich v. New England Life Ins. Co.*, 50 S.E. 68 (Ga. 1905), the Georgia Supreme Court found the state's residents to have a "liberty of privacy" guaranteed by the Georgia constitutional provision: "no person shall be deprived of liberty except by due process of law." The court grounded the right to privacy in the doctrine of natural law:

> The right of privacy has its foundations in the instincts of nature. It is recognized intuitively, consciousness being witness that can be called to establish its existence. Any person whose intellect is in a normal condition recognizes at once that as to each individual member of society there are matters private and there are matters public so far as the individual is concerned. Each individual as instinctively resents any encroachment by the public upon his rights which are of a private nature as he does the withdrawal of those rights which are of a public nature. A right of privacy in matters purely private is therefore derived from natural law.

Id. at 69. The Georgia court's decision in *Pavesich* represented the first time any court of last resort recognized an independent constitutional right to privacy. Over the next fifty years, the majority of states adopted the principle of an individual right to privacy, whether by express constitutional provisions or by interpretation of existing constitutional language.

A.   EXPLICIT RIGHT-TO-PRIVACY CLAUSES

In contrast to the federal constitution, where protection of privacy is inferred from other provisions, at least ten state constitutions contain explicit right-to-privacy clauses.

State	Clause
Alaska	The right of the people to privacy is recognized and shall not be infringed.[179]
Arizona	No person shall be disturbed in his private affairs, or his home invaded, without authority of law.[180]
California	All people ... have inalienable rights. Among these are enjoying and defending life and liberty, acquiring, possessing, and protecting property, and pursuing and obtaining safety, happiness, and privacy.[181]
Florida	Every natural person has the right to be let alone and free from governmental intrusion into his private life except as otherwise provided herein.[182]
Hawaii	The right of the people to privacy is recognized and shall not be infringed without the

---

[179]   ALASKA CONST. art. I, § 22.

[180]   ARIZ. CONST. art. II, § 8.

[181]   CAL. CONST. art. I, § 1.

[182]   FLA. CONST. art. I, § 23.

State	Clause
	showing of a compelling state interest.... The right of the people to be secure in their persons, houses, papers, and effects against unreasonable searches, seizures and invasions of privacy shall not be violated ....[183]
Illinois	The people shall have the right to be secure in their persons, houses, papers, and other possessions against unreasonable searches, seizures, invasions of privacy or interceptions of communications by eavesdropping devices or other means ....[184]
Louisiana	Every person shall be secure in his person, property, communications, houses, papers and effects against ... invasions of privacy.[185]
Montana	The right of individual privacy is essential to the well-being of a free society and shall not be infringed without the showing of a

---

[183]   HAW. CONST. art. I, §§ 6–7.

[184]   ILL. CONST. art. I, § 6.

[185]   LA. CONST. art. I, § 5.

State   **Clause**

                         compelling state interest.[186]

South Carolina   The right of the people to be secure
                         in their persons, houses, papers,
                         and effects against unreasonable
                         searches and seizures and
                         unreasonable invasions of privacy
                         shall not be violated, and no
                         warrants shall issue but upon
                         probable cause, supported by oath
                         or affirmation, and particularly
                         describing the place to be searched,
                         the person or thing to be seized,
                         and the information to be
                         obtained.[187]

Washington   No person shall be disturbed in
                         his private affairs, or his home
                         invaded, without authority of
                         law.[188]

Of these states, California has developed the most extensive body of case law interpreting the scope of its state constitutional right to privacy. The California Supreme Court has consistently interpreted its state constitutional privacy clause as providing its citizens with a greater scope of

---

[186]   MONT. CONST. art. II, § 10.

[187]   S.C. CONST. art. I, § 10.

[188]   WASH. CONST. art. I, § 7.

protection than what the U.S. Supreme Court has found to have been granted by the U.S. Constitution. For example:

1. In California, it is an illegal search and seizure for law enforcement to acquire a bank customer's financial statements from the custody of a bank without a warrant. *Compare Burrows v. Superior Court*, 118 Cal. Rptr. 166 (1974), *with United States v. Miller*, 425 U.S. 435 (1976) (a bank customer has no reasonable expectation of privacy in the confidentiality of his bank statements).

2. A city ordinance that limits the number of unrelated persons who can live together violates California citizens' constitutional right to privacy. *Compare City of Santa Barbara v. Adamson*, 164 Cal. Rptr. 539 (1980), *with Village of Belle Terre v. Borass*, 416 U.S. 1 (1974) (a zoning ordinance that restricts the number of unrelated persons who may live together does not violate the right to privacy).

3. The state of California may not refuse to provide Medicaid recipients' public funds merely because the funds would be used to pay for abortions because abortion is a protected privacy right. *Compare Committee to Defend Reproductive Rights v. Myers*, 172 Cal. Rptr. 866 (1981), *with Contra Harris v. McRae*, 448 U.S. 297 (1980) (states receiving federal funds through the Medicaid program

are not required to fund the costs of medically necessary abortions).

B.   EXTENDING THE RIGHT TO PRIVACY

Many states' constitutions do not have an explicit right-to-privacy clause, but their constitutions do have provisions that mimic the language of the Fourth Amendment of the United States Constitution that protect the right of the people to be free from unreasonable searches and seizures.[189] Privacy rights in these states have largely developed through judicial construction of such search and seizure provisions.[190] Despite the similarities in language between the Fourth Amendment and many states' search and seizure provisions, there have been several occasions when state supreme courts interpreted their constitutions as providing greater privacy protections than what has been granted by the U.S. Supreme Court, as demonstrated in the following examples:

1. The Fourth Amendment does not prohibit law enforcement from conducting a

---

[189]   *Compare* COLO. CONST. art. II, § 7, *and* CONN. CONST. art. I, § 7, *and* IDAHO CONST. art. I, § 17, *and* N.J. CONST. art. I, para. 1, *and* N.Y. CONST. art. I, § 12, *and* N.C. CONST. art. I, § 20, *and* PA. CONST. art. I, § 8, *and* S.D. CONST. art. VI, § 11, *and* UTAH CONST. art. I, § 14, *with* U.S. CONST. amend IV ("The right of the people to be secure in their persons, houses, papers, and effects, against unreasonable searches and seizures, shall not be violated, and no Warrants shall issue, but upon probable cause, supported by Oath or affirmation, and particularly describing the place to be searched, and the persons or things to be seized.").

[190]   Ken Gormley, *One Hundred Years of Privacy*, 1992 WIS. L. REV. 1335, 1427 (1992).

warrantless search of an automobile because automobiles, unlike a home or an office, are subject to more pervasive government regulation and the mobility of the vehicle creates a lower expectation of privacy. *South Dakota v. Opperman*, 428 U.S. 364 (1976). However, in South Dakota, Montana, and Alaska, warrantless searches of automobiles have been found to violate the privacy rights of the people to be free from unreasonable searches under their state constitutions. *State v. Daniel*, 589 P.2d 408 (Alaska 1979); *State v. Sawyer*, 571 P.2d 1131 (Mont. 1977); *State v. Opperman*, 247 N.W.2d 673 (S.D. 1976).[191]

2. Law enforcement is not required under federal constitutional jurisprudence to obtain a warrant before using a pen register because the installation of a pen register is not a search under the Fourth Amendment. *Smith v. Maryland*, 442 U.S. 735 (1979). However, Idaho and Pennsylvania courts have ruled that law enforcement may not use a pen register without obtaining a warrant based on probable cause because the use of a pen register is a search under the search and seizure provisions of their constitutions. *State v. Thompson*, 760 P.2d 1162 (Idaho 1988); *Commonwealth v. Melilli*, 555 A.2d 1254 (Pa. 1989).

---

[191]   *Id.* at 1426.

3. When evidence is illegally obtained, but the person who obtained the search warrant acted in good faith, then the evidence will not be excluded from trial because under the U.S. Constitution the good faith exception to the exclusionary rule applies. *United States v. Leon*, 468 U.S. 897 (1984). However, Connecticut, New Jersey, New York, North Carolina, and Pennsylvania have all ruled that the privacy interests of their citizens in being protected from unlawful searches is so great that the good faith exception to the exclusionary rule does not apply. *State v. Marsala*, 579 A.2d 58 (Conn. 1990); *State v. Novembrino*, 519 A.2d 820 (N.J. 1987); *People v. Bigelow*, 497 N.Y.S.2d 630 (1985); *State v. Carter*, 370 S.E.2d 553 (N.C. 1988); *Commonwealth v. Edmunds*, 586 A.2d 887 (Pa. 1991).[192]

IV.   STATE STATUTES

Due to the lack of comprehensive privacy laws at the federal level, the enactment of privacy laws and regulations has become an increasing priority for state governments over the past decade.

A.   CONSUMER NOTIFICATION OF DATA BREACHES

According to Privacy Rights Clearinghouse, a nonprofit corporation that provides information

---

[192]   *Id.* at 1427.

about privacy, there were 3,722 reported data breaches, *i.e.*, unauthorized or otherwise unlawful exposures of data, involving personal information in the United States between January 1, 2005 and May 7, 2013.[193] This reported number of data breaches is a conservative estimate because data breach reporting requirements vary from state to state.[194] Because of the frequency of data breaches, combined with the fact that they typically affect large numbers of individuals, states have been particularly active in enacting legislation concerning such breaches.

Forty-six states,[195] the District of Columbia, Puerto Rico, and the Virgin Islands have data breach notification laws that require companies or state agencies to notify consumers when a security breach has occurred that has exposed their personal information. The proliferation of these laws has been an important step towards advancing privacy interests, as the notification processes created by them have not just served to alert individuals to the fact that their personal data may have been

---

[193] *Chronology of Data Breaches: Security Breaches 2005 – Present*, PRIVACY RIGHTS CLEARINGHOUSE, http://www.privacyrights.org/data-breach (last visited May 7, 2013).

[194] *Data Breaches: A Year in Review*, PRIVACY RIGHTS CLEARINGHOUSE, https://www.privacyrights.org/data-breach-year-review-2011 (last visited May 7, 2013).

[195] Alabama, Kentucky, New Mexico, and South Dakota do not have consumer security breach notification laws. *State Security Breach Notification Laws*, NAT'L CONF. OF STATE LEGS, http://www.ncsl.org/research/telecommunications-and-information-technology/security-breach-notification-laws.aspx (last updated Aug. 20, 2012).

compromised, but have also raised public awareness of the problem of data breaches.

California enacted the first breach notification law, and it became effective July 1, 2003. The statute requires disclosure of a breach when an unauthorized person acquires, or is believed to have acquired, unencrypted personal information.[196] A breach of personal information occurs when an individual's first name or initial, and last name, are exposed in combination with one or more of the following: (1) Social Security number; (2) driver's license number or California state identification card number; (3) account number, credit or debit card number, in combination with any required security code, access code, or password that would permit access to an individual's financial account; (4) medical information; or (5) health insurance information.[197] California's security breach notification law has become the *de facto* national model for such laws, with most other states modeling their legislation after California's.

B. PREVENTING SECURITY BREACHES

Increasingly, states have acted not just to require reporting of security breaches but, recognizing that many security breaches are the result of incomplete or mishandled disposal of personal data, also to prescribe certain minimum policies that businesses must implement when disposing of personal data.

---

[196]   CAL. CIV. CODE § 1798.82 (2003).

[197]   *Id.*

At least twenty-nine states have enacted such data disposal laws.[198]

For example, Texas passed the Identity Theft Enforcement and Protection Act, which became effective September 1, 2009.[199] This law requires businesses to dispose of personally identifiable information either by: (1) shredding; (2) erasing; or (3) modifying the information so that the information is undecipherable.

Increasingly, states are going even further and requiring businesses to adopt "reasonable" security policies to protect personally identifiable information while it is still being held.[200] The ambiguity of what constitutes a reasonable security policy can frustrate businesses that are trying to ensure compliance with data protection laws, but a few states have enacted statutes or regulations that specify minimum standards.

Massachusetts, for instance, through its Office of Consumer Affairs and Business Regulation (which

---

[198] States with mandatory data disposal laws are: Alaska, Arizona, Arkansas, California, Colorado, Connecticut, Georgia, Hawaii, Illinois, Indiana, Kansas, Kentucky, Maryland, Massachusetts, Michigan, Missouri, Montana, Nevada, New Jersey, New York, North Carolina, Oregon, Rhode Island, South Carolina, Texas, Utah, Vermont, Washington, and Wisconsin. *Data Disposal Laws*, NAT'L CONF. OF STATE LEGS., http://www.ncsl.org/research/telecommunications-and-information-technology/data-disposal-laws.aspx (last updated Mar. 22, 2013).

[199] TEX. BUS. & COM. CODE ANN. § 521.052 (2009).

[200] Massachusetts and Nevada have both fully enacted such laws. At least a dozen other states were considering proposals for such laws or regulations as of 2013.

is empowered by state law to promulgate regulations for the protection of consumer privacy), has set minimum requirements for protecting consumer information from unauthorized access.[201] These requirements include encryption for consumer's personal information, promptly updating or patching relevant software, and requiring that third-party service providers also adopt equivalent security measures.

C. UNAUTHORIZED ACCESS

The rapid expansion and development of computer software and hardware gives hackers new targets to attack and steal information. To combat this threat, states have passed legislation to protect citizens from malicious digital attacks and threats.

Every state has passed a law that addresses unauthorized access to computer systems. Such unauthorized access can cause a wide variety of disruptions or damages to the compromised system, but in many instances the motive of such unauthorized users is to gain access to personal information. Laws penalizing unauthorized access to computer systems thus typically have a collateral privacy-enhancing effect.

Some states have passed laws that address specific types of computer crime that relate to privacy issues. Most notably, seventeen states, and

---

[201]   201 Code Mass. Reg. § 17.04 (2010).

Puerto Rico, have anti-spyware laws.[202] Spyware is software that is covertly installed on a computer, and the software collects information about the browsing habits of the computer users and transmits that information to a third party. State anti-spyware laws typically make it unlawful for a third party to install software on a computer without first disclosing the planned installation to the computer's owner or user.

D. HEALTH INFORMATION

The Health Insurance Portability and Accountability Act of 1996, known as HIPAA, discussed in detail in Chapter 3, Part II.B.2, contains privacy provisions that regulate industry-wide standards for the handling and maintaining the confidentiality of medical records. The HIPPA Privacy Rule sets minimum federal requirements that are applicable in each state, but states may pass laws that grant patients greater protections.[203]

Texas, for example, has amended its medical privacy laws effective September 1, 2012, to impose greater obligations on parties handling personal

---

[202] The states that have enacted spyware laws are: Alaska, Arizona, Arkansas, California, Georgia, Illinois, Indiana, Iowa, Louisiana, Nevada, New Hampshire, Pennsylvania, Rhode Island, Texas, Utah, Virginia, and Washington. *State Spyware Laws*, NAT'L CONF. OF STATE LEGS., http://www.ncsl.org/issues-research/telecom/state-spyware-laws.aspx (last updated Feb. 10, 2012).

[203] *Does the HIPAA Privacy Rule preempt State laws?*, HHS, http://www.hhs.gov/hipaafaq/state/399.html (last updated Dec. 11, 2006).

health information than those required under the HIPPA Privacy Rule.[204] The amendment expanded the definition of a "covered entity" to any entity that engages in the practice of "assembling, collecting, analyzing, storing, or transmitting personal health information," or any entity that "comes into the possession of" or "obtains or stores personal health information." Under the new definition of a covered entity, many businesses otherwise exempt under HIPPA, such as law firms, accounting firms, auditors, and record storage disposal companies, will effectively become subject to the equivalent of HIPPA requirements.

E. SOCIAL MEDIA PRIVACY

Social media continues to grow in popularity, but one of the main challenges to that continued growth has been privacy concerns. These concerns take two principal forms: concerns that the social media operator itself is collecting or using personal information of its users, or both; and concerns that a third party (whether overtly or covertly) may gain access to personal information posted by the users.

The question of operators' use of their users' personal information is presently regulated primarily through website privacy policies, and other terms of use. These are discussed at Chapter 3, Part V.A. Meanwhile, covert access by third parties is typically the result of hacking, spyware, or other forms of software intrusion, which generally

---

[204] *See* Tex. H.B. 300 (May 29, 2011) *amending* TEX. HEALTH & SAFETY CODE § 181.001, *et seq.*

are subject to FTC regulation or criminalized as discussed at Chapter 3, Parts II.E.1.d.(iii)–(iv) and IV.C. A new trend, however, is third parties, especially actual or potential employers, openly demanding that social media users disclose their passwords and other login information to allow those third parties to directly examine the users' accounts. Some employers have justified requesting that employees share their social media username and passwords on the grounds that that accessing these accounts is necessary to protect trade secrets, but many acknowledge that they are simply looking for "undesirable" behavior that could justify not hiring the individual or terminating them if already hired.

Between 2012 and 2013, thirteen states enacted legislation that prohibited employers from requesting or requiring an employee or job applicant to disclose a user name or password for a personal social media account. An additional thirty-six states had such legislation pending or otherwise under consideration by late 2013.[205]

F. DRONES

Another emerging concern in privacy law is the use of unmanned aerial vehicles (UAVs), often called "drones." Drones are predominantly used by

---

[205] Arkansas, California, Colorado, Delaware, Illinois, Maryland, Michigan, Nevada, New Jersey, New Mexico, Oregon, Utah, and Washington. *See Employer Access to Social Media Usernames and Passwords 2013*, NAT'L CONF. OF STATE LEGS., http://www.ncsl.org/issues-research/telecom/employer-access-to-social-media-passwords-2013.aspx (last updated Oct. 23, 2013).

law enforcement for surveillance purposes, but uses for both commercial and scientific purposes have also expanded greatly in recent years. Advocates of the drone industry contend that drones play an important role in law enforcement activities and that other uses will have significant public safety and economic benefits, such as early detection of forest fires or more efficient management of agricultural land. However, many critics have raised concerns that the use of this technology may jeopardize privacy rights, particularly by lowering the cost of surveillance by law enforcement or facilitating private parties bypassing more traditional physical security measures like fences.

As of October 2013, eight states had enacted legislation restricting or regulating the use of drones for surveillance of private property and an additional thirty-four states were considering legislation.[206] However, such legislation has been overwhelmingly focused on law enforcement, particularly imposing a requirement that law enforcement obtain a particularized warrant for drone surveillance. Private drone use remains largely unregulated other than through normal air traffic control rules and common law trespass rules.

---

[206] States with legislation included Florida, Idaho, Illinois, Montana, Oregon, Tennessee, Texas, and Virginia. States considering legislation included Alabama, Alaska, Arizona, Arkansas, California, Georgia, Hawaii, Indiana, Iowa, Kansas, Kentucky, Maine, Maryland, Massachusetts, Michigan, Minnesota, Missouri, Nebraska, Nevada, New Hampshire, New Jersey, New Mexico, New York, North Carolina, North Dakota, Ohio, Oklahoma, Pennsylvania, Rhode Island, South Carolina, Vermont, Washington, West Virginia, and Wyoming.

V.   PRIVATE LAW

Beyond the realm of statutes and regulations that expressly protect privacy rights, there is a considerable range of private law techniques that can be used. All of these operate primarily on contract law principles, although many, including trade secret protections, also have a statutory or tort law component, or both, as well. Private law approaches to protecting privacy rights highlight the complex question of what a "right to privacy" truly means.

A.   PRIVACY POLICIES

The most explicit form of privacy right created by private law is the category of contracts and representations collectively referred to as "privacy policies." These statements range from highly detailed descriptions of what a party's obligations are with regard to particular types of information and what security measures will be in place to assure the appropriate level of protection, to single sentence promises not to "share" an individual's "information" without further definition of those terms. While these policies have become ubiquitous, their enforceability is heavily dependent on how they are drafted and what rights they purport to protect.

Privacy policies may exist in the form of traditional contracts or, especially on the Internet, as statements superficially subject to promissory estoppel principles. Unless clearly stated as not being contractual in nature, the breach of a privacy policy theoretically could give rise to contractual damages. Most efforts at enforcing privacy policies through litigation, however, have failed for one of two reasons. First, in many instances the privacy policy merely recites that a customer or user's information will be protected without sufficiently setting forth what the "protection" will consist of, or what obligations the recipient of the information has with regard to handling the information. The policy thus fails to rise to the level of an enforceable contract because its terms are too vague or otherwise fail to establish the necessary exchange of consideration.[207] Second, even where a privacy policy is determined to be an enforceable contract, courts have found that breach of the policy without specific evidence of quantifiable harm flowing from the breach will not support a breach of contract claim.[208] The ongoing difficulty of enforcing privacy policies through private litigation has been a major factor in driving the activities of the FTC concerning privacy policies discussed above in Chapter 3, Part II(E)(1).

B.   TRADE SECRETS

The intersection between the law of trade secrets and privacy rights demonstrates the paradox of economic interests simultaneously promoting and compromising personal privacy. Personal information may be protected as a trade secret, but

---

[207] *See, e.g.*, *In re* N.W. Airlines Privacy Litig., No. Civ. 04–126(PAM/JSM), 2004 WL 1278459 (D. Minn. June 6, 2004).

[208] *In re* JetBlue Airways Corp. Privacy Litig., 379 F. Supp. 2d 299 (E.D.N.Y. 2005).

rarely by the individual whose personal information is at issue.

The law of trade secrets evolved from the recognition by American courts in the mid-to-late Nineteenth Century that information generated or received by a business could become the property of the business itself and have concrete economic value, rather than simply being something "known" by the individual employees. Early trade secret cases primarily concerned recipes or manufacturing techniques, but by the turn of the Twentieth Century, it became recognized that a list of names and addresses of customers, *i.e.*, personal information, could be a protectable trade secret in and of itself. One of the earliest cases addressing this issue was *Hackett v. A.L. & J.J. Reynolds Co.*, 62 N.Y.S. 1076 (N.Y. Sup. Ct. 1900), which found that a former employee of a grocery delivery business could be barred from contacting its customers:

> The value of the defendant's business consisted not merely of the property invested and the goods sold by it, but, as well, in the knowledge of the location of its routes, and the names of the customers to whom it was accustomed to make sales. This knowledge was in the nature of a trade secret, and was imparted to the plaintiff at the time he was employed by the defendant, solely to enable him to profitably and intelligently attend to the business of the defendant.

Id. at 1078. The employee had signed a contract agreeing not to compete with the employee's former employer, and the customer lists were trade secrets provided only for his use while employed. Therefore, it was a breach of the contract to use the information in a manner that was economically disadvantageous to the employer.

Forty-seven states[209] and the District of Columbia have adopted some form of the Uniform Trade Secrets Act (UTSA). The UTSA defines a "trade secret" as:

> information, including a formula, pattern, compilation, program, device, method, technique, or process, that: (i) derives independent economic value, actual or potential, from not being generally known to, and not being readily ascertainable by proper means by, other persons who can obtain economic value from its disclosure or use, and (ii) is the subject of efforts that are reasonable

---

[209] Including Alabama, Alaska, Arizona, Arkansas, California, Colorado, Connecticut, Delaware, District of Colombia, Florida, Georgia, Hawaii, Idaho, Illinois, Indiana, Iowa, Kansas, Kentucky, Louisiana, Maine, Maryland, Michigan, Minnesota, Mississippi, Missouri, Montana, Nebraska, Nevada, New Hampshire, New Mexico, North Dakota, Ohio, Oklahoma, Oregon, Pennsylvania, Rhode Island, South Carolina, South Dakota, Tennessee, Utah, Vermont, Virgin Islands, Virginia, Washington, West Virginia, Wisconsin, Wyoming. New York, Massachusetts, and Texas have declined to adopt UTSA, but still protect trade secrets either through other statutes or common law.

under the circumstances to maintain its secrecy.[210]

Theft or misappropriation of a secret occurs when an individual or entity, either directly or indirectly, knowingly learns of or discloses a trade secret through improper means or in violation of a duty to the owner of the trade secret.[211] Customer lists may be protectable under the Act even if they consist exclusively of publicly available information, so long as the creator of the list expended significant effort to gather or organize the information and has taken sufficient steps to preserve its confidentiality.[212]

Trade secret law thus expresses in a microcosm the difficulties of protecting personal privacy through traditional legal means. A specific individual's personal information will rarely derive "independent economic value" from being known only to him or herself. Indeed, based on the fact that many businesses are willing to compensate consumers (through "loyalty" card programs, sweepstakes entries, etc.) for providing their personal information, it would appear that for the

---

[210]   Uniform Trade Secrets Act § 1(4) (2007).

[211]   *Id.* at § 1(2).

[212]   *See, e.g.*, Fireworks Spectacular, Inc. v. Premier Pyrotechnics, Inc., 86 F. Supp. 2d 1102 (D. Kan. 2000) ("Customer lists containing merely public information that could be easily compiled by third parties will not be protected as trade secrets; however, where 'the party compiling the customer lists, while using public information as a source, . . . expends a great deal of time, effort and expense in developing the lists and treats the lists as confidential in its business, the lists may be entitled to trade secret protection.") (quoting Robert B. Vance & Assocs., Inc. v. Baronet Corp., 487 F.Supp. 790, 799 (N.D. Ga. 1979)).

vast majority of individuals, their personal information is most valuable when shared. Yet the party that receives the information can, if it has devoted sufficient time and energy to collecting, filtering, and otherwise organizing the information, protect it as a trade secret.

C.   SHRINK-WRAP AND CLICK-WRAP AGREEMENTS

A common type of contract encountered by software users and web surfers is known as "shrink wrap"[213] or "click-wrap"[214] agreements. These agreements can contain privacy policies, but in most instances they actually function as "anti-privacy policies," containing terms expressly allowing the party serving the agreement to collect, use, and distribute the personal information of the user. This may be done candidly through an electronic registration form or surreptitiously through forms of spyware.

---

[213] A "shrink-wrap" agreement is any sort of contract packaged in a container or box that advises the purchaser of the terms of use of the product and is typically only discoverable after having purchased the product. The term is most often applied to "end user license agreements" included with software.

[214] Also known as click-through agreement, point-and-click agreement, user agreement, web-wrap agreement, and browser-wrap agreement. Click-wrap agreements are simply electronic versions of a shrink-wrap agreements. In a typical click-wrap agreement, a user is asked to assent to the terms of an agreement displayed upon reaching a website or running a piece of software by clicking a button, box, or other graphic on the computer screen with the mouse cursor.

Numerous cases challenging the validity of electronically delivered contract terms were brought when businesses began incorporating them into software in the 1990s. The state of the law today is in favor of these agreements so long as they sufficiently comply with traditional contract principles, particularly knowing acceptance of the terms by the user.[215]

D. CONFIDENTIAL SETTLEMENT AGREEMENTS

The term "confidential settlement agreements" refers to a range of practices that result in agreements to resolve a legal dispute between parties with terms not subject to public disclosure. Confidential settlements agreements are a form of contract between the parties and in most instances are not filed with the court. Information that remains private as a result of these agreements can include the allegations, evidence, settlement terms, or even the fact that there was ever a dispute between the parties.

There has been sharp criticism of confidential settlement agreements in recent years, particularly when these agreements are used to resolve litigation that initially attracted significant public attention. The main argument is that confidential settlements conceal misconduct that had an impact on the broader public beyond the specific parties to the

---

[215] *See* ProCD, Inc. v. Zeidenberg, 86 F.3d 1447, 1449 (7th Cir. 1996); Specht v. Netscape Commc'n Corp., 306 F.3d 17, 22 n.4 (2d Cir. 2002).

litigation, and thus others are either left uninformed of the true facts or must file their own litigation. Supporters of confidential settlement agreements contend that this type of contract promotes settlements in many cases where parties might otherwise feel compelled to go to trial simply to "clear their names," with the resulting expense and burden on the judicial system. Most courts eagerly embrace these types of confidential settlements, stating, "secrecy of settlement terms . . . is a well-established American litigation practice."[216] The "well-established" acceptance of confidential settlement agreements has lost ground in recent years, however. Some jurisdictions preclude confidential settlements without court approval.[217] In addition, a number of states regulate confidential settlements out of concern that these agreements may be used to conceal harmful conduct.[218]

---

[216]   Goodyear Tire & Rubber Co. v. Chiles Power Supply, Inc., 332 F.3d 976, 980–81 (6th Cir. 2003) (quoting Palmieri v. New York, 779 F.2d 861, 865 (2d Cir. 1985)).

[217]   *See, e.g.*, Local Rule 5.03(E) of the U.S. District Court for the District of South Carolina.

[218]   *See, e.g.*, Florida Sunshine in Litigation Act, Fla. Stat. Ann. § 69.081(4) (2005) ("Any portion of an agreement or contract which has the purpose or effect of concealing a public hazard, any information concerning a public hazard, or any information which may be useful to members of the public in protecting themselves from injury which may result from the public hazard, is void, contrary to public policy, and may not be enforced.").

E.   CHIEF PRIVACY OFFICERS AND RELATED CONCEPTS

To the extent privacy issues within businesses were specifically addressed at all, they were traditionally handled by several different departments, including legal, human resources, and information technology. Yet as contractual privacy rights have proliferated and compliance with local, state, federal, and international privacy laws has become a critical issue in business operations, companies have increasingly recognized the importance of tasking particular individuals with the responsibility of coordinating privacy protection across different departments.[219] Although these positions are known by many names, the most common descriptor is "Chief Privacy Officer" or "CPO" for short.

A CPO's responsibilities encompass the activities of many different areas of the business, and the CPO should have experience with not just privacy laws but must also understand how and why the company collects personal information, as well as how this information is stored and transmitted. A CPO must work closely with management to balance the benefits of collecting personal information with the legal risks that come with the practice.

---

[219] In 1992, Equifax became the first U.S. company to formally designate a CPO. *Protecting Customer Information: Can You Afford Not to Have a Chief Privacy Officer?*, 3, *available at* http://www.heidrick.com/~/media/Publications%20and%20Report s/PrivacyOfficer.pdf.

For companies that either cannot afford a permanent CPO, or otherwise do not wish to create such a position, there are other solutions intended to accomplish a similar result. Some companies set up a "privacy committee" with members from different departments to discuss privacy and security concerns. Other companies hire outside consultants, including law, accounting, or IT firms, to audit compliance with privacy laws and make recommendations on changes to operations or security measures. Entities specializing in privacy compliance include the Privacy and American Business and the Better Business Bureau, which have developed as consultants to companies to ensure security through the best possible practices.

The International Association of Privacy Professionals (IAPP) was founded in 2000 to define, promote, and improve the privacy profession. Growing very rapidly, the IAPP is the world's largest association of privacy professionals, with over 12,000 members from 78 countries. The IAPP provides a forum to allow members to share best practices, issues, and trends with other privacy professionals and offers training and certification programs on privacy law.

VI. PROFESSIONAL PRIVACY ETHICS

In stark contrast to the numerous discrete statutory provisions outlining privacy law in the United States, are the ethical considerations governing the practices of law and medicine. The legal profession's requirement of client privacy and confidentiality is imposed in a largely self-governing manner,[220] while the medical profession adheres to a similar code of ethical conduct designed to protect and benefit the patient.[221]

A.   LEGAL ETHICS

At the intersection of legal ethics and client privacy is the concept of the attorney-client privilege. "Privilege," generally, refers to the right to withhold information from a legal proceeding. The attorney-client privilege acts to protect a client's private information at the expense of the court's truth-seeking process; the privilege is a balance between the rights of, and to, the clients, and the courts. The attorney-client privilege has been characterized as the most widely respected and applied common-law privilege. It applies to confidential client communications made to an attorney for the purpose of seeking legal services. As the U.S. Supreme Court has stated, the "privilege is intended to encourage 'full and frank communication between attorneys and their clients and thereby promote broader public interests in the observance of law and the administration of justice.'" *Swidler & Berlin v. United States*, 524 U.S. 399, 403 (1998).

The extent of the attorney-client privilege can be shaped by statute, but it has been carved from the

---

[220]   MODEL RULES OF PROF'L CONDUCT pmbl. (2005).

[221]   *Principles of Medical Ethics*, AM. MED. ASS'N, http://www.ama-assn.org/ama/pub/category/2512.html (last revised June 2001).

common law. While the heart of the attorney-privilege lies within innumerable state and federal court decisions and state rules of professional conduct, its basics tenets of respecting a client's right to privacy are enumerated in both the Model Rules of Professional Conduct, and the *Restatement (Third) of the Law Governing Lawyers*. These works set forth the ethical standards that lawyers are bound to abide by concerning the protection of client communications. While these rules do not create an independent basis for criminal or civil liability (although in some jurisdictions it may be considered as evidence), violation of the ethical rules of conduct will subject an attorney to professional discipline from the governing bar.

1. Model Rules of Professional Conduct

The ABA Model Rules of Professional Conduct (Model Rules) are the main "influence on the rules of professional conduct governing lawyers in the United States."[222] The Model Rules do not bind lawyers to maintain a specific level of conduct, rather, the Model Rules must be adopted by a jurisdiction to become enforceable, although many courts and disciplinary bodies have found them to be persuasive authority even when not formally adopted. Although no jurisdiction has adopted the Model Rules in their entirety, close analogues to the Model Rules regarding attorney-client confidentiality and privacy are in effect in all U.S. jurisdictions. The Model Rules set standards for

---

[222]   MODEL RULES OF PROF'L CONDUCT pmbl. (2005).

attorney conduct concerning current,[223] former,[224] and prospective clients.[225]

Lawyers have a duty to not reveal private or confidential information relating to the representation of a current client unless the client provides "informed consent."[226] Absent informed consent, an attorney may reveal confidential information in only limited situations, namely:

(1) to prevent reasonably certain death or substantial bodily harm;

(2) to secure legal advice about the lawyer's compliance with these [Model] Rules;

(3) to establish a claim or defense on behalf of the lawyer in a controversy between the lawyer and client, to establish a defense to a criminal charge or civil claim against the lawyer based upon conduct in which the client was involved, or to respond to allegations in any proceedings concerning the lawyer's representation of the client; or

(4) to comply with other law or court order.[227]

Trust is fundamental to the attorney-client relationship. For assistance of counsel to be

---

[223]   *Id.* at R. 1.6.

[224]   *Id.* at R. 1.9.

[225]   *Id.* at R. 1.18.

[226]   "Informed consent" is agreement by a client to allow certain conduct after the attorney has fully explained and communicated the nature of the proposal, and explained the risks and alternatives. *Id.* at R. 1.0(e).

[227]   *Id.* at R. 1.6(b)(1)–(4).

effective, an attorney needs the client to fully and frankly disclose private information necessary to the representation. To facilitate this discourse, attorneys are bound by the rules of ethics to not disclose such private information in a manner adverse to clients' interests. Attorneys must act with competence to safeguard clients' information against "inadvertent or unauthorized disclosure," and must take reasonable precautions when transmitting the clients' private information.[228]

The duty to protect confidential client information extends even after completion of the attorney-client relationship. This continuing duty prevents an attorney from using a former clients' private information to the client's disadvantage, or to the benefit of a new client whose interests are adverse to the former client. Essentially, absent informed consent by the former client, the lawyer is forever barred from utilizing private information of a former client to the former client's detriment or for the benefit of another.

In addition to current and former clients, the attorney also has a duty to protect some, but not all, communications with prospective clients. Any discussions with an attorney regarding the possibility of forming an attorney-client relationship are considered communications with a prospective client.[229] Regardless of whether an attorney-client relationship is formed after the initial discussion,

---

[228]   *Id.* at R. 1.6 cmt. 15–16.

[229]   *Id.* at R. 1.18(a).

the attorney has a duty not to reveal private information learned through these consultations.

2. Restatement (Third) of the Law Governing Lawyers

The *Restatement (Third) of the Law Governing Lawyers* (*Restatement*) is the American Law Institute's attempt to define the prevailing ethical rules and standards applied to lawyers.[230] As with the Model Rules, the *Restatement* defines the lawyers' duty to keep client information private and confidential for current, former, and prospective clients. With the exception of duties to prospective clients, the professional duty of confidentiality usually does not adhere to lawyers in the absence of an attorney-client relationship. Under the *Restatement*, an attorney-client relationship arises when the client intends for the lawyer to provide legal services, and the lawyer either consents to provide such service, or fails to consent to service when he knows that the client is relying on him for legal service. While the attorney-client relationship is normally "a consensual one," the "consent requirement . . . is not symmetrical."[231] It is the client's manifestation of intent to form an attorney-client relationship that controls. Intent does not need to be reduced to writing, and may be inferred from the surrounding circumstances, conduct, or communication from the client or its agent. In this

---

[230] *See generally* RESTATEMENT (THIRD) OF THE LAW GOVERNING LAWYERS § 1 (2000).

[231] *Id.* at § 14 cmt. b.

respect, the legal profession displays a unique trait: duties of privacy and confidentiality that bind attorneys may be created without explicit acts of acceptance and consent on the part of the attorney.

The attorney-client privilege set forth in the *Restatement* applies to confidential communications between "privileged persons" made with the intent of extending or receiving legal services. A "communication" includes "any expression . . . undertake[n] to convey information to another privileged person and any document or other record revealing such an expression."[232] Parties to the privilege include current, prospective, and former clients, the attorneys, and agents of those parties. The privilege remains in effect, unless waived through agreement or disclosure, both during and after the representation of a client.

Once a duty of confidentiality arises, it becomes necessary to consider what exactly qualifies as confidential client information. The *Restatement* defines confidential client information as being "information relating to the representation of a client, other than information that is generally known."[233] Information can be in any form, whether written, oral, electronic recording, or others. The information must also be protected regardless of the ultimate source of the information, including whether or not the source itself is protected by the attorney-client privilege.

---

[232]   *Id.* at § 69.

[233]   *Id.* at § 59.

A lawyer's duty to maintain the confidential status of a client's information arises from the lawyer's status as a fiduciary of the client, which requires a commitment of loyalty to the client. The lawyer ordinarily must not use or disclose a client's confidential information and is required to "take reasonable measures to safeguard" the information.[234] A lawyer may disclose confidential client information in certain limited situations. A lawyer is allowed to disclose confidential client information:

1. if the lawyer reasonably believes that disclosure is necessary to protect or advance the client's interests;

2.   if ordered to by a court or pursuant to a subpoena or similar legal document, so long as the lawyer first "takes reasonably appropriate steps to assert that the information is privileged or otherwise protected against disclosure;"[235]

3. if the lawyer reasonably determines that the disclosure is necessary to defend against a claim that the lawyer committed malpractice or otherwise engaged in bad conduct in the course of the representation, but only to the extent necessary to rebut the claim;

4. if the lawyer reasonably determines that the disclosure is necessary to resolve a billing dispute with the client; or

---

[234]   *Id.* at § 16 cmt. e.
[235]   *Id.* at § 63.

5. if the lawyer reasonably believes the disclosure is "necessary to prevent reasonably certain death or serious bodily harm to a person;"[236] or to prevent the future commission of a crime or fraud by the client or its agent which "threatens substantial financial loss," and which would result from the client's use of the lawyer's services.[237]

Alternatively, the lawyer may almost always disclose a client's confidential information if the client has agreed after having been provided a sufficiently detailed explanation of the planned disclosure, to permit a reasoned determination as to whether to permit the lawyer to proceed, *i.e.*, "informed consent."

When the attorney-client relationship terminates, the attorney must take reasonable steps to protect the client's interests. As with present clients, in most instances an attorney cannot use a former client's confidential information without first seeking the former client's informed consent. These requirements are applied regardless of the reason for the termination, and regardless of which party initiates the termination.

The duties to prospective clients arise as soon as the lawyer begins discussing the *possibility* of forming an attorney-client relationship. Even if following the discussion, no actual attorney-client relationship forms, the duties still attach to the

---

[236]   *Id.* at § 66.

[237]   *Id.* at § 67(1).

attorney. Most relevant to privacy concerns is the lawyer's duty not to disclose confidential information that was learned in the course of the initial consultation and other preparatory communications. Under the *Restatement*, the duty of confidentiality to prospective clients exists no matter how brief the initial consultation or screening.

3. Unauthorized Disclosure

While instances of civil liability for breach of the attorney's duty of confidentiality are rare, the doctrinal basis supporting a claim is sound and can result in awards for monetary or injunctive relief, or both. In *Prudential Insurance Co. of America v. Massaro*,[238] for example, equitable relief in the form of a permanent injunction barring further disclosure was granted following the unauthorized disclosures of an attorney acting in an in-house capacity. As the court explained, essential to the attorney-client privilege is the requirement that "lawyers must not themselves voluntarily divulge information covered by their client's . . . privilege."[239] In *Perez v. Kirk & Carrigan*, 822 S.W.2d 261 (Tex. Ct. App. 1991), disclosure of confidential client information was held to allow for tort based recovery upon proof of damages. Perez was employed by Coca-Cola as a truck driver and was involved in a tragic automobile accident resulting in the death of 21 children.[240]

---

[238]   Civ. Act. No. 97–2022, 2000 WL 1176541 (D.N.J. Aug. 11, 2000).

[239]   *Id.* at *7.

[240]   *Perez*, 822 S.W.2d at 263.

Coca-Cola attorneys represented to Perez that they would represent him in the ensuing legal action, and with this understanding, Perez provided a sworn statement regarding the accident. Without the consent of Perez, the Coca-Cola attorneys disclosed this statement to the District Attorney resulting in a grand jury indictment for involuntary manslaughter. The statement was found to be a protected attorney-client communication revealed without client consent, and thus, the mental anguish and emotional distress that Perez suffered as a result of his conviction created a valid claim for damages.

4. The Brobeck Closed Archive

The "Brobeck Closed Archive" represents a unique challenge to traditional principles of client confidentiality, but it bears discussion due to the possibility that similar situations will arise in the future. Brobeck, Phleger & Harrison (Brobeck) was a large, national law firm founded in San Francisco in 1926. In the 1990s, the growth of Brobeck's business was driven by the wave of dot-com companies through its representation of numerous technology startups. Following the burst of the dot-com bubble, mismanagement and the loss of key personnel forced the firm to announce its intention to liquidate in February 2003, and ultimately filed for liquidation through a Chapter 7 bankruptcy proceeding.

What exactly is the Brobeck Closed Archive? Pursuant to the terms of its bankruptcy plan, "[t]he

Brobeck Closed Archive is a secure digital repository authorized by Order of Judge Dennis Montali, United States Bankruptcy Court, Northern District of California, San Francisco Division on August 9, 2006."[241] Judge Montali's Order effectively places confidential client records, previously private and clearly protected by the attorney-client privilege in most instances, into a digital repository sponsored by the Library of Congress and its National Digital Information Infrastructure Preservation Program (NDIIPP). Former clients have been given the opportunity to opt-out of the program, but absent affirmative communication from the former clients, their private information will automatically become available to researchers. Written notice was sent to former clients, and a notification was published in the Wall Street Journal and the San Francisco Chronicle.[242]

Strangely, through the course of bankruptcy proceedings, previously confidential client information has been transformed into a historical "artifact" containing, in the words of the Archive's managers, "a wealth of historical information" which must be preserved at the expense of any existing privilege.[243] Justification for this sweeping abrogation of settled principles of client confidentiality include: "if no action is taken to

---

[241] *Frequent Questions*, BROBECK CLOSED ARCHIVE, http://brobeckclosedarchive.org/faq.html (last visited Nov. 15, 2013).

[242] *Id.*

[243] BROBECK CLOSED ARCHIVE, http://brobeckclosed archive.org (last visited Nov. 15, 2013).

preserve these records, they will be lost to history forever"; "these digital records document one of the most extraordinary episodes in the history of capitalism, the explosion of internet technology companies in the 1990s"; and, lastly, Congress has charged the "Library of Congress to develop a national strategy for digital preservation" of "non-public digital objects."[244]

The Archive purports to keep access to the client files limited to "a small number of archivists or scholars who have signed strict non-disclosure agreements," with physical access taking "place in an on-site institutional setting, and only for specific . . . purposes [approved] . . . by the Court."[245] Given today's digital economy and appetite for sensationalized news, there is a high risk that this archived information will be leaked to the public. More importantly, the events surrounding the formation of the Archive suggest critical questions for both law firms and their clients concerning what steps should be taken to preserve the confidentiality of client information beyond the life of a particular law firm. While the Brobeck Closed Archive perhaps represents a truly extreme and unique situation, it still serves to unsettle the very foundation of the legal tradition: communication between attorney and client will be private, confidential, and privileged forever.

---

[244] *Frequent Questions*, BROBECK CLOSED ARCHIVE, http://brobeckclosedarchive.org/faq.html (last visited Nov. 15, 2013).

[245] *Id.*

B.   MEDICAL ETHICS

The medical profession has long been governed by ethical rules directed to the benefit of the patient. Physicians adhere to ethical rules in the form of an accepted standard of conduct; these rules are not legally binding and typically exceed any legal duty imposed.[246]

1. Ethical Rules

The medical profession arguably has the longest tradition of protecting privacy rights of any group or organization. The importance of promising patients confidentiality in order to provide effective medical care was recognized as early as the classical Greek Oath of Hippocrates.[247]

This principle continues to be reflected in the modern Hippocratic Oath:

I will respect the privacy of my patients, for their problems are not disclosed to me that the world may know.[248]

In 2001, the American Medical Association House of Delegates adopted the Revised Principles of Medical

---

[246]   *Opinion 1.02 - The Relation of Law and Ethics*, AM. MED. ASS'N,   http://www.ama-assn.org/ama/pub/physician-resources/medical-ethics/code-medical-ethics/opinion102.page?   (last updated June 1994).

[247]   *See* Peter Tyson, *The Hippocratic Oath Today*, NOVA (Mar. 27, 2001), http://www.pbs.org/wgbh/nova/body/hippocratic-oath-today.html.

[248]   *Definition of Hippocratic Oath*, MEDICINENET.COM, http://www.medterms.com/script/main/art.asp?articlekey=20909 (last updated Aug. 28, 2013).

Ethics.[249] The Revised Principles continue to emphasize that the privacy of patient information remains a paramount concern:

A physician shall respect the rights of patients, colleagues, and other health professionals, and shall safeguard patient confidences and privacy within the constraints of the law.[250]

In addition to the American Medical Association's Principles of Medical Ethics, the Judicial Council of the Association has issued opinions related to the privacy of patient information.[251] Opinion 5.05 states in part:

The information disclosed to a physician by a patient should be held in confidence. The patient should feel free to make a full disclosure of information to the physician in order that the physician may most effectively provide needed services. The patient should be able to make this disclosure with the knowledge that the physician will respect the confidential nature of the communication. The physician should not reveal confidential information without the express consent of the

---

[249] *Principles of Medical Ethics*, AM. MED. ASS'N, http://www.ama-assn.org/ama/upload/mm/369/2001_principles.pdf (last revised June 2001).

[250] *Id.*

[251] *See generally AMA's Code of Medical Ethics: 5.00— Opinions on Confidentiality, Advertising and Communications Media Relations*, AM. MED. ASS'N, http://www.ama-assn.org/ama/pub/physician-resources/medical-ethics/code-medical-ethics.page (last visited Nov. 15, 2013).

patient, subject to certain exceptions which are ethically justified because of overriding considerations.[252]

2. Doctor-patient Privilege

Patient confidentiality and privacy is a fundamental principle of the medical profession. The doctor-patient privilege allows candid discussion, ensuring the patient's medical needs are met. The privilege is not absolute, however, the doctor-patient privilege may fall where concerns over public health are raised (*e.g.*, to warn partners of sexually transmitted diseases), or where a legal duty requires disclosure of information.

Doctors must maintain procedural safeguards on private patient information, and public discussion of patients' medical problems without their consent represents a grave breach of professional ethics. Only with a patient's explicit consent may their personal information be disclosed outside of an academic medical setting. Doctors are also encouraged to be advocates for improving measures and procedures for protecting the confidentiality of patients' information.

---

[252] *Opinion 5.05 – Confidentiality*, AM. MED. ASS'N, http://www.ama-assn.org/ama/pub/physician-resources/medical-ethics/code-medical-ethics/opinion505.page? (last updated June 2007).

3. Unauthorized Disclosure

Recovery for unauthorized disclosure of medical information is based, in part, on the implied contract between doctor and patient.

> Any time a doctor undertakes the treatment of a patient, and the consensual relationship of physician and patient is established, two jural obligations . . . are simultaneously assumed by the doctor. Doctor and patient enter into a simple contract, the patient hoping that he will be cured and the doctor optimistically assuming that he will be compensated. As an implied condition of that contract, . . . the doctor warrants that any confidential information gained through the relationship will not be released without the patient's permission. Almost every member of the public is aware of the promise of discretion contained in the Hippocratic Oath, and every patient has a right to rely upon this warranty of silence. . . . Consequently, when a doctor breaches his duty of secrecy, he is in violation of part of his obligations under the contract.[253]

In order to be entitled to the doctor-patient confidentiality, the patient must specifically be seeking medical care or treatment from the doctor.[254] Discussion of a non-present, third party's

---

[253] Hammonds v. Aetna Cas. & Sur. Co., 243 F. Supp. 793, 801 (N.D. Ohio 1965).

[254] Howes v. United States, 887 F.2d 729, 732 (6th Cir. 1989).

medical concerns between doctor and patient is not covered by the doctor-patient privilege. On the other hand, disclosing confidential patient information during litigation without having at least notified the patient of the planned disclosure, even if it would appear to fall within an exception to the privilege, can be considered a breach of doctor-patient privilege.[255] These disclosures may create tort liability.[256] The privilege, however, can be compromised even without notice in extreme situations. Where a patient is considered a danger to himself and others, a physician's disclosure of confidential information does not amount to breach of the duty of confidentiality, nor commission of a tort; "[t]he protective privilege ends where the public peril begins."[257] Thus the court in *McDonald v. Clinger*, ruled that "disclosure of confidential information by a psychiatrist to a spouse will be justified whenever there is a danger to the patient, the spouse or another person."[258]

---

[255] Sorensen v. Barbuto, 143 P.3d 295, 300 (Utah Ct. App. 2006).

[256] *See id.* at 301–02.

[257] Tarasoff v. Regents of Univ. of Cal., 551 P.2d 334, 347 (Cal. 1976).

[258] 446 N.Y.S.2d 801, 805 (N.Y. App. Div. 1982).

CHAPTER FOUR
INTERNATIONAL PRIVACY

As the "right to privacy" has evolved from a "right to be let alone" to the right to control other's use and dissemination of one's personal data, so too has the economic and technological background of the world changed. Now that global data networks are ubiquitous, personally identifiable data is no longer tied to the locality of its owner or even to the owner's nation of residence. Exchanges of personal data regularly cross national borders, often between countries where the "right to privacy" means two different things. This chapter considers how international and non-U.S. privacy protection regimes operate, both on their own and where they intersect with U.S. privacy law.

I.   INTERNATIONAL AGREEMENTS

A true binding international agreement protecting privacy does not exist. The differences in national legal systems are a clear obstacle to any agreement, but the many types and forms of data that might be considered "personal" further exacerbate these legal differences. Over the past several decades, however, there has been increasing progress toward identifying and agreeing on at least certain foundational issues. The single most influential document on this subject has been the Guidelines on the Protection of Privacy and

Transborder Flows of Personal Data (Guidelines)[1] produced by the Organization for Economic Co-operation and Development (OECD).

1. OECD Privacy Guidelines

The OECD is a group of 30 countries committed to the promotion of democratic governance and economic development. As part of these efforts, the members of the OECD collaborate to produce various documents, including model treaties, reports, and recommendations to promote an orderly international system and facilitate trade not just between its members, but between all interested nations.

The realization that market forces would create both challenges and opportunities for privacy rights happened during the 1970s, when the OECD began to see arguments over national privacy laws in the context of trade negotiations. On September 23, 1980, after several years of negotiations, the OECD Council approved its proposed Guidelines, which aspired to harmonize national data protection legislation, protect human rights, and facilitate international data transfers. The Guidelines try to bring commonality to the *mechanisms* of privacy protections in participating countries without attempting to design a complete regulatory

---

[1]   *OECD Guidelines on the Protection of Privacy and Transborder Flows of Personal Data*, ORG. FOR ECONOMIC COOPERATION & DEV. (Sept. 23, 1980), http://www.oecd.org/sti/ieconomy/oecdguidelinesontheprotectionofprivacyand transborderflowsofpersonaldata.htm [hereinafter *Guidelines*].

framework. The Guidelines are only a "soft law" agreement and do not legally bind the signatories; however, these Guidelines also represent a pragmatic consensus that inconsistent privacy laws can be a barrier to economic development.

The OECD Council Recommendation concerning the 1980 Guidelines recognizes that:

- although national laws and policies may differ, Member countries have a common interest in protecting privacy and individual liberties, and in reconciling fundamental but competing values such as privacy and the free flow of information;

- automatic processing and transborder flows of personal data create new forms of relationships among countries and require the development of compatible rules and practices;

- transborder flows of personal data contribute to economic and social development;

- domestic legislation concerning privacy protection and transborder flows of personal data may hinder such transborder flows.[2]

The Guidelines set out eight basic principles that data protection legislation should follow:

---

[2]   *Id.*

1. **Collection Limitation:** Personal data should be obtained by lawful means, preferably with the knowledge or consent of the individual whose data is being collected.

2. **Data Quality:** Controllers of personal data (data controllers) should strive to maintain records, which are accurate, complete, and up-to-date, as well as being relevant to the purposes for which the data is collected.

3. **Purpose Specification:** Data controllers should disclose the purposes for which personal data will be collected no later than the time of collection, with subsequent use of the data limited to the disclosed purposes or use in a manner not incompatible with the original purposes, although compatible alternative uses should be disclosed when implemented.

4. **Use Limitation:** Personal data should not be disclosed or used for purposes other than those specified prior to or upon collection unless approved by the individual or to comply with the directions of a legal authority.

5. **Security Safeguards:** Once collected, if personal data is stored, it should be subject to reasonable security precautions.

6. **Openness:** Data controllers should provide a readily available means for individuals to determine whether and what type of personal data of theirs is held by the data controller. This should include facilitating the

identification of the data controller and the purposes for which the data is being used.

7. **Individual Participation:** Individuals should have the ability to obtain information from a data controller within a reasonable time regarding any personal data held by the collector and be able to have errors or omissions in the data corrected.

8. **Accountability:** A means should be provided by which data controllers can be accountable for compliance with the Guidelines' principles.[3]

The 1980 Guidelines also set out four Basic Principles of International Application concerning Free Flow and Legitimate Restrictions, which are the OECD's recommendations for applying data protection legislation to international transfers of personal data:

1. Member countries should take into consideration the implications for other Member countries of domestic processing and re-export of personal data.

2. Member countries should take all reasonable and appropriate steps to ensure that transborder flows of personal data, including transit through a Member country, are uninterrupted and secure.

---

[3]   *Id.* at ¶¶ 7–14.

3. A Member country should refrain from restricting transborder flows of personal data between itself and another Member country except where the latter does not yet substantially observe these Guidelines or where the re-export of such data would circumvent its domestic privacy legislation. A Member country may also impose restrictions in respect of certain categories of personal data for which its domestic privacy legislation includes specific regulations in view of the nature of those data and for which the other Member country provides no equivalent protection.

4. Member countries should avoid developing laws, policies, and practices in the name of the protection of privacy and individual liberties, which would create obstacles to transborder flows of personal data that would exceed requirements for such protection.[4]

While the Guidelines have served as the foundation for other agreements concerning transborder data flows, numerous countries continue to have contrary and incompatible data protection legislation. Subsequent efforts, especially the U.S./E.U. Safe Harbor, have been directed at both harmonization of protection regimes and providing for effective enforcement.

---

[4]   *Id.* at ¶¶ 15-18.

2. Revision of the OECD Guidelines

In 2013, the OECD Council adopted a major revision to the 1980 Guidelines (Revised Guidelines).[5] This is the first revision since the Guidelines were adopted in 1980 and stems from a call by participants in the 2008 *Seoul Declaration for the Future of the Internet Economy*[6] to review the Guidelines in light of "changing technologies, markets and user behaviour, and the growing importance of digital identities."[7]

In 2011, the OECD Working Party on Information Security and Privacy (WPISP) agreed on Terms of Reference for that review.[8] The Terms of Reference highlighted the fact that in the past 30 years, there has been a profound change of scale in terms of the role of personal data in the economy, society, and in daily life. The WPISP recognized that the environment in which the traditional privacy

---

[5]   OECD, RECOMMENDATION OF THE COUNCIL CONCERNING GUIDELINES GOVERNING THE PROTECTION OF PRIVACY AND TRANSBORDER FLOWS OF PERSONAL DATA (2013), http://www.oecd.org/sti/ieconomy/2013-oecd-privacy-guidelines. pdf [hereinafter *Revised Guidelines*] (last visited Nov. 5, 2013).

[6]   DIRECTORATE FOR SCI., TECH. & INDUS. COMM. FOR INFO., COMPUTER AND COMMC'NS POLICY, OECD, THE SEOUL DECLARATION FOR THE FUTURE OF THE INTERNET ECONOMY (2008), *available at* http://www.oecd.org/internet/consumer/ 40839436.pdf (last visited Nov. 5, 2013).

[7]   *Id.* at 10.

[8]   WPISP, OECD, TERMS OF REFERENCE FOR THE REVIEW OF THE OECD GUIDELINES GOVERNING THE PROTECTION OF PRIVACY AND TRANSBORDER DATA FLOWS OF PERSONAL DATA (2011), *available at* http://www.oecd.org/sti/ieconomy/48975226. pdf.

principles are now implemented has undergone substantial changes especially in:

- The *volume of personal data* being collected, used and stored;

- The *range of analytics* involving personal data, providing insights into individual and group trends, movements, interests, and activities;

- The *value of the societal and economic benefits* enabled by new technologies and responsible uses of personal data;

- The *extent of threats* to privacy;

- The *number and variety of actors* capable of either putting privacy at risk or protecting privacy;

- The *frequency and complexity of interactions* involving personal data that individuals are expected to understand and negotiate; and

- The *global availability* of personal data, supported by communications networks and platforms that permit continuous, multipoint data flows.[9]

Two themes run through the Revised Guidelines. First, is a focus on privacy protection centered on risk management.[10] Second, is the need for

---

[9]   *Id.* at 3 (emphasis in original).
[10]   *See generally Revised Guidelines, supra* note 5, at 19–30.

increased efforts to address the global aspects of privacy by improving interoperability.[11]

The Council introduced a number of new concepts in the Revised Guidelines, including a focus on national privacy strategies at the highest levels of government, implementation of privacy management programs, and data breach notification requirements.[12] Other revisions modernized the OECD approach to transborder data flows, detailed the key elements of what it means to be an accountable organization, and strengthened privacy enforcement.[13]

3. Additional OECD Guidelines

In the 1990s, the Guidelines were joined by two more agreements from the OECD that demonstrated the continuing evolution of the attitude toward privacy protection.

In 1992, the OECD published its Guidelines for the Security of Information Systems and Networks (Security Guidelines).[14] The OECD reviewed the Security Guidelines in 1997 and concluded that they remained adequate to address the issues and

---

[11]   *Id.* at 33–34.

[12]   *Id.* at 22.

[13]   *Id.* at 17.

[14]   *OECD Guidelines for the Security of Information Systems, 1992*, OECD (Nov. 26, 1992), http://www.oecd.org/sti/ieconomy/oecdguidelinesforthesecurityofinformationsystems1992.htm [hereinafter *1992 Security Guidelines*].

purposes for which they were designed.[15] In 2000, the OECD initiated a second review of the Security Guidelines focused on "the development of interconnected and interdependent information systems which are fundamental to modern economies," and the collection of "information on existing threats, vulnerabilities and actions taken by governments and the private sector."[16]

In anticipation of the second review, Japan offered to host a "Workshop on Information Security in a Networked World" in Tokyo on September 12–13, 2001 to facilitate review efforts, exchange and share information, develop an understanding of information security, and increase involvement in this area.[17]

This review was marked by a sense of urgency, which resulted from: (1) the recognition that developments affecting the security of information systems in a world characterized by global ubiquitous networks significantly reduced the relevance of the 1992 Guidelines; and (2) the events of September 11, which took place the day before the Tokyo Workshop.[18]

---

[15] *The Role of the 2002 Security Guidelines: Towards Cybersecurity for an Open and Interconnected Economy*, WPISP, OECD 4 (Nov. 16, 2012), http://search.oecd.org/officialdocuments/publicdisplaydocumentpdf/?cote=DSTI/ICCP/REG(2012)8/FINAL&docLanguage=En.

[16] *Id.*

[17] *Id.*

[18] *See id.* (citing Summary Record of the WPISP meeting on October 9–10, 2001 (OECD, 2001c) where "delegates concurred

In November 2012, the OECD initiated a third review of the Security Guidelines.[19] As of this publication, the OECD has not released the details of this third review.

The OECD published its Guidelines for Cryptography Policy in 1997.[20] Subsequent reviews of these guidelines have concluded that they "continue to be adequate to address the issues and purpose for which they were developed."[21]

The implementation of these guidelines signaled a shift in the OECD's thinking. The rise of the Internet meant that international commerce was becoming more important and more democratized as increasing numbers of consumers began dealing directly with businesses in other nations. Yet, at the same time, consumers were also becoming increasingly concerned about the privacy of personal information they might transmit in the course of such transactions. Maintaining the privacy of personal data was recognized as something that encouraged people to use electronic networks

---

that, particularly in light of the events of September 11, a thorough and expedited review should be conducted . . . .")

[19]   See Terms of Reference for the Review of the OECD Guidelines for the Security of Information Systems and Networks (OECD Digital Economy Papers, No. 210, Nov. 16, 2012), available at http://www.oecd-ilibrary.org/science-and-technology/terms-of-reference-for-the-review-of-the-oecd-guidelines-for-the-security-of-information-systems-and-networks_5k8zq92zhqhl-en.

[20]   Guidelines for Cryptography Policy, OECD (Mar. 27, 1997),   http://www.oecd.org/internet/ieconomy/guidelinesfor cryptographypolicy.htm.

[21]   See id.

thereby increasing transborder dataflows, rather than halting them.

II.   NATIONAL LAWS

A.   CANADA

1. Constitutional Protection

Canada, like the United States, has no explicit right to privacy in its constitution. Section Eight of the Canadian Charter of Rights and Freedoms, enacted as part of the Canada Act of 1982, however, has been interpreted by Canadian courts to guarantee a reasonable right to privacy.[22] Section Eight, which is much like the U.S. Constitution's Fourth Amendment, thus governs any constitutional privacy concerns.

2. Statutory Protection

a. Personal Privacy in the Public Sector

Canada's Privacy Act governs personal privacy in the public sector. The Act was passed in 1983 to "extend the present laws of Canada that protect the privacy of individuals with respect to personal information about themselves held by a government institution and that provide individuals with a right of access to that information."[23]

---

[22]   *See* Hunter v. Southam, Inc., [1984] 2 S.C.R. 145, 159–60 (Can.).

[23]   Privacy Act, R.S.C. 1985, c. P-21 § 2 (Can.).

Canadian law allows government institutions to collect information only if it relates directly to an operating program or activity of the institution.[24] With few exceptions, government agencies must inform individuals that their personal information is being collected and the purpose for which it is being collected. Moreover, any information gathered by an institution must be used solely for the purpose for which it was gathered.[25] Personal information collected by the government, in most instances, cannot be disclosed without the permission of the individual who is the subject of the information.[26]

Every Canadian citizen has the right to access the information that is "reasonably retrievable" by the governmental institution storing the information for the purpose of correcting the information if it is inaccurate.[27] Any individual can complain to the Privacy Commissioner if the individual was denied access to his or her information.[28] An individual who is denied access to information has a right to bring suit in the Canadian Federal Court for review of the denial.[29] The Privacy Commissioner also receives and investigates any other complaints submitted under the Privacy Act.

---

[24]   *Id.* at § 4.

[25]   *Id.* at § 7(a).

[26]   *Id.* at § 8(1).

[27]   *Id.* at § 12(1)(b).

[28]   *Id.* at § 16(1).

[29]   *Id.* at § 41.

b. The Privacy Commissioner

The Canadian Privacy Commissioner is a representative who is appointed by the Canadian Federal Cabinet, with the appointment being approved by resolution in the Canadian House of Commons and Senate.[30] The position was created pursuant to the Privacy Act, but now has significantly broader authority because of the enactment of additional privacy legislation discussed below. The Commissioner serves for a seven-year term and can be reappointed.[31]

The Privacy Commissioner, who is considered an agent of Parliament, reports directly to the House and Senate on issues dealing with privacy. The Commissioner is responsible for ensuring that the federal government, as well as the private sector, collect, use, and disclose personal information in a manner that is responsible and consistent with applicable laws and regulations.

The Privacy Commissioner has broad authority within the subject area he or she has been tasked with overseeing.[32] The Commissioner can initiate audits of an organization's information collection, management, and disclosure practices to determine whether adequate protective measures are in place and to verify that the information is being used in a

---

[30]   *Id.* at § 53(1).

[31]   *Id.* at § 53(2)–(3).

[32]   *Id.* at § 34(1); *see also About the Office of the Privacy Commissioner,* OFFICE OF THE PRIVACY COMM'R OF CAN., http://www.priv.gc.ca/au-ans/index_e.asp#cn-tphp (last modified Jul. 19, 2010).

lawful manner. When conducting an audit, any person with relevant information can be summoned to appear before the Commissioner.[33] The Commissioner also has the power to administer oaths and receive sworn testimony and evidence in quasi-judicial hearings.[34]

Despite the Privacy Commissioner's far-reaching investigatory power, the office lacks the ability to issue orders or impose penalties for any violations.[35] The Commissioner instead usually arrives at decisions calculated to resolve problems through negotiated settlements. If the Commissioner determines that the violation is sufficiently severe, the office can file litigation against the offender in the Federal Court and proceed through the judicial process.[36] As an alternative for disputes that cannot be resolved through a negotiated agreement but are not sufficiently grave to merit the Commissioner pursuing litigation on its own, the Commissioner can, in some situations, provide the results of its investigation to private individuals who have been injured by the privacy breach to facilitate them bringing private litigation against the bad actor.[37]

c. Personal Privacy in the Private Sector

The main legislation governing personal privacy in the Canadian private sector is the Personal

---

[33]   Privacy Act § 34(1)(a).

[34]   *Id.* at § 34(1)(c).

[35]   *Id.* at § 42(a)–(c).

[36]   *Id.*

[37]   *Id.* at § 35(5).

Information Protection and Electronic Documents Act (PIPEDA).[38] Beginning with its 1992–93 annual report, the Privacy Commissioner began urging the adoption of legislation extending protection to personal information held by the private sector. Two years later, Canada's Information Highway Advisory Council joined this call. Contemporaneously with these developments, the European Union (E.U.) was starting to take steps to restrict transmission of its citizens' personal information to parties in non-E.U. nations with inadequate privacy protections, which would have seriously affected Canadian business.[39] In 1998, the supporting bill for PIPEDA was introduced, ultimately passing in 2000.[40]

Rather than implementing the entire legislation at once, PIPEDA had a tiered implementation schedule. In January of 2001, PIPEDA implementation included all personal information excluding health information held by federally regulated private sector entities. A year later, in January 2002, the act began regulating personal health information. Finally, in January 2004 the act reached full-implementation status. The 2004 implementation encompasses all organizations that

---

[38] Personal Information Protection and Electronic Documents Act, S.C. 2000, c. 5 (Can.) [hereinafter PIPEDA].

[39] The European Union's efforts at privacy protection are discussed in detail in Chapter 4, Part II(B).

[40] *Legal Information Related to PIPEDA*, OFFICE OF THE PRIVACY COMM'R OF CAN., http://www.privcom.gc.ca/legislat ion/02_06_02b_e.asp (last modified Apr. 1, 2004).

commercially collect, use, or disclose personal information.[41]

Personal information under PIPEDA includes "information about an identifiable individual."[42] The name, title, business address, or telephone number of an employee within an "organization," however, is not considered personal information. "Organization" is broadly defined to include associations, partnerships, and unions.[43] PIPEDA does not cover Canadian government institutions that are otherwise subject to the Privacy Act.[44] Information that is collected, used, or disclosed by individuals for personal purposes or for "journalistic, artistic, or literary purposes" is also not included.[45] Provinces may enact their own privacy legislation provided that it meets or exceeds the level of protection afforded by PIPEDA. The provinces of Alberta, British Columbia, Ontario, Manitoba, and Quebec have enacted such legislation.[46]

---

[41]   *Id.*

[42]   PIPEDA § 2(1).

[43]   *Id.* at § 2(1).

[44]   *Id.* at § 4(2)(a).

[45]   *Id.* at § 4(2)(b)–(c).

[46]   Personal Information Protection Act, S.A. 2003, c. P-6.5 (Can. Alta.); Personal Information Protection Act, S.B.C. 2003, c. 63 (Can. B.C.); An Act Respecting the Protection of Personal Information in the Private Sector, R.S.Q., c. P-39.1 (Can. Que.); Personal Information Protection and Identity Theft Prevention Act, S.M. 2013, c. 17 (Man. Can.); *see also Fact Sheets, Questions and Answers regarding the application of PIPEDA, Alberta and British Columbia's Personal Information Protection Acts*, OFFICE OF THE PRIVACY COMM'R OF CAN., http://www.privcom.gc.ca/fs-fi/02_05_d_26_e.asp (last modified Nov. 05, 2004).

PIPEDA sets forth specific individual rights as well as requiring organizations to follow certain guidelines. PIPEDA gives individuals the right to know why an organization collects, uses, or discloses personal information.[47] PIPEDA also gives individuals the right to expect that organizations collect, use, or disclose personal information reasonably and appropriately and only for the purpose for which the individual has consented.[48] Individuals have the right to know who in the organization is collecting the personal information, and who is responsible for protecting that information.[49] Individuals have the right to expect an organization to implement adequate security measures to protect personal information.[50] Individuals are also entitled to expect that the personal information an organization holds is accurate, complete, and up-to-date.[51] PIPEDA, like the Privacy Act, allows individuals to obtain access to personal information and make corrections if necessary.[52]

Under PIPEDA, organizations that commercially use personal information, or make other non-exempt uses of it, are required to follow ten principles of fair information practices, which are modeled on the OECD Guidelines. The principles are: (1)

---

[47]   PIPEDA § 7; PIPEDA sch. 1, cl. 4.9.
[48]   PIPEDA sch. 1, cl. 4.3.
[49]   *Id.* at sch. 1, cl. 4.8.
[50]   *Id.* at sch. 1, cl. 4.7.
[51]   PIPEDA § 5; PIPEDA sch. 1, cl. 4.6.
[52]   PIPEDA § 8; PIPEDA sch. 1, cl. 4.9.

accountability; (2) identifying purposes; (3) consent; (4) limiting collection; (5) limiting use, disclosure, and retention; (6) accuracy; (7) safeguards; (8) openness; (9) individual access; and (10) challenging compliance.[53] If an organization has safeguards in place to insure compliance with these principles then it is likely fulfilling all its duties under PIPEDA.

PIPEDA requires organizations to obtain consent from the individual, when collecting, using, or disclosing personal information. Organizations must supply an individual with a service or product even if the individual refuses to consent to the collection, use, or disclosure of personal information. Beyond merely collecting information in a lawful fashion, organizations must have personal information policies that are clear, understandable, and readily available.[54]

PIPEDA has specific procedures for individuals to make complaints to the Office of the Privacy Commissioner concerning violations of PIPEDA. If the Commissioner determines that certain types of violations have occurred the complainant will have a cause of action against the violator, which can be pursued in the Federal Court.[55] PIPEDA requires the Commissioner to commence an investigation upon receipt of a properly filed complaint.[56] Once an investigation has been opened, the Commissioner

---

[53]   PIPEDA sch. 1.

[54]   *Id.* at sch. 1, 4.8.1.

[55]   PIPEDA § 14(1)–(3).

[56]   *Id.* at § 12(1)(a)–(c).

has one year to complete the investigation and issue a written report, although it may be determined in certain situations that a written report is unnecessary.[57]

(i) Trans-border data flows under PIPEDA

As previously mentioned, a significant motivating factor for enacting PIPEDA was to assure the European Union that Canada's privacy laws were strict enough to protect the interests of the citizens of the European Union.[58] Currently, Canada and the European Union allow certain personal data to flow freely to Canada from the European Union, subject to PIPEDA, without additional safeguards. This, however, does not include data held by national agencies.[59]

The Privacy Commissioner has determined that PIPEDA not only governs the collection, use, and disclosure of personal information within Canada, but the law also controls the transmission of personal information internationally pursuant to

---

[57]   *Id.* at § 13(1).

[58]   ARTICLE 29-DATA PROTECTION WORKING PARTY, OPINION 2/2001 ON THE ADEQUACY OF THE CANADIAN PERSONAL INFORMATION AND ELECTRONIC DOCUMENTS ACT (2001), *available at* http://ec.europa.eu/justice/policies/privacy/docs/wpdocs/2001/wp39en.pdf (last visited Nov. 5, 2013).

[59]   Commission Decision of 20 December 2001 pursuant to Directive 95/46/EC of the European Parliament and of the Council on the Adequate Protection of Personal Data Provided by the Canadian Personal Information Protection and Electronic Documents Act, 2002/2/EC, 2002 O.J. (L 2/13) (2002), *available at* http://eur-lex.europa.eu/LexUriServ/LexUriServ.do?uri=OJ:L:2002:002:0013:0016:EN:PDF (last visited Nov. 5, 2013).

the federal government's power over international trade and commerce.[60]

The Privacy Commissioner has given some guidelines to individuals wishing to protect their personal information from inappropriate disclosure to foreign parties.[61] Individuals are encouraged to report concerns about the collection or use of their personal information to the Commissioner. Although the Commissioner lacks power to act directly against foreign parties, the Commissioner can raise the issue with the national government of the state where the foreign party is located. Even more powerfully, if a Canadian organization or a multi-national organization with a Canadian presence is cooperating with, or otherwise assisting, the foreign party; it can be subject to regular proceedings under the PIPEDA complaint process.[62]

(ii) PIPEDA and the Patriot Act

Following the terrorist attacks of September 11, 2001 the United States Congress passed the USA

---

[60]   *A Privacy Handbook for Lawyers, PIPEDA and Your Practice,* OFFICE OF THE PRIVACY COMM'R OF CAN., http://www.priv.gc.ca/information/pub/gd_phl_201106_e.pdf (last modified Aug. 16, 2011).

[61]   *Fact Sheets, What Canadians Can Do to Protect Their Personal Information Transferred Across Borders,* OFFICE OF THE PRIVACY COMM'R OF CAN., http://www.privcom.gc.ca/fs-fi/02_05 _d_23_e.asp (last modified Aug. 18, 2004).

[62]   *A Privacy Handbook for Lawyers, PIPEDA and Your Practice,* OFFICE OF THE PRIVACY COMM'R OF CAN., http://www.priv.gc.ca/information/pub/gd_phl_201106_e.pdf (last modified Aug. 16, 2011); *see also* Lawson v. Accusearch Inc., 2007 FC 125.

PATRIOT Act of 2001 (Patriot Act). The Patriot Act is discussed at length in Chapter 3, which addresses U.S. privacy law; however, certain of its provisions are relevant to PIPEDA, specifically the Patriot Act's expansion of the U.S. Treasury Secretary's powers to regulate and monitor financial transactions that involve foreign individuals and entities.[63]

Canada is the United States' largest trading partner. As a result, many of the databanks used to store personal information of Canadian residents are located in the United States, thus making them subject to the provisions of the Patriot Act. However, if a U.S.-based company makes a disclosure of a Canadian resident's personal information to U.S. authorities under the Patriot Act without the consent of the individual who is named, this could result in the Canadian organization that originally transferred the information being liable for a breach of PIPEDA unless the disclosure meets an exception in the applicable Canadian law.

One of the exceptions found in PIPEDA is for investigations of criminal activity under the laws of Canada or foreign jurisdictions.[64] Specifically, the statute provides that personal information may be

---

[63]   Uniting and Strengthening America by Providing Appropriate Tools Required to Intercept and Obstruct Terrorism Act [USA PATRIOT Act], Pub. L. 107-56, U.S.C.C.A.N. (115 Stat.) 272. (2001) (codified as amended in scattered sections 8, 12, 15, 18, 20, 31, 42, 47, 49, and 50 U.S.C.).

[64]   See PIPEDA, S.C. 2000, c. 5 § 7(2)(a) (Can.).

disclosed without the knowledge of the subject where "required to comply with a subpoena or warrant issued or an order made by a court . . . with jurisdiction to compel the production of information."[65] It is unclear; however, from the face of the statute whether PIPEDA only allows disclosure under Canadian court orders or if a U.S. court order would apply.

The office of the Privacy Commissioner recognizes this issue and has urged Canadian organizations to take a number of steps that are intended to assist them in avoiding this dilemma.[66] These steps include: (1) informing Canadian residents that their personal information may be transferred to locations in the United States and be subject to search; (2) entering into contracts with United States-based organizations which require them to provide the same level of protection for the personal information of Canadian residents as would be required by PIPEDA; (3) limiting the amount of personal information that is transferred into the United States; and (4) limiting the ability of United States-based organizations to access personal information of Canadian residents stored in Canada.[67]

---

[65]   *Id.* at § 7(3)(c).

[66]   Heather Black, Assistant Privacy Comm'r of Can., The Latest Developments in Privacy Compliance: PIPEDA Review and the USA PATRIOT Act, Address at the 11th Annual Meeting on Regulatory Compliance for Financial Institutions (Nov. 18, 2005), *available at* http://www.privcom.gc.ca/speech/2005/sp-d_051118_hb_e.asp (last modified Nov. 18, 2005).

[67]   *Id.*

These are only recommendations; therefore Canadian organizations likely to be transacting business with U.S. organizations must balance the potential risks of violating Canadian privacy legislation against the benefits of working within the United States.

In 2009, the Privacy Commissioner released guidelines for processing personal data across borders. These guidelines explain how PIPEDA applies to personal information that is transferred to third parties for processing, including those located outside of Canada.[68] The guidelines do not cover transfers of personal information for processing by federal, provincial, or territorial public sector entities. Nor do these guidelines address any specific rules governing transfers for processing that may be found in provincial private sector privacy laws. However, organizations not governed by PIPEDA for commercial activities within a province need to be aware that PIPEDA applies to transborder transfers.[69]

d. Updating Privacy Legislation

In May of 2013, the Privacy Commissioner released a position paper (Position Paper) calling for

---

[68]   *Processing Personal Data Across Borders: Guidelines*, OFFICE OF THE PRIVACY COMM'R OF CAN., http://www.priv.gc.ca/ information/guide/2009/gl_dab_090127_e.pdf (last visited Nov. 15, 2013).

[69]   *Id.*

substantial changes to PIPEDA in keeping with changes to the global landscape.[70]

The Position Paper outlines four important recommendations for changes to PIPEDA, most of which focus on increasing the accountability of data controllers and processors. Those changes include expanding the Commissioner's enforcement powers, implementing mandatory breach reporting and notification requirements, requiring notification to consumers of warrantless disclosures of their personal information to government authorities, and providing the Commissioner with the authority to enter into and enforce agreements similar to the use of consent decrees in the U.S. Under these "enforceable agreements," an organization found to be in violation of law would agree to comply with the Commissioner's recommendations and to demonstrate such compliance within a set period; otherwise, the Commission would be able to seek judicial enforcement.[71]

Legislators have attempted to amend PIPEDA several times but ultimately the law has remained unchanged. Most recently, Bill C-12 was proposed. That bill would amend PIPEDA to require organizations to report material breaches of safeguards involving personal information and would require organizations to notify the affected

---

[70]   *The Case for Reforming the Personal Information Protection and Electronic Documents Act*, OFFICE OF THE PRIVACY COMM'R OF CAN. (May 2013), http://www.priv.gc.ca/parl/2013/pipeda_r_201305_e.pdf.

[71]   *Id.*

individuals if the breach creates a risk of significant harm. The Privacy Commissioner, however, has argued that Bill C-12 is "behind the times" and does not sufficiently address challenges resulting from the massive aggregation of personal data.[72] As of this publication, Bill C-12 is awaiting its second reading before the House of Commons.

B.   EUROPEAN UNION

Since the Second World War, Western European nations have shown an increasingly strong commitment to protecting individual privacy. Long before the Internet boom of the 1990s, European countries were focusing on protection of personal privacy by limiting data access. The German state of Hesse, for example, passed the first law granting individuals control of their personal information in 1970.[73] Indeed, the term "data protection" entered the European lexicon from the German word "Datenschutz." Three years later, Sweden was the first country to pass a privacy protection law.[74] While much of the underlying public concern that motivated these early efforts grew from historical concerns about the possible abuses of compilations

---

[72]   Address by Jennifer Stoddart, Privacy Commissioner of Canada, Privacy protection in Canada – Keeping Pace with Advancing Global Norms, Remarks at the 2012 Access and Privacy Conference, organized by University of Alberta, June 14, 2012 Edmonton, Alberta, http://www.priv.gc.ca/media/sp-d/2012/sp-d_20120614_e.asp.

[73]   Hessisches Datenschutzgesetz [HDSG] [Data Protection Act of the German Federal State of Hessen], Sept. 30 1970, v 7.10.1970 GVB1, Hesse I § 625 (Ger.).

[74]   Datalag (1973:289) [Data Act] (Swed.).

of personal information, technological developments were the immediate stimulus, as both statutes were enacted in response to proposals to combine separate government archives into computerized databases.

The process of political integration in Europe has advanced considerably since the era of these first attempts at legislating protections for personal information. The governing bodies of the European Union now wield considerably more influence over patterns of economic regulation in the E.U. Member States than the national governments do. While individual member states of the European Union still maintain separate laws addressing privacy issues, the scope of European privacy protection has been driven mainly by the European Union for the past decade or more. The European Union's privacy regime will be reviewed as a "national" policy, notwithstanding its many member states.

1. The Data Protection Directive

The mainstay of privacy protection in the European Union arises from Directive 95/46 (Data Protection Directive).[75] The Data Protection Directive was an outgrowth of the national regulatory schemes promoted by the OECD

---

[75] Council Directive 95/46/EC of the European Parliament and of the Council of 24 October 1995 on the Protection of Individuals with Regard to the Processing of Personal Data and on the Free Movement of Such Data, 1995 O.J. (L 281) 31, *available at* http://eur-lex.europa.eu/LexUriServ/LexUriServ.do?uri=OJ:L:1995:281:0031:0050:EN:PDF [hereinafter *Data Protection Directive*].

Guidelines, which had produced a patchwork of different privacy regimes throughout Europe. The Data Protection Directive was designed to harmonize Member States' data protection legislation, thereby reducing obstacles to economic activity within the European Union while preserving (or even enhancing, depending on the preexisting level of national data protection) the privacy rights of individual residents.

The Data Protection Directive encompasses "personal data" of E.U. residents, meaning "information relating to an identified or identifiable natural person,"[76] where that data is processed[77] "wholly or partly by automatic means" or where the data will form part of a filing system, or both.[78] A person is "identifiable" if the individual "can be identified, directly or indirectly, in particular by reference to an identification number or to one or more factors specific to [their] physical, physiological, mental, economic, cultural, or social

---

[76]   Data Protection Directive, 95/46/EC, ch. I, art. 2(a), 1995 O.J. (L281) 31, 38.

[77]   "Processing of personal data" is defined as any operation pertaining to personal data including "collection, recording, organization, storage, adaptation or alteration, retrieval, consultation, use, disclosure by transmission, dissemination or otherwise making available, alignment or combination, blocking, erasure or destruction." Data Protection Directive, 95/46/EC, art. 2(b), 1995 O.J. (L281) 31, 38.

[78]   A "filing system" is "any structured set of personal data which are accessible according to specific criteria, whether centralized, decentralized, or dispersed on a functional or geographical basis." Data Protection Directive, 95/46/EC, ch. I, art. 2(c), 1995 O.J. (L281) 31, 38.

identity."[79] An exception is provided for "purely personal" use by a natural person and for government purposes relating to security, defense, and criminal law.[80]

The laws enacted in accordance with the Data Protection Directive must apply to data "controllers"[81] or "processors"[82] located in a Member State, a territory subject to a Member State's laws, or located elsewhere but relying on equipment located within a Member State for any purpose other than transmission.[83]

Data must be collected only for "specified, explicit and legitimate purposes," without any further processing that would be "incompatible with those purposes."[84] The data collected must be "adequate, relevant, and not excessive" given the purposes for

---

[79] Data Protection Directive, 95/46/EC, ch. I, art. 2(a), 1995 O.J. (L281) 31, 38.

[80] Id. at art. 3(2), 1995 O.J. (L281) 31, 39.

[81] A data "controller" is any "natural or legal person, public authority, agency or any other body which alone or jointly with others determines the purposes and means of the processing of personal data." Id. at art. 2(d), 1995 O.J. (L281) 31, 38.

[82] A data "processor" is any "natural or legal person, public authority, agency or any other body which processes personal data on behalf of the controller." Id. at art. 2(e), 1995 O.J. (L281) 31, 38. A data processor may not legitimately process personal data unless instructed by the data controller or otherwise required by law to process the data. Id. at ch. II, § 7, art. 16, 1995 O.J. (L281) 31, 43.

[83] Id. at ch. I, art. 4(1)(a)–(c), 1995 O.J. (L281) 31, 39.

[84] Processing of previously collected personal data for "historical, statistical or scientific purposes" is permissible with "appropriate safeguards." Id. at ch. II, art. 6(1)(b), 1995 O.J. (L281) 31, 40.

which it was acquired.[85] Data must not only be accurate, but "every reasonable step must be taken" to delete or correct inaccurate and incomplete data.[86] The data must not be "kept in a form which permits identification of data subject" for any longer than is necessary for the original purpose it was collected for, except where Member States provide for safeguards if the data is to be retained for "historical, statistical or scientific purposes."[87] Compliance with these requirements is the responsibility of the data controller.

Absent certain legal circumstances, personal data may only be processed if the subject "has unambiguously given . . . consent."[88] Further protections are required for particularly sensitive personal data,[89] which may even override explicit consent by subjects to the use of their personal data.[90] These added protections do not apply where that data is necessary for medical care, law enforcement, or other "reasons of substantial public interest" if an exemption has been provided for by the Member State's data protection legislation.[91]

---

[85]   *Id.* at ch. II, § I, art. 6(1)(c), 1995 O.J. (L281) 31, 40.

[86]   *Id.* at art. 6(1)(d), 1995 O.J. (L281) 31, 40.

[87]   *Id.* at art. 6(1)(e), 1995 O.J. (L281) 31, 40.

[88]   *Id.* at ch. II, § II, art. 7(a)–(f), 1995 O.J. (L281) 31, 40.

[89]   Referred to as "special categories of data," this includes data "revealing racial or ethnic origin, political opinions, religious or philosophical beliefs, trade-union membership . . . [or] concerning health or sex life." *Id.* at art. 8(1), 1995 O.J. (L281) 31, 40.

[90]   *Id.* at ch. II, § III, art. 8(2)(a), 1995 O.J. (L281) 31, 40.

[91]   *Id.* at art. 8(3)–(5), 1995 O.J. (L281) 31, 41.

Exceptions based on law enforcement and public interest needs must be notified to the European Commission (Commission). If necessary to avoid unreasonable restrictions on free expression, Member States may provide exemptions for journalism, artistic, or literary works.[92]

The data controller or its representative must provide subjects from whom data has been collected with "at least" the identity of the controller and any representatives, the intended purposes for which the data will be processed, and any further relevant information necessary to "guarantee fair processing" of the subject's data.[93] If the data has not been obtained directly from the subject, the data controller must provide the same information as above to the subject, either when the personal data is initially recorded or no later than when the data is first disclosed to a third party. In the latter case, particularly if the data has been obtained for historical, statistical, or scientific purposes, the controller does not need to provide such notice if doing so would "involve a disproportionate effort," or is otherwise exempted by law, providing that proper safeguards are undertaken.[94]

---

[92]   Id. at art. 9, 1995 O.J. (L281) 31, 41.

[93]   Other information can include the recipients of the data, whether providing the data is voluntary or mandatory (including the consequences of not providing the data), and the existence of the right to review and correct the data. Id. at ch. II, § IV, art. 10(a)–(c), 1995 O.J. (L281) 41.

[94]   Id. at ch. II, § IV, art. 11(2), 1995 O.J. (L281) 31, 42.

A data subject must have the right to obtain from the controller confirmation of whether data about the subject is being processed, the purposes of the processing, the types of data involved, and the identities of the data recipients.[95] The subject also has the right to receive communications pertaining to the processing that describe the data "in an intelligible form," the source of the data, and "knowledge of the logic" used in automatic processing of the data, if applicable.[96] The subject has the right to rectify, erase, or block data where processing has not complied with the terms of the Data Protection Directive, and of notification to third-party recipients of the data of such corrections or deletions unless doing so would involve a disproportionate effort. Member States, however, have the power to adopt legislation restricting these rights if the limitations are a necessary part of protecting national security, public safety, or law enforcement investigations. Finally, the subject has the right to object "on compelling legitimate grounds" to processing performed because of the public interest exception or the exception provided for processing in the legitimate interest of the controller or third parties, or both.[97] If those grounds are found to be justified, the subject has the

---

[95]   *Id.* at ch. II, § V, art. 12(a)–(c), 1995 O.J. (L281) 31, 42. This right must be able to be exercised at "reasonable intervals and without excessive delay or expense."

[96]   *Id.* at ch. II, § V, art. 12(a), 1995 O.J. (L281) 31, 42.

[97]   This is so unless national legislation provides otherwise. *Id.* at ch. II, § VII, art. 14(a), 1995 O.J. (L281) 31, 42-43.

right to have the processing halted.[98] If the data is to be used for direct marketing purposes, there is an implicit presumption the objection is legitimate and justified.[99]

Data controllers must "implement appropriate technical and organizational measures" for protecting personal data from "accidental or unlawful destruction," loss, alteration, disclosure, or theft.[100] The measures must provide a reasonable level of security for the type of data, as determined by the state of the art and cost of implementation, and the risks posed by its processing. The controller is responsible for ensuring that any data processors working on its behalf provide adequate technical and organizational measures to protect the personal data being processed. Agreements between controllers and processors must be by contract or other binding legal act, and the provisions relating to data protection and the protective measures must be in writing or "equivalent form."[101]

The controller or its representative must notify the appropriate national supervisory authority of

---

[98]   *Id.*

[99]   *See generally Id.* at ch. II, § VII, art. 14(b), 1995 O.J. (L281) 31, 43 (bestowing a right to object upon the data subject where the information will be used for direct marketing).

[100]   *Id.* at ch. II, § VIII, art. 17(1), 1995 O.J. (L281) 31, 43.

[101]   The Data Protection Directive itself does not stipulate what an "equivalent form" would be, indicating that it is left to the Member States to determine that point. For example, Austria does not recognize an "equivalent form," requiring all such contracts to be in writing. *Id.* at ch. II, § VIII, art. 17(4), 1995 O.J. (L281) 31, 43.

any intent to carry out a wholly or partially automatic data processing operation.[102] Member States may make exceptions to the notification requirement, or allowances for simplified notice, under certain circumstances. An exception of particular significance exists where a data controller, in compliance with national law, appoints a "personal data protection official," who is responsible for independently guaranteeing the internal application of the terms of the Data Protection Directive and keeping a record of processing operations directed by the controller. If notification is required, it must at least include:

1. The name and address of the controller and, if appropriate, its representative;

2. The purpose of the processing;

3. A description of the categories of data subjects and the categories of data pertaining to them;

4. The recipients who may receive the data;

5. Proposed transfers to non-Member States; and

6. A general description of the security measures employed to guard the data

---

[102]   *Id.* at ch. II, § IX, art. 18(1), 1995 O.J. (L281) 43. Member States are required to establish or empower one or more independent public agencies to be responsible for monitoring the implementation of the Data Protection Directive. *Id.* at ch. VI, art. 28(1), 1995 O.J. (L281) 31, 47.

processing sufficient to allow a preliminary determination of their adequacy.[103]

Member States must also determine which processing operations are likely to pose particular risks to the rights and freedoms of their residents and carry out examinations of these operations prior to their commencement. These examinations are to be carried out by the supervisory authority after notification by the data controller or its data protection official. If the controller or the official cannot decide whether the operation would pose particular risks, the supervisory authority must be consulted. Member States may enact more restrictive pre-implementation notification requirements.[104]

A public record available for inspection by any person must be kept of all processing operations for which the Member State has received notification.[105] Data controllers, or another body appointed by the Member State, must also make available to any person, upon request, records of all processing operations other than those for which notice was required.[106] Member States may make an exception for processing done solely for keeping a register mandated by law or regulation, and which

---

[103]   *Id.* at ch. II, art. 19(1)(a)–(f), 1995 O.J. (L281) 31, 44.

[104]   *Id.* at ch. II, § IX, art. 20(1)–(3), 1995 O.J. (L281) 31, 44.

[105]   This record must contain at least the notification information required by the Data Protection Directive, with the exception of a description of the security measures used to protect the data. *See Id.* at ch. II, art. 21(2), 1995 O.J. (L281) 31, 44–45.

[106]   *Id.* at ch. II, § IX, art. 21(3), 1995 O.J. (L281) 31, 45.

is intended to provide information to the public, whether generally or for those who can prove a legitimate interest.[107]

In addition to any administrative remedies provided by the supervisory authority, every person is to have access to a judicial remedy for the breach of any rights incorporated in the Member State's data protection legislation.[108] Some Member States have gone even further and have provided for criminal penalties for breach of their national data protection legislation in addition to civil penalties. Sweden, for example, allows for a fine and a six-month term of imprisonment, with imprisonment up to two years "if the offence is grave."[109] Austria provides for a maximum of one-year imprisonment "unless the offence shall be subject to a more severe punishment pursuant to another provision."[110] The injured party is entitled to damages from the controller for loss, unless the controller can prove it is not responsible for the events leading to the loss.

Of particular significance in the Data Protection Directive are its provisions on extraterritorial application of its requirements. Personal data undergoing processing, or to be processed, may only be transferred to a party in a non-Member State, such as the United States, if the non-Member State

---

[107]   *Id.* at ch. II, § IX, art. 21(3), 1995 O.J. (L281) 31, 45.

[108]   *Id.* at ch. III, § IX, art. 22, 1995 O.J. (L281) 31, 45.

[109]   49 § Personuppgiftslagen (1998:204) [Personal Data Act] (Swed.).

[110]   Datenschutzgesetz [DSG] [Federal Act Concerning the Protection of Personal Data] No. 165/1999, § 51 ¶ 1 (Austria).

"ensures an adequate level of protection."[111] Adequacy of protection is determined by reference to all the circumstances pertaining to a data transfer operation, particularly the nature of the data, the purpose of the proposed processing operation, the duration of the operation, the countries of origin and destination, as well as the laws, professional rules, and security measures employed by the non-Member State.[112] Member States and the Commission must keep each other informed of evidence showing a non-Member State is failing to provide a satisfactory level of security.[113] If the Commission determines that a non-Member State is failing to provide adequate protection for personal data originating from the European Union, then Member States must take measures to block further transfer of the same type of data to the non-Member State in question.[114] Where such a determination has been made, the Commission must enter into negotiations with the non-Member State to remedy the situation.[115]

Member States, however, may provide exceptions to the transfer restrictions on the condition that the data subject has given unambiguous consent to the transfer, or meets other criteria.[116] Member States

---

[111]   Data Protection Directive, 95/46/EC, ch. IV, art 25(1), 1995 O.J. (L281) 31, 45.

[112]   *Id.* at ch. IV, art 25(2), 1995 O.J. (L281) 31, 45.

[113]   *Id.* at ch. IV, art 25(3), 1995 O.J. (L281) 31, 46.

[114]   *Id.* at ch. IV, art 25(4), 1995 O.J. (L281) 31, 46.

[115]   *Id.* at ch. IV, art 25(5), 1995 O.J. (L281) 31, 46.

[116]   *Id.* at ch. IV, art 26(1)(a), 1995 O.J. (L281) 31, 46.

may also permit transfers to data controllers in non-Member States that have failed to comply legislatively with the Data Protection Directive if the controller itself guarantees adequate safeguards, particularly by contract.[117] Member States must inform the Commission of any authorizations they grant under self-certification criteria, and these may be challenged by any other Member State or the Commission itself. The Commission may also decide that a standard contractual clause provides adequate protection, in which case the Member States must permit data transfers made pursuant to contracts containing this type of clause.[118]

2. Problems Implementing the Data Protection Directive

As noted above, the Member States of the European Union enforce the terms of the Data Protection Directive by implementing their own laws—the Directive is not self-executing. Member States were required under the terms of the Directive to have "laws, regulations and administrative provisions" in force no later than three years after the adoption of the directive.[119] Member States were to have had their compliant data protection legislation in place by October 24, 1998. Member States were also allowed to grant an exemption for an additional nine years to manual

---

[117]   *Id.* at ch. IV, art 26(2), 1995 O.J. (L281) 31, 46.

[118]   *Id.* at ch. IV, art 26(3), 1995 O.J. (L281) 31, 46.

[119]   *Id.* at ch. VII, art. 32(1), 1995 O.J. (L281) 31, 49.

filing systems. A number of Member States, however, delayed passing the necessary implementing legislation, leading the Commission to file suit in the European Court of Justice in December 1999 against France, Ireland, Germany, the Netherlands, and Luxembourg. Even under the pressure of litigation, it was not until July 1, 2003, when Ireland's national data protection legislation became effective that all Member States were compliant.[120]

Getting all Member States to enact the necessary legislation was by no means the only challenge to implementation. Member States' various approaches to implementing the Directive have resulted in national requirements sufficiently different to mean that compliance with the bare terms of the Directive will not automatically mean a company is in compliance with the laws of any given Member State. The United Kingdom defines "personal data" as information that may be used to identify a living, natural individual.[121] Information concerning deceased individuals, thus, is not ordinarily protected. Austria, on the other hand, protects the information of not just natural persons

---

[120]   Member States joining the European Union subsequent to the Directive taking effect were obligated to enact compliant legislation as a condition of entry. *See Justice, Status of Implementation of Directive 95/46 on the Protection of Individuals with Regard to the Processing of Personal Data,* EUROPEAN COMM'N, http://ec.europa.eu/justice/data-protection/law/status-implementation/index_en.htm (last updated July 16, 2013).

[121]   Data Protection Act, 1998, c. 29, § 1(1) (Eng.), *available at* http://www.legislation.gov.uk/ukpga/1998/29/data.pdf.

regardless of their vital status, but legal persons as well.[122]

3. Updates to the Data Protection Directive

One of the strong points of the Data Protection Directive is that it is adaptable across a wide range of industries and service providers. The Directive is calculated to avoid technological or economic obsolescence by not depending on the specific details of collection or processing, but rather by focusing on the nature of the data to determine how it should be protected. The Data Protection Directive, did however, focus exclusively on the uses of personal data by "collectors" and "processors." It did not address the question of transmission of data via third parties who served neither as collectors nor as processors, but who could potentially compromise the security of the data whether deliberately or inadvertently.

The European Union's response was the E.U. Electronic Communications Directive (Communications Directive).[123] The

---

[122] Bundesgesetz über den Schutz Personenbezogener Daten [DSG 2000] [Federal Act Concerning the Protection of Personal Data] Bundesgesetzblatt I [BGB1] No. 165/1999, *amended by* [BGB1] No. 135/2009, § 4(1), (3) (Austria), *available at* http://www.ris.bka.gv.at/Dokumente/Erv/ERV_1999_1_165/ERV_1999_1_165.pdf.

[123] Council Directive 2002/58/EC of the European Parliament and of the Council of 12 July 2002 Concerning the Processing of Personal Data and the Protection of Privacy in the Electronic Communications Sector, 2002 O.J. (L 201) 37, *available at* http://eur-lex.europa.eu/LexUriServ/LexUriServ.do?uri=OJ:L:2002:201:0037:0037:EN:PDF [hereinafter *Communications Directive*].

Communications Directive creates privacy rules for the telecommunications industry that implement the principles of the Data Protection Directive with respect to communications channels. The Communications Directive speaks specifically to communications privacy in Article 5:

> Member States shall ensure the confidentiality of communications and the related traffic data by means of a public communications network and publicly available electronic communications services, through national legislation. In particular, they shall prohibit listening, tapping, storage, or other kinds of interception or surveillance of communications and the related traffic data by persons other than users, without the consent of the users concerned, except when legally authorized to do so in accordance with Article 15(1). This paragraph shall not prevent technical storage, which is necessary for the conveyance of a communication without prejudice to the principle of confidentiality.[124]

Of note is the mention to Article 15(1) in the preceding text. Article 15(1) demonstrates the limits of the strong privacy rights created by the Data Protection Directive:

> Member States may adopt legislative measures to restrict the scope of the rights and obligations provided for in Article 5 . . . of this

---

[124] Communications Directive, 2002/58/EC, art. 5(1), 2002 O.J. (L 201) 37, 43.

Directive when such restriction constitutes a necessary, appropriate and proportionate measure within a democratic society to safeguard national security, defense, public security, and the prevention, investigation, detection and prosecution of criminal offences or of unauthorized use of the electronic communication system, as referred to in Article 13(1) of [the Data Protection Directive]. To this end, Member States may adopt, *inter alia*, legislative measures providing for the retention of data for a limited period justified on the grounds laid down in this paragraph.[125]

Article 15(1) of the Communications Directive, when combined with legislation enacted pursuant to Article 13(1) of the Data Protection Directive effectively created an exception with the potential to swallow the rule depending on the actions of the Member States.

Almost immediately after the passage of the Communications Directive, the Member States began enacting national legislation with significant variations in data monitoring and retention requirements for communications providers. In response to the numerous incompatible and in some instances contradictory national legislative schemes, the European Union responded with yet

---

[125]   *Id.* at art. 15(1), 2002 O.J. (L 201) 37, 46.

another Directive, this time attempting to set uniform limits on data retention policies.[126]

The preamble clauses of the Data Retention Directive acknowledge the non-uniformity of the Member States' actions, and the technical problems this was causing service providers:

> (5) Several Member States have adopted legislation providing for the retention of data by service providers for the prevention, investigation, detection, and prosecution of criminal offences. Those national provisions vary considerably. (6) The legal and technical differences between national provisions concerning the retention of data for the purpose of prevention, investigation, detection and prosecution of criminal offences present obstacles to the internal market for electronic communications, since service providers are faced with different requirements regarding the types of traffic and location data to be retained and the conditions and periods of retention.[127]

---

[126] Council Directive 2006/24/EC of the European Parliament and of the Council of 15 March 2006 on the Retention of Data Generated or Processed in Connection with the Provision of Publicly Available Electronic Communications Services or of Public Communications Networks and Amending Directive 2002/58/EC, 2006 O.J. (L 105) 54, *available at* http://eur-lex.europa.eu/LexUriServ/LexUriServ.do?uri=OJ:L:2006:105:005 4:0063:EN:PDF [hereinafter *Data Retention Directive*].

[127] Data Retention Directive, 2006/24/EC, (5) & (6), 2006 O.J. (L105) 54.

While uniformity may be welcome to some degree, the Data Retention Directive also serves to further legitimize and institutionalize data collection:

> (10) On 13 July 2005, the Council reaffirmed in its declaration condemning the terrorist attacks on London the need to adopt common measures on the retention of telecommunications data as soon as possible. (11) Given the importance of traffic and location data for the investigation, detection, and prosecution of criminal offences, as demonstrated by research and the practical experience of several Member States, there is a need to ensure at European level that data that are generated or processed, in the course of the supply of communications services, by providers of publicly available electronic communications services or of a public communications network are retained for a certain period, subject to the conditions provided for in this Directive.[128]

The Data Retention Directive in fact not only permits Member States to derogate from the privacy protections of the Data Protection and Electronic Communications Directives, but also affirmatively requires the Member States to do so on several points. Member States must enact legislation which compels service providers to retain "data necessary to trace and identify" the source and destination of electronic communications, including the telephone numbers, IP addresses, or other identifiers of both

---

[128]   *Id.* at (10) & (11), 2006 O.J. (L105) 54, 55.

sending and receiving parties. Service providers are also required to preserve information concerning the date, time, and duration of electronic communications as well as the communications protocols used, the transmitting and receiving equipment, and the actual physical location of a mobile device at the time of the communication.[129] Service providers may be required to retain the information for between six months to two years. Member States were given until September 15, 2007 to pass implementing legislation, although they were given the right to exempt certain types of Internet communication from the retention requirements until March 15, 2009.

Some countries have either refused to adopt the Data Retention Directive, or have struck down their national data retention laws implementing the directive for violating human rights.

The Data Retention Directive was adopted in Romania, but declared unconstitutional in 2009.[130] In 2011, Cyprus declared their national data retention law unconstitutional.[131] The Courts in

---

[129]   *Id.* at art. 5(1)(a)–(f), 2006 O.J. (L105) 54, 57–58.

[130]   *Romanian Senate Rejects the new Data Retention Law,* Digital Civil Rights in Europe, EDRI, (Jan. 18, 2012), http://edri.org/edrigramnumber10-1romanian-senate-rejects-data-retention/ (last visited January 11, 2014).

[131]   Retention of Telecommunication Data for Purposes of Investigation of Serious Criminal Offences Law of 2007, 183(I)/2007 (Cyprus); *see also Data retention law provisions declared unlawful in Cyprus,* Digital Civil Rights in Europe, EDRI, (Feb. 9, 2011), http://edri.org/edrigramnumber9-3data-retention-un-lawful-cyprus/ (last visited January 11, 2014).

Bulgaria also declared their mandatory data retention laws unconstitutional.[132] Nations now fighting the Directive include Cyprus, Czech Republic, Germany, Greece, and Romania.[133]

On November 7, 2013, the Advocate General of the European Court of Justice was scheduled to announce a decision in concerning the constitutionality of the Data Retention Directive. The case stems from a challenge brought by Ireland and Austria's highest courts and seeks clarification of the purposes, effectiveness, and necessity of the Data Retention Directive in light of Articles 7, 8, and 11 of the European Union Constitution.

In 2012, the European Commission proposed a comprehensive reform to the 1995 data protection rules, in order to strengthen online privacy rights and boost Europe's "digital economy."[134]

Rooted in the European concept that personal data privacy is a human right, the updated directive is intended to modernize the principles enshrined in

---

[132] *Bulgarian Court Annuls a Vague Article of the Data Retention Law*, Digital Civil Rights in Europe, EDRI, (Dec. 17, 2008), http://edri.org/edri-gramnumber6-24bulgarian-administrative-case-data-retention/ (last visited January 11, 2014).

[133] *European Union*, ELEC. FRONTIER FOUND., https://www.eff.org/issues/mandatory-data-retention/eu (last visited Nov. 7, 2013).

[134] Press Release, European Commission, Commission Proposes a Comprehensive Reform of Data Protection Rules to Increase Users' Control of their Data and to Cut Costs for Businesses (Jan. 25, 2012), *available at* http://europa.eu/rapid/press-release_IP-12-46_en.htm?locale=en (last updated Sept. 19, 2013).

the 1995 Directive and to ensure privacy rights in the future. The suggested reforms include legislative proposals, including a regulation setting out a general framework for data protection.[135] This reform is not scheduled to take effect until 2014.[136]

4. Safe Harbor

A key part of the Data Protection Directive is its strong restrictions on the transfer of E.U. residents' data outside of the European Union—recipients of the transferred data must either be subject to national regulations providing protection equivalent to that of the Directive or otherwise enter into certain contractual arrangements guaranteeing an equivalent level of protection. The United States did not have (and still lacks) a comprehensive privacy protection regime, let alone one that provided equivalent protections to the Data Protection Directive. Some compromise solution had to be reached or E.U.-U.S. trade would be severely impacted. The U.S. Department of Commerce entered into negotiations with the E.U. Commission concerning what steps could be taken to avoid U.S. businesses being summarily cut off from access to E.U. residents' data.

The result of these negotiations is the agreement called the "Safe Harbor." The Safe Harbor, which is administered by the U.S. Department of Commerce, is a self-certification system for U.S. businesses to confirm that they have implemented internal

---

[135]   *Id.*

[136]   *Id.*

procedures sufficient to ensure E.U. residents' data receives protections equivalent to those required by the Data Protection Directive. The E.U. Commission approved the use of the Safe Harbor in July 2000 pursuant to its authority under Article 25 of the Data Protection Directive to certify non-Member States as complying with the provisions of the Directive.[137] As a result, U.S. businesses that meet the requirements of the Safe Harbor may safely receive and process data from E.U. residents. The Safe Harbor itself is analyzed in greater detail in Chapter 4, Part III(A)(1) below concerning transborder data flows.

C.   MEXICO

1. Constitutional Protection

The Mexican Constitution contains privacy guarantees similar to those found in the Fourth Amendment of the U.S. Constitution. Article 16 of the Mexican Constitution sets up the framework for personal privacy: "No one shall be molested in his person, family, domicile, papers, or possessions except by virtue of a written order of the competent authority stating the legal grounds and justification

---

[137]   *See* Commission Decision 2000/520/EC of 26 July 2000 Pursuant to Directive 95/46/EC of the European Parliament and of the Council on the Adequacy of the Protection Provided by the Safe Harbor Privacy Principles and Related Frequently Asked Questions Issued by the US Department of Commerce, art. 1(1), 2000 O.J. (L 215) 7, 8, *available at* http://eur-lex.europa.eu/ LexUriServ/LexUriServ.do?uri=CELEX:32000D0520:EN:HTML [hereinafter *Safe Harbor Decision*].

for the action taken."[138] This is essentially the "right to be let alone"; the Mexican Constitution does not expressly provide protection for personal data.

2. Statutory Protection

Mexico has numerous statutes that address privacy and data protection. In 2010, Mexico enacted its first comprehensive data protection statute, the Federal Law on the Protection of Personal Data held by Private Parties (Federal Law), and related regulations were issued in 2011.[139]

The Federal Law applies to all private individuals or entities that obtain, use, divulge, or store the personal data of third parties, unless the data is (1) collected by credit bureaus acting under the laws regulating them, or (2) collected exclusively for personal use and without the purpose of divulging it or using it for commercial purposes.

On September 10, 2013, Mexico's Data Protection Authority (Instituto Federal de Acceso a la Información Pública y Protección de Datos (IFAI))

---

[138] Constitución Política de los Estados Unidos Mexicanos [C.P.], art. 16, Diario Oficial de la Federación [D.O.], 5 de Febrero de 1917 (Mex.), *available at* http://www.oas.org/juridico/mla/en/mex/en_mex-int-text-const.pdf (English translation).

[139] Ley Federal de Protección de Datos Personales en Posesión de Particulares [L.F.P.D.P.P.P.][Federal Protection of Personal Data in Possession of Private Parties Law] Diario Oficial de la Federación [D.O.], 5 de Julio de 2010 (Mex.), *available at* https://www.privacyassociation.org/media/pdf/knowledge_center/Mexico_Federal_Data_Protection_Act_July2010.pdf (Unofficial English Translation).

published their draft Data Security Guidelines for public consultation. The guidelines recommend companies adopt a Personal Data Safety Management System, as well as internationally accepted standards issued by the International Organization for Standardization (ISO) (discussed in more detail below) and the OECD (discussed above).[140]

The Federal Law incorporates eight general principles that data controllers must follow in handling personal data: legality, consent, notice, quality, purpose limitation, fidelity, proportionality, and accountability.[141] The Federal Law also addresses data retention, providing that personal data must be deleted when no longer necessary for the purposes set out in the privacy notice and applicable law. Under the Federal Law, data processors must:

- Designate an individual or department to be in charge of securing the personal data obtained by the processor and to handle requests from data subjects;

- Prepare and deliver privacy notices to each data subject (Privacy Notice);

---

[140] *Mexico: IFAI Publishes Security Guidelines for Public Consultation,* DATAGUIDANCE, http://www.dataguidance.com/news.asp?id=2105 (last updated Sept. 12, 2013).

[141] Ley Federal de Protección de Datos Personales en Posesión de Particulares [L.F.P.D.P.P.P.][Federal Protection of Personal Data in Possession of Private Parties Law], art 6, Diario Oficial de la Federación [D.O.], 5 de Julio de 2010 (Mex.).

- Obtain the consent of data subjects before collecting, processing, or transferring "sensitive" information;

- Limit the use of the personal data collected to those uses listed in the Privacy Notice; and

- Ensure that the personal data in its databases is pertinent, correct, and current for the purposes the data was collected.[142]

In 2013, Mexico's Ministry of Economy, in collaboration with the IFAI, published its *Lineamientos del Aviso de Privacidad* (Privacy Notice Guidelines).[143] These guidelines impose notice and opt-out requirements for the use of cookies and similar technology, and impose broad requirements on the content and delivery of Privacy Notices.

Mexico has also passed laws that address privacy protection in different sectors of the economy and that relate to specific business practices. The Federal Consumer Protection Law, for example, gives consumers the right to request that their personal information be deleted from direct

---

[142] *See generally* Ley Federal de Protección de Datos Personales en Posesión de Particulares [L.F.P.D.P.P.P.][Federal Protection of Personal Data in Possession of Private Parties Law], art. 30, Diario Oficial de la Federación [D.O.], 5 de Julio de 2010 (Mex.).

[143] Lineamientos del Aviso de Privacidad, [Privacy Notice Guidelines], Diario Oficial de la Federación [D.O.], 17 de Enero de 2013 (Mex.), *available at* http://www.dof.gob.mx/nota_detalle.php?codigo=5284966&fecha=17/01/2013.

marketing lists,[144] while the Law of Protection and Defense of the User of Financial Services protects the personal information of individuals engaged in banking and securities transactions.[145] Many of these statutes were updated as part of the passage of the E-Commerce Act in 2000 and have been updated periodically since 2000 with no major changes to the data privacy aspects of the legislation. The E-Commerce Act updated the language of the Federal Civil Code, the Federal Rules of Civil Procedure, the Commercial Code, and the Federal Consumer Protection Law. This update added language that provides protection to electronic documents, digital signatures, and online activity.

3. Other Organizations & Enforcement

The focus on data privacy in Mexico centers on the government. The IFAI is an independent body, which serves to both facilitate citizens' access to information about the internal operations of the government and reviews government activities that affect the privacy interests of Mexican citizens.

Recently, a group of college professors founded the first Non-Governmental Organization (NGO)

---

[144] Ley Federal de Protección al Consumidor [L.F.P.C.] [Federal Consumer Protection Law], *as amended*, 16 de Enero de 2013, Diario Oficial de la Federación [D.O.], 24 de Diciembre de 1992 (Mex.).

[145] Ley de Protección y Defensa al Usuario de Servicios Financieros [L.P.D.U.S.F.] [Financial Services User Protection and Defense Law], *as amended*, 4 de Septiembre de 2012, Diario Oficial de la Federación [D.O.], 18 de Enero de 1999 (Mex.).

focusing on privacy rights and personal information held by private entities. Founded in 2011, SonTusDatos [It's Your Data], has been developing an advocacy program and continues to be the only NGO in Mexico focusing on data protection and privacy.[146] SonTusDatos' objectives include raising public awareness, educating and empowering internet users, acting as an intermediary between legislative institutions and the public, and reporting violations of the data privacy laws.[147]

Criminal prosecution of companies that violate data privacy laws is being openly discussed in Mexico, especially following the discovery of an illegal transfer of personal data to U.S. government agencies, which appears to have been used at least in part by U.S. immigration officials to locate and remove Mexican nationals unlawfully in the United States.

Federal Law also classifies some activities as crimes that can be punished by imprisonment. For example, a person who is authorized to handle personal data and causes a breach of security measures with the intent of gaining a pecuniary benefit could receive a sentence of between three months and three years in prison. Likewise, a person who collects and handles personal data fraudulently with the aim of gaining a pecuniary

---

[146] SONTUSDATOS, ACERA DE, ANTECEDENTES, http://sontusdatos.org/acerca-de/antecedentes/ (last visited Nov. 5, 2013).

[147] *Id.*

benefit can be punished by imprisonment between six months and five years.[148]

D. JAPAN

1. Constitutional Protection

Like the Fourth Amendment to the U.S. Constitution, the Japanese Constitution provides the basis of personal privacy (right to be let alone). Article 35 provides, "The right of all persons to be secure in their homes, papers, and effects against entries, searches, and seizures shall not be impaired except upon warrant issued for adequate cause and particularly describing the place to be searched and things to be seized . . . ."[149] Article 21 maintains secrecy of communications providing, "No censorship shall be maintained, nor shall the secrecy of any means of communication be violated."[150] In 2000, the Japanese Diet established a body called the Research Commission on the Constitution to consider possible amendments to the Japanese Constitution. The Research Commission's report was released in 2005 and included a

---

[148] Ley Federal de Protección de Datos Personales en Posesión de Particulares [L.F.P.D.P.P.P.][Federal Protection of Personal Data in Possession of Private Parties Law] Diario Oficial de la Federación [D.O.], 5 de Julio de 2010 (Mex.), *available at* https://www.privacyassociation.org/media/pdf/ knowledge_center/Mexico_Federal_Data_Protection_Act_July201 0.pdf (Unofficial English Translation).

[149] NIHONKOKU KENPŌ [KENPŌ] [CONSTITUTION], art. 35, para. 1 (Japan), *available at* http://www.kantei.go.jp/foreign/ constitution_and_government_of_japan/constitution_e.html (English translation).

[150] *Id.* at art. 21, para. 2.

recommendation that an amendment concerning personal privacy be added,[151] but the Diet has not yet taken action.

2. Statutory Protection

Personal data collected by the government is regulated by the 1988 Act for the Protection of Computer Processed Personal Data Held by Administrative Organs.[152] This law implements the OECD Guidelines of security, access, and correction, and it limits subsequent uses of data for purposes other than those for which the data was originally gathered.

Japan, historically, has allowed businesses and private organizations to self-regulate the handling of personal information. This began to change in 1997, when the Ministry of International Trade and Industry (MITI) issued a set of guidelines concerning data collections in the private sector.[153] The momentum toward regulating the private sector continued when Japan enacted the Personal Information Protection Law[154] (PIPL) in May 2003,

---

[151] RESEARCH COMM'N ON THE CONST., HOUSE OF COUNCILLORS, HANDBOOK ON THE RESEARCH REPORT ON THE CONSTITUTION OF JAPAN 21 (2005), *available at* http://www.sangiin.go.jp/eng/report/ehb/ehb.pdf.

[152] Act on the Protection of Computer Processed Personal Information held by Administrative Organs, Act No. 58 of 2003.

[153] MITI, *Guidelines Concerning the Protection of Computer Processed Personal Data in the Private Sector*, Mar. 4, 1997.

[154] Act on the Protection of Personal Information, Law No. 57 of 2003 (Japan) *available at* http://www.cas.go.jp/jp/seisaku/hourei/data/APPI.pdf (English translation).

which took effect in April 2005. PIPL extends the notice, security, access, and correction principles to the private sector, protecting information both in electronic and in print form.

It is important to note, however, that the PIPL is merely a set of implementing guidelines, and Japan's government ministries are ultimately responsible for issuing specific administrative guidelines to the business sectors under their respective authority.[155] Various Japanese ministries have in fact issued guidelines on the use of personal information pursuant to PIPL. The activities of a majority of businesses are covered by the guidelines promulgated by one of the following agencies: the Ministry of Economy, Trade and Industry (METI)[156]; the Ministry of Health, Labor and Welfare (MHLW)[157], the Financial Services Agency (FSA)[158], the Ministry of Internal Affairs and Communications (MIAC)[159], and the Ministry of

---

[155] David A. Laverty, *JAPAN: Internet Privacy and Related Developments*, INTERNATIONAL COUNSEL (Mar. 2000), http://www. internationalcounsel.com/pubs/updates/update008.htm.

[156] Eric Kosinski, *Japanese Privacy Guidelines Require Tighter Oversight of Data Processors*, PRIVACY LAWS AND BUS. INT'L NEWSLETTER, Issue 92 (April 2008).

[157] *Section 4. Promotion of Information-Oriented Society*, MINISTRY OF HEALTH, LABOUR AND WELFARE, http://www. mhlw.go.jp/english/wp/wp-hw2/part2/p2c11s4.pdf (last visited Nov. 15, 2013).

[158] *Guidelines for Personal Protection in the Financial Field*, FIN. SERVS. AGENCY, http://www.fsa.go.jp/frtc/kenkyu/event/ 20070424_02.pdf (unofficial English translation) (last visited Nov. 5, 2013).

[159] *Guideline on Protection of Personal Information in Telecommunications Business-Efforts with Security Control*

Land, Infrastructure, and Transport (MLIT).[160] As of 2007, these ministries have established 35 sets of guidelines, covering 22 business areas.[161]

3. Other Organizations & Enforcement

A recent series of high profile database breaches and cases of identity theft have prompted an attitude of increased vigilance on the part of the Japanese government and the private sector. The Ministry of Justice revised its internal regulations to place greater emphasis on prosecuting privacy violations and identity theft. Meanwhile Japanese businesses have moved quickly to adopt the data security management best practices reflected in ISO 27001, with more Japanese businesses being certified as compliant as of December 2006 than the rest of the world combined.[162] In 2012, Japanese

---

Measures to Prevent Personal Information Leakage, MINISTRY OF INTERNAL AFFAIRS AND COMMC'NS, http://www.soumu.go.jp/main_sosiki/joho_tsusin/eng/Resources/others/110214_1.pdf (last visited Nov. 15, 2013).

[160] MINISTRY OF LAND, INFRASTRUCTURE AND TECH., http://www.mlit.go.jp/en/index.html (search "guidelines") (last visited Nov. 15, 2013).

[161] *International Privacy and Data Protection Laws; Japan*, MCAFEE, http://www.mcafee.com/us/regulations/apac/japan.aspx (last visited Nov. 15, 2013); *see also Privacy International, Report: Japan*, PRIVACY INT'L, https://www.privacyinternational.org/reports/japan/iii-privacy-issues#footnote1_w1ifmyj (last visited Nov. 5, 2013).

[162] INT'L ORG. FOR STANDARDIZATION (ISO), The ISO Survey—2006, 40–41 (2006), *available at* http://www.iso.org/iso/survey2006.pdf.

businesses continued to hold more than one-third[163] of the world's certifications.[164]

E.   REPUBLIC OF KOREA (SOUTH KOREA)

1. Constitutional Protection

The constitution of South Korea contains provisions guaranteeing the traditional "right to be let alone," as well as an express right of privacy. Article 16 states: "All citizens are free from intrusion into their place of residence. In case of search or seizure in a residence, a warrant issued by a judge upon request of a prosecutor has to be presented."[165] Article 17 provides that the "privacy of no citizen may be infringed"[166] and Article 18 provides secrecy of communication: "The secrecy of correspondence of no citizen may be infringed."[167]

2. Statutory Protection

South Korea has both comprehensive and sectoral legislation addressing the use of personal information. The comprehensive Protection of Personal Information Act (PIPA) went into effect on

---

[163]   In 2012, Japanese businesses held 7,199 of 19,577 ISO certifications, or 1 out of every 2.71 certifications issued worldwide.

[164]   Certifications by country can be accessed at http://www.iso.org/iso/home/standards/certification/iso-survey.htm.

[165]   Constitution of the Republic of Korea, ch. 1, art. 16, *available at* http://www.ccourt.go.kr/home/att_file/download/Constitution_of_the_Republic_of_Korea.pdf (English translation).

[166]   *Id.* at art. 17.

[167]   *Id.* at art. 18.

September 30, 2011.[168] In addition, to the extent that they have not been superseded by any specific provision of PIPA, personal data in the private sector is protected through many laws, each covering different categories of business. These laws include the Protection of Communications Secrets Act,[169] the Telecommunications Business Act,[170] the Framework Act on Electronic Commerce,[171] and the Digital Signatures Act.[172]

Like the statutes of many other countries, PIPA adopts an approach to regulation that follows the OECD privacy principles. PIPA sets forth eight Personal Information Protection Principles that encompass the concepts of transparency, accuracy, fair use and collection, and security.[173] Under PIPA, data subjects have the right to receive notice of processing of their personal information, the right to consent or not to such processing, the right to demand access to, or correction of their personal

---

[168]   BUSINESS SOFTWARE ALLIANCE (BSA), COUNTRY REPORT: KOREA (2012), *available at* http://cloudscorecard.bsa.org/ 2012/assets/PDFs/country_reports/Country_Report_Korea.pdf. English version of the Personal Information Protection Act is available at http://koreanlii.or.kr/w/images/9/98/DPAct1110en. pdf.

[169]   Protection of Communications Secrets Act (1993), Act No. 4650, *amended by* Act No. 8867, February 29, 2008.

[170]   Telecommunications Business Act (1991), Act No. 4394, last amended by Act No. 8867, February 29, 2008.

[171]   Framework Act on Electronic Commerce (1999), Act No. 5834, *amended by* Act No. 8979, March 21, 2008.

[172]   Digital Signatures Act (1999), Act No. 5792, *amended by* Act No. 8852, February 29, 2008.

[173]   Personal Information Protection Act, ch. I, art. 3 (S. Kor.) [hereinafter *PIPA*].

information, and the right to terminate the processing of their information.[174]

Also like many other statutory regimes, PIPA provides additional protections related to "sensitive" data about an individual, such as that related to ideology, health, or other categories of information that could be used to do harm to the privacy of the data subject.[175] Additionally, PIPA requires the processor of personal information to issue a privacy policy[176] and to designate an officer in charge of processing personal information.[177] Following an international trend, PIPA also includes a requirement that data processors notify data subjects in the event of a data breach.[178]

3. Other Organizations & Enforcement

The Minister of Public Administration and Security (MPAS) is the enforcement authority for PIPA, and public entities that process data are required to register with the authority.[179] Under PIPA, MPAS may request reports from processors on their handling of personal information and issue orders relating to compliance.[180] On July 30, 2013, the MPAS announced amendments to PIPA addressed at strengthening protections for Korean

---

[174]   *Id.* at ch. I, art. 3.

[175]   *Id.* at ch. III, sec. 2, art. 23.

[176]   *Id.* at ch. IV, art. 30.

[177]   *Id.* at ch. IV, art. 31.

[178]   *Id.* at ch. IV, art. 34.

[179]   *Id.* at ch. IV, art. 32.

[180]   *Id.* at ch. IV, arts. 61–64.

resident registration numbers, including a provision allowing for a maximum fine of up to .5 billion Korean won on a processor of personal information who fails to protect resident registration numbers.

F.   THE PEOPLE'S REPUBLIC OF CHINA (CHINA)

1. Constitutional Protection

The Chinese Constitution has a number of provisions dedicated to personal privacy. Article 37 protects individuals from unlawful searches, while Article 39 provides the same protection for private residences.[181] Article 40 expressly protects the privacy of correspondence from both public and private actors, but includes an express reservation of the power "to censor correspondence in accordance with procedures prescribed by law."[182] In addition to this rather significant derogation, the Chinese government has admitted that its domestic law enforcement agencies are not always consistent in applying procedural protections and that any constitutional guarantees may not be applied evenly or systematically.

2. Statutory Protection

Provisions relating to personal data protection are found in various Chinese laws and regulations, but

---

[181]   XIANFA [CONSTITUTION] ch. 2, arts. 37, 39 (1982) (China), *available at* http://www.purdue.edu/crcs/itemResources/PRCDoc/pdf/Constitution.pdf (English translation).

[182]   *Id.* at ch. 2, art. 40.

China does not yet have comprehensive national legislation regulating the use and protection of personal data. In the past few years, however, China has passed numerous rules related to data privacy protection in telecommunications and on the Internet.

In 2011, China's Ministry of Industry and Information Technology promulgated the "Several Regulations on Standardizing Market Order for Internet Information Services,"[183] which created nationwide privacy standards specific to Internet information service providers, including general disclosure, consent, secure storage, and breach reporting requirements.[184] In 2012, China's Standing Committee of the National People's Congress issued a decision further strengthening online personal data protection. The 2012 directive creates more stringent requirements for Internet service providers such as the adoption of technological measures to prevent the breach of individual information and more stringent breach reporting requirements. Additionally, under the

---

[183] *Several Regulations on Standardizing Market Order for Internet Information Services*, MINISTRY OF INDUS. AND INFO. TECH. OF THE PEOPLE'S REPUBLIC OF CHINA, http://www.miit.gov.cn/n11293472/n11293832/n12771663/ 14417081.html (Chinese language version) (last visited Nov. 16, 2013).

[184] *China: New Measures to Standardize Internet Services and Protect Users Launched*, LIBRARY OF CONG., http://www.loc.gov/lawweb/servlet/lloc_news?disp3_l205403038_ text (last updated Mar. 19, 2012).

2012 directive, Internet users must use their real names to identify themselves to service providers.[185]

Finally, in mid-2013, China's Ministry of Industry and Information Technology released the "Rules on Protecting Personal Information of Telecommunication and Internet Users," which heightens protection in the areas of collection and use of personal information, information security measures, supervision, and inspection by relevant Chinese authorities, and liability for breach of the rules.[186]

Outside of the areas of telecommunications and the Internet, privacy breaches in China, when they are addressed, are handled through tort law, local ordinances, and criminal law. For example, Shanghai's consumer protection rules provide some limited guidance on information privacy and there are Articles of the Chinese criminal code that penalize physical intrusions of privacy, including illegally inspecting mail or entering a private residence,[187] but there is no general law that

---

[185] Laney Zhang, *China: NPC Decision on Network Information Protection*, LIBRARY OF CONG., http://www.loc.gov/lawweb/servlet/lloc_news?disp3_l205403445_text (last updated Jan. 4, 2013).

[186] *Telecommunication and Internet Personal User Data Protection Regulations*, CHINA COPYRIGHT AND MEDIA (July 16, 2013), http://chinacopyrightandmedia.wordpress.com/2013/07/16/telecommunications-and-internet-user-individual-information-protection-regulations/ (English translation) (last visited January 11, 2014).

[187] Criminal Law of China, pt. I, ch. IV, arts. 245 & 252 (1997), *available at* http://www.procedurallaw.cn/english/law/200807/t20080724_40992.html (English translation).

prohibits personal data collection. The Chinese government is essentially unfettered in its ability to collect, store, and use all manner of personally identifiable data, and service providers are unlimited in their ability to use data related to electronic communications, whether telephonic or Internet.

3. Other Organizations & Enforcement

The Chinese tradition has long been one of keeping close track of its citizens. As far back as the 4th century B.C.E., Chinese provinces kept accurate records of their populations in order to tax and conscript their subjects, and unquestionably, the Chinese legal system has for the past several decades shown little concern for "privacy rights" under any definition one might apply to the term. However, in an implicit recognition of the economic advantages privacy protections can confer, the Chinese government is beginning to research adopting measures, including electronic signature certification authorities and database protection standards, in an attempt to increase the level of e-commerce in China. Several municipalities and provinces have also adopted "Open Government" acts, which allow citizens to check on their personal data stored by the municipal government and request that errors be corrected. Critics, however, have suggested that these experiments with privacy protection are likely to be undermined by broad national security exceptions contained within them.

G.　INDIA

1. Constitutional Protection

Article 21 of the Indian Constitution states, "No person shall be deprived of his life or personal liberty except according to procedure established by law."[188] Although this provision most closely resembles the Fifth Amendment to the U.S. Constitution, which is not generally considered a source of privacy rights in U.S. jurisprudence, the Indian Supreme Court found in *Rajgopal v. State of Tamil Nadu* (1994)[189] and *PUCL v. Union of India* (1996)[190] that the right to privacy is implicitly encompassed within the term "personal liberty" and "life." In *Shashank Shekhar Mishra v. Ajay Gupta* (2011),[191] the New Delhi High Court confirmed that money damages were available for invasion of the right to privacy under Article 21.

2. Statutory Protection

The concept of privacy as the "right to be let alone" is protected in tort and criminal law in India; India has no specific legislation directed at the protection and use of personal information. In the last few years, however, pressure from both E.U. and U.S. firms, who rely on Indian companies for

---

[188]　INDIA CONST. art. 21.

[189]　Rajagopal v. State of T.N. (1994) 6 S.C.C. 632, 649 (India).

[190]　PUCL v. Union of India, A.I.R. 2003 S.C. 2363 (India).

[191]　Shashank Shekhar Mishra v. Ajay Gupta (2011) 184 DLT 675 (Del.).

business outsourcing, has resulted in significant though incremental changes in India's privacy landscape.

India's Information Technology Act of 2000 did not initially address information privacy, but it was amended in 2008 to provide the Indian Government with the power to enact rules and regulations in line with the 2000 Act.[192] From this enabling legislation, in 2011, India's Ministry of Communications and Information Technology implemented the Information Technology (Reasonable security practices and procedures and sensitive personal data or information) Rules (IT Rules).[193] These IT Rules establish data collection, processing, and transfer requirements for sensitive personal data or other information of any person located anywhere in the world that is collected or processed in India.[194]

The IT Rules are in line with the E.U. Directive and other global data protection regulations, and require that data subjects be apprised of, and affirmatively consent to the collection, processing, and transfer of their personal information, amongst other requirements for retention, collection, and

---

[192]   Information Technology Amendment Act of 2008, Act. No. 10 of 2009, *available at* http://deity.gov.in/sites/upload_files/dit/files/downloads/itact2000/it_amendment_act2008.pdf (India).

[193]   Information Technology (Reasonable security practices and procedures and sensitive personal data or information) Rules, 2011, MINISTRY OF COMMC'N AND INFO. TECH., *available at* http://deity.gov.in/sites/upload_files/dit/files/GSR313E_10511(1).pdf (India).

[194]   *Id.* at §§ 3–8.

transfer of data.[195] The IT Rules also set forth
requirements that companies protect against the
negligent and intentional disclosure of sensitive
personal information.[196]

Notably, a clarification to the IT Rules carves out
an exception to required adherence for entities
providing certain services under contractual
obligation with a legal entity located within or
outside India, provided the outsourcing company
does not have direct contact with the data subject.[197]
Accordingly, outsourcing service providers in India
should be exempt from obtaining consent from the
individuals whose data they process. Additionally,
India has some sectoral privacy protection,
including the Public Financial Institutions Act of
1993, which mandates confidentiality in bank
transactions.

A more comprehensive Indian data privacy law is
in the works. The Indian Government has
established a planning commission on privacy law to
study international privacy laws, analyze existing
Indian legal provisions, and make specific proposals
for incorporation into future Indian law.[198] In

---

[195]   *Id.* at §§ 5, 7.

[196]   *Id.* at § 6.

[197]   Press Release, Press Information Bureau, Government of
India, Clarification on Information Technology (Reasonable
Security Practices and Procedures and Sensitive Personal Data
or Information) Rules, 2011 Under Section 43A of the
Information Technology ACT, 2000 (Aug. 24, 2011), *available at*
http://pib.nic.in/newsite/erelease.aspx?relid=74990.

[198]   Ajit Prakash Shah, *Report of the Group of Experts on
Privacy*, GOV. OF INDIA PLANNING COMM. (Oct. 16, 2012),

October 2012, the group released a report and informal draft privacy legislation making recommendations for a regulatory framework, but the legislation is still under consideration.

3. Other Organizations & Enforcement

Indian law enforcement agencies have not prioritized data protection issues. The National Association of Software and Service Companies (NASSCOM), a trade group composed of businesses in the information technology field, is actively engaged in lobbying for more stringent legislation, as well as developing mechanisms for self-regulation in the interim. For example, NASSCOM has established the National Skills Registry, which is a centralized database of information technology workers who have been subject to background checks and whose employment histories have been verified. While the National Skills Registry itself presents challenges to employee privacy (as NASSCOM acknowledges), it serves as an important check on individuals potentially planning on committing serial identity theft or other violations of consumer privacy by moving from job to job.

III.   TRANS-BORDER DATA FLOWS AND PRIVACY

With the advent of the Internet, information has been sent across borders in greater volumes and

available   at   http://planningcommission.nic.in/reports/genrep/rep_privacy.pdf.

with greater frequency than ever before. This transfer of information is typically referred to as "trans-border data flows" or "cross-border data flows." In the context of privacy protection, these transfers pose challenges and opportunities to the public and private sectors.

A. GOVERNMENTAL DEVELOPMENTS

Two major inter-governmental attempts have been made to deal with the issue of trans-border data flows: The OECD Guidelines on Privacy, discussed at Section I.1 above, and the E.U./U.S. Safe Harbor.

1. U.S./E.U. Safe Harbor

Unlike the United States, the European Union has effectively adopted the OECD principles into its law. As discussed earlier in Chapter 4, the European Union has enacted Directive 95/46/EC, commonly called the "Data Protection Directive," modeled on the OECD Guidelines, which required the Member States of the European Union to enact national legislation for the protection of E.U. residents' personal data. The Data Protection Directive included restrictions on the ability of parties inside the European Union to transfer the personal data of E.U. residents to recipients in non-Member States. Given the extremely expansive nature of what constitutes "personal data" subject to protection under the Directive, this posed a serious threat to the viability of inter-U.S./E.U. trade, particularly in services. Shortly after the passage of the Directive, representatives of the U.S. Department of Commerce (DOC) began negotiating with the E.U. Commission over what steps the United States could take to receive recognition that it was providing sufficient levels of privacy protection for personal data transferred from the European Union.

Although the parties agreed that improvements in data protection were necessary, the DOC and the Commission were divided on the best solution. The DOC concurred with a report by the FTC that found, given the fluid, evolving nature of the "information economy," self-regulation by industry was the superior method by which to achieve maximum protection with minimal constraint on future development.[199] The Commission stood at the opposite extreme, arguing that anything less than comprehensive data protection legislation of the sort Member States were required to enact was insufficient. Through 1998 and into 1999, the DOC submitted multiple proposed self-regulation schemes (referred to as "safe harbors"), all of which were rejected by the E.U. Working Party on the Protection of Individuals with Regard to the Processing of Personal Data (Working Party). The Working Party was established pursuant to Article 29 of the Data Protection Directive to give the Commission opinions on the level of data protection

---

[199]   For the text of the report, *see* FTC, SELF-REGULATION AND PRIVACY ONLINE: A REPORT TO CONGRESS (1999), *available at*   http://www.ftc.gov/news-events/press-releases/1999/07/self-regulation-and-privacy-online-ftc-report-congress (last visited Jan. 11, 2014).

both within the European Union and in other nations. As the Working Party stated in its last opinion on the subject, We "deplore[ ] that most of the comments made in . . . previous position papers do not seem to be addressed in the latest version of the US documents."[200]

By the summer of 2000, however, the DOC had worn down the Commission's resistance to permitting some form of self-regulation. With extensive behind the scenes lobbying, and despite the strenuous objections of the Working Party, the Commission issued a decision on July 26, 2000 confirming the adequacy of the draft Safe Harbor proposal submitted by the DOC on July 21 of that year.[201] The decision of the Commission means that national data protection agencies in Member States can only restrict the transmission and processing of personal data by a U.S. business subject to the Safe

---

[200] Working Party on the Protection of Individuals with Regard to the Processing of Personal Data, Opinion 7/99 on the Level of Data Protection Provided by the "Safe Harbor" Principles as Published together with the Frequently Asked Questions (FAQs) and other Related Documents on 15 and 16 November 1999 by the US Department of Commerce, 5146/99/EN/final at 3 (Dec. 3, 1999), *available at* http://ec.europa.eu/justice/policies/privacy/docs/wpdocs/1999/wp27en.pdf.

[201] Commission Decision of 26 July 2000 Pursuant to Directive 95/46/EC of the European Parliament and of the Council on the Adequacy of the Protection Provided by the Safe Harbour Privacy Principles and Related Frequently Asked Questions Issued by the US Department of Commerce, 2000/520/EC, art. 1(1), 2000 O.J. (L 215) 7, 8, *available at* http://eur-lex.europa.eu/LexUriServ/LexUriServ.do?uri= CONSLEG:2000D0520:20000825:en:PDF [hereinafter *Adequacy Decision*].

Harbor under two circumstances.[202] The first is if either the DOC or another authorized U.S. government agency notifies the agency that the business breached the terms of the Safe Harbor.[203] The second situation is where there is a likelihood that the Safe Harbor has been, or will be, breached.[204] The Commission thus effectively surrendered enforcement of the Data Protection Directive to the DOC as it pertained to businesses within the United States. The decision recognizing the Safe Harbor went into effect on November 1, 2000.

a. Structure of the Safe Harbor

The Safe Harbor consists primarily of two parts: the Safe Harbor Privacy Principles (Principles) and the Safe Harbor Frequently Asked Questions (FAQ), which offer additional high-level interpretation by the DOC on the meaning of the Principles.[205] Together, the two provide "authoritative guidance" to U.S. organizations that receive personal data from the European Union.[206] Compliance with the Safe Harbor is considered sufficient to meet the requirements of the Data Protection Directive.

---

[202]   *Id.* at art. 3, 2000 O.J. (L215) 7, 10.

[203]   *Id.* at art. 3(1)(a), 2000 O.J. (L215) 7, 10.

[204]   *Id.* at art. 3(1)(b), 2000 O.J. (L215) 7, 10.

[205]   *See* Issuance of Safe Harbor Principles and Transmission to European Commission, 65 Fed. Reg. 45,666 (July 24, 2000) [hereinafter *Safe Harbor*].

[206]   Only "U.S. organizations" may qualify for inclusion in the Safe Harbor; however, what constitutes a "U.S. organization" is not defined. Safe Harbor, 65 Fed. Reg. at 45,666–67.

Issued under the DOC's general power to "foster, promote, and develop international commerce," compliance with the Safe Harbor is voluntary and no specific methodology is prescribed.[207] Joining an existing self-regulatory privacy program that complies with the Principles or developing an internal privacy policy that meets the Principles are both acceptable. To fall within the Safe Harbor, these programs or policies must be drafted to make organizations subject to action under Section 5 of the Federal Trade Commission Act concerning unfair or deceptive trade practices. Compliance with the Safe Harbor becomes effective immediately upon self-certifying adherence to the Principles.

(i) The Principles

The Principles cover all "personal data" or "personal information" received by a U.S. organization from the European Union, in any recorded form, which is defined as "data about an identified or identifiable individual that are within the scope of the [Data Protection] Directive."[208] The Principles are based on the OECD Guidelines and are divided into the following seven categories: (1) Notice, (2) Choice, (3) Onward Transfer, (4) Security, (5) Data Integrity, (6) Access, and (7) Enforcement.[209]

Under the principle of "Notice," an organization is obliged to tell individuals about the purposes for

---

[207] Safe Harbor, 65 Fed. Reg. at 45,667.

[208] Id.

[209] Id. at 45,667–68.

which data is to be collected and how that data is to be used.[210] The organization must also explain how individuals can make complaints or inquiries, the types of third parties to which the data may be disclosed, and the opportunities individuals have to limit such disclosure. The notice must be presented in "clear and conspicuous language" at the time individuals are asked to give personal information or as soon afterwards as feasible, but notice must be given before the organization employs the information for a purpose other than for which it was originally collected or discloses it to a third party. Notice is not required if disclosure or transfer is being made to an agent of the organization, although the Onward Transfer Principle would apply.

In regards to the principle of "Choice," the organization must provide individuals with an opportunity to decide on an opt-out basis whether their personal information can be disclosed to a third party or be used for a purpose other than one related to those that have previously been authorized.[211] For "sensitive information,"[212] the individual must affirmatively opt-in before that information may be disclosed to third parties or be used for an alternative purpose.

---

[210]   *Id.* at 45,667.

[211]   *Id.*

[212]   This is equivalent to the Data Protection Directive's "special categories of data," *see* Data Protection Directive, 95/46/EC, art. 8(1), 1995 O.J. (L281) 31, 40.

The principle of "Onward Transfer" applies where the original data controller intends to disclose personal information to a third party. All of the following Onward Transfer rules are found in the Safe Harbor as reported in the Federal Register.[213] The controller may only disclose personal information to a third party acting as an agent after having determined whether the third party meets the requirements of the Safe Harbor, the Data Protection Directive or another adequate measure of data protection. This provision of the Safe Harbor implies that if the intended recipient is bound by another nation's personal data protection scheme, which has been found acceptable by the Commission, then the requirements of the Onward Transfer principle have been satisfied. Alternatively, the controller may enter into a written agreement with the third party, which guarantees that the recipient of the data will offer at least the same level of data protection as the Safe Harbor. If the original controller makes the determination or otherwise enters into an agreement with the third party, the original controller will not be held at fault if the third party breaches the terms of the Safe Harbor, provided that the original controller did not know and should not have known that the third party would commit the breach.

Under the principle of "Security," data controllers must "take reasonable precautions" to guard against "loss, misuse and unauthorized access, disclosure,

---

[213]   Safe Harbor, 65 Fed. Reg. at 45,668.

alteration and destruction." The "security" principle is the least developed part of the Safe Harbor's Principles, meriting only a single-sentence description. The fifth principle, "Data Integrity," holds that personal data collected must be relevant to its specified purpose. The data controller must not process data "in a way that is incompatible with the purposes for which it has been collected or subsequently authorized by the individual." Controllers are required to take reasonable steps to ensure the integrity of the data.

"Access" is the next principle, stipulating that data subjects must be able to examine personal data concerning them and "be able to correct, amend, or delete" the data if found inaccurate. If the financial and temporal costs to the controller, however, would be disproportionate to the risks posed to the subject's privacy, controllers are not obliged to provide access. Controllers may also withhold personal data where access could threaten the rights of individuals other than the requesting party.

The final principle is "Enforcement." For data protection to be considered effective, data controllers must implement measures to guarantee compliance with the Principles, provide recourse for data subjects whose personal data may have been compromised, and make clear the consequences of failure to comply with the Principles. The measures implemented by the controller must at least include "readily available and affordable independent recourse mechanisms" which will allow a subject's complaint to be investigated and resolved in accordance with the Principles, including damage awards if applicable. There must also be procedures to verify that the controller is in fact complying with the Principles and a commitment to remedy the problems that led to the breach of the Principles. There must be adequate sanctions to make certain that the controller complies. The FTC and the U.S. Department of Transportation (DOT) are recognized by the European Union as being competent to investigate complaints of unfair or deceptive practices that are in breach of the Principles.

(ii) The FAQ

The FAQ is divided into fifteen parts, covering the Principles and related issues. The first FAQ asks, "Must an organization always provide explicit (opt-in) choice with respect to sensitive data?"[214] The opt-in choice is not required if the data processing operation meets any of six criteria. These include situations where the processing is in the vital interests of the data subject, is necessary for medical treatment, is done by a non-profit organization as part of its mission, involves personal data that has been made public by the subject, is necessary for establishing a legal claim or defense, or where the organization is required to process the information to comply with other statutes or regulations. The second FAQ asks, "Do the Safe Harbor Principles apply to personal information gathered, maintained, or disseminated for

---

[214]   *Id*. Each FAQ is found in this section.

journalistic purposes?" Due to First Amendment concerns, journalistic interests in data will typically trump privacy interests, although common law privacy torts, contractual obligations, or other regulations of the sort discussed elsewhere in this text might impose independent restrictions. Personal information, which has been previously published or otherwise made available to the public through another outlet, may be republished without violating the Principles.

The third FAQ asks, "Are Internet service providers (ISPs) . . . or other organizations liable under the . . . Principles when on behalf of another organization they merely transmit, route, switch or cache information that may violate their terms?" The answer is no, the Principles do not give rise to any secondary liability where a party merely acts as a conduit for data transmission. The fourth FAQ asks, "Under what circumstances is [the processing of personal data by auditors and investment bankers] permitted by the Notice, Choice, and Access Principles?" Auditors and investment bankers are permitted to process personal data without the data subject's approval only for the duration and to the extent necessary to comply with other legislation or to meet the legitimate needs of the auditor or banker. These needs include verifying compliance with legal obligations and accounting practices, along with transactions concerning mergers, acquisitions, and joint ventures.

The fifth FAQ asks, "How will companies that commit to cooperate with European Union Data

Protection Authorities (DPAs) make those commitments and how will they be implemented?" Data controllers may make these commitments by declaring in their Safe Harbor certification that they will comply with all terms of the Enforcement Principle, cooperate with data protection agencies in investigating and resolving complaints related to the Principles, comply with the advice from the agencies on remedies and compensation, and provide written confirmation of their action to the agencies. The data protection agencies in turn will give their advice through a panel operating at the supra-national level within the European Union that will consider both complaints by E.U. residents and submissions by controllers who have joined the Safe Harbor. In the event of a complaint, both the E.U. resident and the U.S. controller will have the opportunity to present their case before the panel, with a non-binding decision to be issued within sixty days where possible. Failure to comply with the panel's decision within twenty-five days of its delivery will result in notification by the panel to the FTC or other federal or state agencies with the power to enforce laws against deceptive trade practices. The panel may also choose to notify the DOC about the controller's failure to meet the terms of the Principles and request that the controller be stricken from the roster of Safe Harbor participants.

The sixth FAQ asks, "How does an organization self-certify that it adheres to the Safe Harbor Principles?" Certification becomes effective immediately after the following information is submitted:

1. The name of the data controller, mailing address, e-mail address, telephone and fax numbers;

2. A description of the controller's activities with regard to personal data received from the European Union;

3. A description of the controller's privacy policy, including where the policy is available for public viewing, the date of its implementation, a contact for handling Safe Harbor-related issues, the government agency under whose authority the controller is subject; any privacy programs the controller is part of, method of verifying compliance with the Safe Harbor, and the mechanism for investigating unresolved complaints.[215]

If the controller wants to gain Safe Harbor protection for its E.U.-based human resources information, it may do so only if a government body has jurisdiction over claims relating to that data. The controller also must indicate a desire to include human resources data in its self-certification and make itself subject to relevant E.U. authorities.

The DOC maintains a list of all data controllers who have self-certified. The list is updated using annual statements from controllers certifying that they are still in compliance with the Principles and noting any changes that have occurred. Data received while a controller is certified under the

---

[215] *Id.* at 45,669–70.

Safe Harbor must continue to receive Safe Harbor protections even if the controller later leaves the Safe Harbor. Where a data controller that is currently operating under the Safe Harbor will be merged into, or taken over by, another organization which does not enjoy Safe Harbor status, the DOC must be notified in advance as to whether the new controller will continue the existing Safe Harbor protections, make a new self-certification, or provide some other safeguards such as creating a written guarantee of adherence to the Principles. If the new controller does not wish to comply, it must delete all personal data received under the terms of the Safe Harbor.

A critical point about this process is that it relies entirely on the honesty of the party making the certification. As the DOC states on the Safe Harbor website:

> In maintaining the [Safe Harbor] list, the Department of Commerce does not assess and makes no representation as to the adequacy of any organization's privacy policy or its adherence to that policy. Furthermore, the Department of Commerce does not guarantee the accuracy of the list and assumes no liability for the erroneous inclusion, misidentification, omission, or deletion of any organization, or

any other action related to the maintenance of the list.[216]

The seventh FAQ asks, "How do organizations provide follow up procedures for verifying [compliance] . . . with the Safe Harbor Principles?"[217] A data controller may meet the verification requirements of the Enforcement Principle through either self-assessment or a compliance audit by a third party. A self-assessment must indicate that the controller's privacy statement is "accurate, comprehensive, prominently displayed, completely implemented, and accessible." Furthermore, the self-assessment must show the controller's privacy policy meets the conditions of the Principles, that data subjects are informed as to how they may make complaints, that employees are trained in the privacy policy and are disciplined for failing to follow it, and that there are internal means for "conducting objective reviews of compliance" with the aforementioned requirements. Annually, a corporate officer or other authorized representative of the controller must sign a statement confirming the self-assessment. This document must be kept on file and be made available to individuals upon request or in the event of an investigation concerning whether the company's conduct and certification were proper.

---

[216] *See Safe Harbor Workbook*, U.S. DEP'T OF COMMERCE, *available at* http://export.gov/safeharbor/eg_main_018238.asp (last updated July 1, 2013).

[217] Safe Harbor, 65 Fed. Reg. at 45,670.

A compliance audit must demonstrate that the controller's privacy policy conforms to the Principles, is being complied with, and that data subjects are told how they may make complaints. There is no prescribed method for how such a review should be conducted. An annual statement confirming that the audit has been satisfactorily completed should be signed by the reviewer or an authorized representative of the controller and made available upon request or in case of investigation.

The eighth FAQ is divided into eleven sub-questions concerning the Access Principle. Summarized briefly, there is not an absolute right of access.[218] Instead, data subjects are limited by questions of "proportionality or reasonableness." The Access Principle does not require the same degree of thoroughness as a response to a subpoena. Rather, the controller should work to provide only the information specifically requested by the subject. If a request for information is vague or extremely broad, it is appropriate for the controller to ask the subject questions that will help narrow the focus of the request. Importantly, individuals requesting access to their own personal data are under no obligation to justify their petitions. The amount of effort expended by the controller should be dependent upon the significance of the request by

---

[218]   *See id.* at 45,670–72.

the subject. "Confidential commercial information"[219] may be denied to a subject.

"Access" merely means disclosure of information to the subject.[220] The controller does not have to permit literal physical access to databases or other repositories of information. The controller may deny information to a subject where important public interests, such as law enforcement investigations, would be impacted or where other limitations on disclosure, such as professional privilege, would apply. Access may also be refused where the costs or efforts involved would be disproportionate or excessive, although controllers are entitled to charge reasonable fees for providing information to the subject and may limit requests to a certain number of times per period. The burden is on the controller to demonstrate why access should be restricted. An example of a legitimate reason for denying access exists where personal data is inextricably bound up with confidential commercial information, such as marketing data. Responses to access requests should be made "within a reasonable time period."[221]

The ninth FAQ concerns human resources information and is divided into four sub-

---

[219] "Confidential commercial information" is defined as "information which an organization has taken steps to protect from disclosure, where disclosure would help a competitor in the market." *Id.* at 45,671.

[220] *Id.*

[221] *Id.* at 45,672.

questions.[222] The Safe Harbor covers personal data collected as part of an employment relationship in the EU and transmitted to the United States. A data controller may only disclose such information, or use it for a purpose other than for which it was originally collected, if it conforms to the Notice and Choice Principles. The data collected may be subject to specific national data protection legislation that will impose additional restrictions on its use beyond the limitations of the Safe Harbor. Controllers "should make reasonable efforts to accommodate employee privacy preferences," including anonymizing data or otherwise dissociating it from the employee's identity if feasible. Complaints about misuse of E.U. employee data are to be handled according to the national data protection legislation where the employee is located.

The tenth FAQ asks, "[w]hen data is transferred from the [European Union] to the United States only for processing purposes, will a contract be required, regardless of participation by the processor in the Safe Harbor?" The answer is yes; however, data controllers are instructed to remember that the contract is intended for their own protection from liability in the event that the data processor mishandles the data. A U.S. processor is not directly responsible for applying the Principles, as they will be encapsulated in the required contract with the E.U. controller. However, processors that are not enrolled in the Safe Harbor

---

[222]   *Id.* All references to the ninth and tenth FAQs are found in the Safe Harbor.

may be subject to pre-authorization requirements by the Member States, substantially delaying operations. By joining the Safe Harbor, the processor may enjoy faster approval of such contracts.

The eleventh FAQ asks, "How should the dispute resolution requirements of the Enforcement Principle be implemented, and how will an organization's persistent failure to comply with the Principles be handled?" A data controller may meet the Enforcement Principle's requirements in any of three ways:

> (1) Compliance with private sector developed privacy program that incorporate the Safe Harbor Principles in their rules and that include effective enforcement mechanisms . . . ; (2) compliance with legal or regulatory supervisory authorities that provide for handling of individual complaints and dispute resolution; or (3) commitment to cooperate with data protection authorities located in the European Union or their authorized representatives.[223]

Controllers should encourage data subjects to raise concerns with them before proceeding to contact other enforcement bodies. The enforcement process should function with great independence from the controller or processor, as demonstrated by such matters as "transparent composition and financing or a proven track record."

---

[223]   *Id.* at 45,673.

Any remedies provided must have the effect of reversing or correcting the breach of the Principles vis-à-vis the data subject and ensure that future processing will be in compliance. A range of penalties would best serve private sector regulatory bodies so that they may respond with some finesse based on how egregious the breach is. A private sector regulatory body must alert the appropriate government agency if a controller subject to the Safe Harbor refuses to comply with its rulings. The FTC will review referrals by such regulatory bodies and E.U. Member States to determine whether a controller has violated Section 5 of the FTC Act concerning unfair or deceptive trade practices.[224] These reviews are to be made on a priority basis. If the FTC determines a violation has occurred, it may obtain an administrative cease-and-desist order addressing the bad conduct or file a complaint with a federal district court. As discussed above in Chapter 3, Part II(E)(1), the FTC may assess its own penalties. The FTC is required to notify the DOC of any action it takes to penalize a failure to comply with the Safe Harbor's Principles.

If a data controller "persistently fails to comply with the Principles," then it is no longer entitled to the benefits of the Safe Harbor.[225] "Persistent failure to comply" results when a controller refuses to obey a final determination by any private sector regulatory body or a government agency or where such an organization has found that the controller

---

[224] *Id.*

[225] *Id.* at 45,674.

has failed to comply with the Principles so frequently that its claim of compliance is no longer credible. The DOC must be notified by the controller about the finding, and failure to do so may be punishable under the Fraud and False Statements Act, 18 U.S.C. § 1001. After receiving notice of a persistent failure to comply, the DOC must grant the controller thirty days to respond, after which, assuming the matter is not resolved satisfactorily, the controller will be cited on the Safe Harbor list for persistent failure to comply and be stripped of Safe Harbor benefits. A controller that has received a citation and later seeks enrollment in another private sector regulatory body must provide that body with a complete accounting of its previous participation in the Safe Harbor. The exact dynamics of the enforcement of the Safe Harbor remain unclear. In over seven years of operation, no entity registered with the Safe Harbor has been subject to an enforcement action or otherwise cited for failure to comply.

The twelfth FAQ asks, "Does the Choice Principle permit an individual to exercise choice only at the beginning of a relationship or at any time?" A data subject should have the right to opt out of having her data used for direct marketing at any time, subject to reasonable limits related to processing. A controller may also request information to confirm the identity of the subject before permitting the subject to opt out. If it is not feasible to contact subjects before using their data for direct mailings, the mailing itself should offer them a means to opt out of future mailings.

The thirteenth FAQ asks, "When can . . . travel information, such as frequent flyer or hotel reservation information . . . be transferred to organizations located outside the [European Union]?" If a data controller has joined the Safe Harbor such data may be automatically transferred, subject only to specific national data protection legislation. If the controller has not joined the Safe Harbor, then the transfer must be "necessary to provide the services requested by the consumer or to fulfill the terms of an agreement" or, alternatively, the transfer can be made if the data subject (traveler) has given unambiguous consent. An example of a transfer "necessary to provide the services requested by the consumer," would be participation in a frequent flyer program.

The fourteenth FAQ deals with medical privacy concerns and is divided into seven sub-questions.[226] Medical data gathered from individual E.U. residents is subject to the national data protection legislation of the Member State where they reside and becomes subject to the Principles when transmitted to the United States. To minimize the likelihood of breaching the Safe Harbor, data controllers are instructed to anonymize personal data concerning medical care and conditions when possible. Where the data has been gathered as part of a particular medical research project, the Notice and Choice Principles must be met before the data is employed in a different research project. Since future lines of research are not always predictable, a

---

[226]   *Id.* at 45,674–75.

general clause stating that the personal data collected from the subject may be used in other forms of research is acceptable unless the purposes of the new research project prove inconsistent with the original purpose.[227]

Finally, the fifteenth FAQ asks, "[i]s it necessary to apply the Notice, Choice and Onward Transfer Principles to public record information or publicly available information?"[228] The answer is no, so long as the public data is not combined with personal data and there are no restrictions imposed by specific national data protection legislation. Data controllers suffer no liability under the Principles if they obtain data from published sources, but if controllers intentionally publish personal data for the purpose of removing it from the scope of the Safe Harbor, they will lose their Safe Harbor certification.

b. The Safe Harbor's Scope

The Safe Harbor is a voluntary self-regulatory program, thus no entity is legally required to join it under U.S. law. Because of the scope of the Data Protection Directive any business that has contact with E.U. residents on anything other than an anonymous cash-only basis, has effectively collected some form of personal data and thus would be subject to the Data Protection Directive. In the realm of e-commerce, any organization that operates a Web site and collects information from web-

---

[227]   *Id.* at 45,674.
[228]   *Id.* at 45,667.

surfers for commercial purposes, including serving advertising to them, will be at risk of violating the Directive if an E.U. resident should happen to visit the site. On the other hand, the Safe Harbor is limited to only those entities that are subject to FTC or DOC regulatory jurisdiction, since they are the only two U.S. administrative agencies recognized to enforce it. Certain types of businesses, including telecommunications common carriers or insurance companies are ineligible and must pursue alternative means of complying with the Data Protection Directive.[229]

2. Regulation of Airline Passenger Data

Following the terrorist attacks of September 11, 2001, Congress passed the Aviation and Transportation Security Act (ATSA).[230] ATSA required the Department of Homeland Security (DHS) to promulgate regulations to be followed by airlines for international flights landing at U.S. airports. Among the regulations implemented by DHS is 19 C.F.R. § 122.49(a)–(d), collectively referred to as the "Passenger Manifest provision."

The Passenger Manifest provision requires that an airline provide to the U.S. Commissioner of Customs, or other designee, a passenger and crew

---

[229] *See Safe Harbor Workbook*, U.S. DEP'T OF COMMERCE, http://export.gov/safeharbor/eg_main_018238.asp (last visited Oct. 15 2013) (identifying types of businesses not subject to FTC or DOT authority).

[230] Aviation and Transportation Security Act, Pub. L. No. 107–71, 115 Stat. 597 (2001) (codified as amended in scattered sections of Title 5, 26, 31, and 49 U.S.C.).

manifest for any international flight bound for the United States prior to the departure of the flight. As part of this manifest, airlines are required to provide the full names of passengers, date of birth, sex, nation of citizenship and residence, passport information, and other personal data. Airlines that fail to provide the information required face fines or the possibility of losing landing rights at all of the United States' airports.[231]

The adoption of the Passenger Manifest provision immediately caused tension with the European Union, as it set up a sharp conflict with the E.U. Data Protection Directive's restrictions on the collection and use of E.U. residents' personal information. In 2003, as the DHS pressed forward with plans to begin enforcement of the Passenger Manifest provision, the E.U. Parliament passed a resolution denouncing both the scope of the data collected and the apparent inadequacy of protection against misuse of personal information once received by U.S. authorities.[232] Airlines operating flights between points in the United States and the European Union were naturally put in the awkward position of deciding whether to disclose passenger information and face fines or even criminal penalties from E.U. Member States, or to withhold the information and face fines in the United States and possible revocation of their landing rights.

---

[231] 19 C.F.R. § 122.49(b) (2011).

[232] European Parliament Resolution on Transfer of Personal Data by Airlines to the US Immigration Service, 2003 O.J. (C 61), 381 (2003), *available at* http://eur-lex.europa.eu/LexUriServ/ LexUriServ.do?uri=OJ:C:2004:061E:0381:0384:EN:PDF.

The conflict seemed to be resolved in May of 2004 when the United States and the E.U. Commission and Council reached agreements, which made the sharing of passenger information subject to usage limitations and retention policies.[233] Yet still dissatisfied with the level of protection afforded E.U. residents' personal data, the E.U. Parliament sued the Commission and the Council in a proceeding before the European Court of Justice arguing that the agreements were in conflict with the Data Protection Directive, and beyond the scope of authority conferred on the Commission to negotiate agreements with other nations concerning the handling of personal data. The Court of Justice agreed with the Parliament's analysis and annulled the agreements in a 2006 ruling.[234]

The Court of Justice decision compelled the United States and E.U. Council to negotiate further and establish a new agreement governing the transfer of airline passenger information. Adopted July 23, 2007, the new agreement permits DHS to collect personal information pursuant to the Passenger Manifest provision, but places greater

---

[233] Commission Decision of 14 May 2004 on the Adequate Protection of Personal Data Contained in the Passenger Name Record of Air Passengers Transferred to the United States Bureau of Customs and Border Protection, 2004/535/EC, 2004 O.J. (L235) 11, ¶¶ 15, 31, 46, *available at* http://eur-lex.europa.eu/LexUriServ/LexUriServ.do?uri=OJ:L:2004:235:0011:0022:EN:PDF.

[234] Joined Cases C-317/04 and C-318/04, *European Parliament v. Council of the European Union and Comm'n of the European Communities*, 2006 ECJ CELEX LEXIS 239 (May 30, 2006).

restrictions on its ability to use or retain such information beyond an initial screening of passenger identities.[235] The E.U. Parliament registered an objection to the agreement before it even took effect, but the Parliament did not commence litigation to try to set it aside.[236] A new agreement, the Passenger Name Records Agreement (PNR), was adopted by the E.U. Council on April 26, 2012.[237] The PNR replaces the 2007 agreement, which had been applied on a provisional basis. The PNR has strict controls over the retention of personally identifiable information, requiring such information to be "masked" after six months.

B.   BUSINESS DEVELOPMENTS

1. Outsourcing

Outsourcing may be defined as the transfer of responsibility for execution of a business activity from one organization to an external service provider that assumes a primary role in performing the activity and returns a value-added product or

---

235 Agreement between the European Union and the United States of America on the Processing and Transfer of Passenger Name Record (PNR) Data by Air Carriers to the United States Department of Homeland Security (DHS) (2007 PNR Agreement), 2007 O.J. (L204) 18.

236 European Parliament Resolution on the Passenger Name Records (PNR) Agreement with the United States of America, Bulletin EU 7/8–2007, §§ 1.10.17-18, 1.20.22-23 (2007), available at http://www.eulib.com/documents/bulletin200707en.pdf.

237 Press Release, Council of the European Union, Council Adopts New EU-US Agreement on Passenger Name Records (PNR) (Apr. 26, 2012), available at http://consilium.europa.eu/uedocs/cms_data/docs/pressdata/en/jha/129806.pdf.

service. Historically, outsourcing was primarily associated with manufactured products, but with declining communication costs and the ability to transmit documents at near instantaneous speeds, services are increasingly subject to outsourcing as well. Outsourcing services on an international basis has become particularly attractive given "transportation" costs are almost non-existent, thus profit margins realized from wage differentials can be even greater than for manufactured products.

While outsourcing is, all things being equal, generally a good strategy for increasing profits in those service sectors that can be performed remotely, it also poses significant privacy challenges. Many of the services businesses consider outsourcing, including medical transcription, payroll record management, or insurance claim processing, which may implicate personal information of customers or employees. Compounding this situation further is that, given the increasingly multinational nature of many businesses, personal information (both customer and employee) may have been collected in multiple nations and be subject to different privacy protection regimes. This poses the possibility of a business inadvertently committing violations of numerous laws. For example, if an E.U. resident purchases shares listed on the Toronto Stock Exchange through the Canadian branch of a U.S.-headquartered brokerage house, and the brokerage house transmits the information concerning that transaction to an outside vendor in India for processing, it is possible the brokerage house has almost simultaneously violated (a) the

E.U. Member State's national data protection legislation enacted pursuant to the Data Protection Directive, (b) PIPEDA; and (c) the Gramm-Leach-Bliley Act.[238] Strategies for dealing with this challenge break down into four principle approaches.

The first is the "ostrich" approach. Companies using this approach, assuming they are even fully aware of the intricacies of the statutes and regulations affecting their collection, use, or retransmission of personal information, ignore the problems they are facing and simply proceed with their activities. Although no systematic study has been made of business strategies for coping with the challenge of international transfers of personal information, what evidence exists suggests this approach is the most popular. By way of example, although the U.S./E.U. Safe Harbor has been open for registration for over seven years, fewer than 1,400 businesses are currently enrolled in it. While this approach may seem surprising in light of the general reputation of businesses being cautious with regard to liability exposure, it is a rational approach in the short term. Enforcement of privacy laws in the context of international transactions has been limited, except in cases of serious criminal conduct. The cost of compliance, thus, can be significantly greater than the costs of non-compliance when the latter is adjusted for the very low risk of being held

---

[238] In this example, the U.S./E.U. Safe Harbor is not implicated because the SEC rather than the FTC would regulate the customer's transaction and thus be outside the Safe Harbor's scope.

accountable for violations. Anecdotal accounts suggest that many European corporate entities actually take this approach, retain appropriate privacy counsel, and ultimately pay whatever fines are assessed. How viable this approach will remain in the end is questionable though, as agencies within the European Union increase enforcement activity.

A second approach has been termed the "Just in Time" approach. Companies using this approach deal with privacy issues in outsourcing as problems are brought to their attention. A typical example of this sort of approach arises when a Canadian customer informs a U.S.-based vendor that it will require compliance with PIPEDA from the vendor before continuing to do business. This approach allows companies to deal with challenges on a more manageable level, but at the risk of creating contradictory or incomplete internal processes. The vendor in the example above, after making the requested changes, would still be at risk of violating the Data Protection Directive if it was also collecting personal information from E.U. customers, since PIPEDA compliance by a U.S. business has no impact on the legality of transfers between the European Union and the United States.

The third approach sometimes called the "E.U. Gambit," has companies simply complying with the Data Protection Directive, relying on the fact that there is substantial overlap between the Directive and most other data protection regimes. While of course this strategy is effective when dealing with parties located in E.U. Member States, it is still an incomplete approach.[239] National variations still result in compliance gaps and, when the onward transfer restrictions of the Data Protection Directive are factored in, a business relaying personal information from E.U. residents to a third party in another country might still be violating the Directive even if its internal compliance is sufficient.

The final approach is the "audit" strategy. Under this approach, companies conduct audits on their privacy compliance. The audits analyze three things: (1) the privacy protection regime in each jurisdiction where the company collects or processes personal information; (2) the categories of personal information the company collects; and (3) the internal procedures the company employs for handling the information and the procedures its outsourcing vendors use in handling transferred information. The purpose of the audit approach is to permit a company to segregate personal information by its point of origin and treat each category of information with the necessary level of care to comply with the law of the country of origin. This approach can be characterized as a "best practice" and, anecdotally, seems to be on the rise.

---

[239] It bears mention that even in that instance the strategy is not completely safe. As discussed in Chapter 4, Part II.B. concerning the Data Protection Directive and the Safe Harbor, each E.U. Member State has enacted its own variant of the Directive and compliance with the bare terms of the Directive without Safe Harbor certification or being subject to PIPEDA (or equivalent legislation approved by the E.U. Commission) will be insufficient.

CHAPTER FIVE

CURRENT PRIVACY CHALLENGES, DEVELOPING TECHNOLOGIES & FUTURE TRENDS

With the quickening pace of technological development, any attempt to divide challenges to privacy into concrete categories of present, imminent, and remote-but-approaching, threats, is by its very nature an exercise in artifice. However, there are certain issues that are clearly more manifest than others. This chapter explores these ongoing and upcoming challenges and contemplates what lies ahead in the field of privacy law.

I. CURRENT PRIVACY CHALLENGES

A. IDENTITY THEFT

Identity theft occurs when someone poses as another person by using that person's personal information without his or her permission. Although the term "identity theft" was coined relatively recently, the concept of impersonating an individual to realize undeserved gain has existed since ancient times, being reflected in such sources as the biblical account of Jacob impersonating his brother Esau to gain their dying father's blessing. What has made identity theft an increasing problem is the ease with which it can now be committed on a massive scale due to technological changes. Identity theft once required such risky acts as physically stealing a limited number of paper records or actually entering a financial institution in person to complete a transaction with forged documents. Today it can be accomplished remotely and with minimal risk of apprehension. Complaints filed with the FTC concerning identity theft topped the list of consumer complaints for the thirteenth consecutive year, with complaints rising from 31,117 in 2000, to 369,132 in 2012. Furthermore, while identity theft is usually thought of as a crime perpetrated against individuals, it is also an increasing problem for corporations and other organizations.

The difficulty of actually finding and prosecuting identity thieves (who are commonly located in a different country than their victims, judgment proof, or both), in recent years, has led to litigation against institutions from which the personal information used to commit identity theft was stolen. The central theory behind this litigation is one of shifting "externalities," *i.e.*, costs, to the party best able to bear them. Institutions, particularly those operating domestically in the United States, traditionally had little financial incentive to protect customer or employee information since the theft of information had minimal impact on the institution that actually had the information stolen. It was the customer or employee who usually suffered the greatest injury, along with third parties deceived by the identity thief. However, the institutions that hold personal information are, generally, the parties most able to protect the information in their custody. Consequently, litigation against institutions for failure to adequately protect personal information is arguably one of the most dynamic areas of privacy law to develop in recent years.

1. Causes of Action Relating to Identity Theft

a. Negligence

The most common type of action brought in litigation resulting from identity theft is a negligence claim. The tort of negligence requires a breach of duty, which causes, both actually and proximately, an injury to the party whom the duty was owed. Identity theft negligence claims typically are predicated on one or both of two duties. The first duty is to take precautionary measures to protect the plaintiff's personal information, while the second is to eliminate or correct any incorrect information that has already been attributed to the plaintiff. Courts have found that this duty may arise even in situations where the individual whose personal information is held by the institution is not a customer, employee, or other category of person whom one might expect to be owed a duty.

Remsburg v. Docusearch, 816 A.2d 1001 (N.H. 2003), was a seminal case concerning negligence claims based on a failure to take adequate precautions in the handling of personal information. In *Remsberg*, a stalker employed the help of a company called Docusearch to locate a woman with whom he had become obsessed. The stalker obtained several pieces of personal information concerning the woman from Docusearch, including her Social Security number and work address. Docusearch itself had obtained the information from other sources or from the woman herself under false pretenses. Shortly after receiving the information, the stalker drove to the woman's place of employment and killed her.

The victim's estate sued Docusearch on several theories of liability, including negligence. The New Hampshire Supreme Court found that, given the serious and pervasive threat of stalking and identity theft, "the risk of criminal misconduct is sufficiently foreseeable so that an investigator has a duty to exercise reasonable care in disclosing a third person's personal information to a client." *Id.* at 1008. A claim for negligence could be based on the unauthorized disclosure of another party's personal information.

b. Privacy Torts

A second theory of liability analyzed in *Remsburg* was whether Docusearch's conduct and that of contractors in its employ could constitute the tort of intrusion, *i.e.*, an invasion of the victim's privacy interests in a manner as to be offensive to persons of ordinary sensibilities. *See id.* The New Hampshire Supreme Court concluded that a person could have a protectable privacy interest in a Social Security number, but that the question of whether any particular use or distribution of the number without the permission or knowledge of the number's holder was a sufficiently egregious violation of the victim's privacy interests to be actionable would be a question of fact. The court, however, rejected the argument that the plaintiff could have a claim based on the disclosure of the victim's place of employment because, while individuals could reasonably expect their Social Security numbers to be kept private, places of employment are usually public in nature and thus the victim could not reasonably assume that information was private.

An alternative privacy tort that has been pled with some success in the context of identity theft, even in the absence of specific evidence that identity theft has occurred, is that of public disclosure of private facts. In *Shqeirat v. United States Airways Group*, 515 F. Supp. 2d 984 (D. Minn. 2007), a plaintiff included a claim for disclosure in a lawsuit against the Minneapolis Metropolitan Airport Commission. Following an altercation at the Minneapolis airport, the Commission published a police report containing the plaintiff's Social Security number on its official website. *See id.* at 998. The Commission did not dispute that it had made the plaintiff's Social Security number publicly available, but instead moved to dismiss on the grounds that the plaintiff had not sufficiently pled an injury. The United States District Court for the District of Minnesota, applying Minnesota tort law, declined to dismiss the plaintiff's claim on a motion to dismiss, finding that the emotional distress resulting from the threat of identity theft could constitute a sufficient injury to support a claim for disclosure.

c. Breach of Contract

As discussed in Chapter 3, privacy policies are becoming more prevalent and even mandatory in a number of states. These privacy policies are intended to inform the consumer of how the company will use and store any personal information that it collects during the business relationship. Consumers, however, are using this privacy policy in some instances as a cause of action in identity theft suits against these companies, arguing that the policies create a contract between the consumer and the company. Under a breach of contract claim, the consumer must prove a legal obligation on the part of the company defendant to the consumer plaintiff, a breach of that obligation, and an injury resulting from such breach.

In *Kuhn v. Capital One Fin. Corp.*, 855 N.E.2d 790 (Mass. App. Ct. 2006), a plaintiff brought suit after a hacker compromised certain financial account information, including Social Security numbers, which resulted in fraudulent charges to the plaintiff's account. The plaintiff alleged a breach of contract claim stemming from the "Privacy Notice and Customer Agreement" that plaintiff had received from Capital One. The court found that this was enough to establish a contract between the parties.

Alternatively, plaintiffs have had limited success in pleading a cause of action for breach of implied contracts. In *Anderson v. Hannaford Bros. Co.*, 659 F.3d 151 (1st Cir. 2011), a plaintiff brought suit alleging that Hannaford breached an implied contract between itself and its customers. The plaintiff alleged that there was an implied contract with Hannaford that it would not allow unauthorized access to its customers' credit card data. The court agreed with the plaintiff, finding, at the pleading stage at least, that under Maine law it was reasonable to conclude that when customers provide a merchant with their credit card numbers they are providing that information to the merchant only, and the merchant has an implicit duty to safeguard that information from unauthorized third-party access.

d. Breach of Fiduciary Duty

Several cases alleging claims premised on identity theft have included the claim of breach of fiduciary duty. A fiduciary duty arises in a transaction when one party has placed trust and confidence in another's judgment or advice. A fiduciary duty has been commonly found to exist between an attorney and client, an employer and employee, and a trustee and beneficiary. In the identity theft context, this has proven to be a difficult theory under which to succeed. *See Anderson*, 659 F.3d at 157–58; *Meadows v. Hartford Life Ins. Co.*, 492 F.3d 634 (5th Cir. 2007); *but see Jones v. Commerce Bank, N.A.*, No. 06 Civ. 835 (HB), 2007 WL 672091, at *3 (S.D.N.Y. Mar. 6, 2007) (finding an implied fiduciary duty may exist).

e. Infliction of Emotional Distress

Several courts have entertained claims for infliction of emotional distress as a result of identity theft, but there are as yet no reported instances of a plaintiff having successfully brought such a claim.[1] The difficulty of establishing the elements of intentional infliction of emotional distress in an identity theft situation is the reason these claims have failed so far. In most jurisdictions, a plaintiff must prove that the defendant acted with malice, ill will, or in an extremely outrageous manner and that an actual physical injury, or apprehension of physical harm, resulted. Because identity theft is usually not accompanied by these facts, the claims are typically struck on a motion to dismiss or for summary judgment.

f. Constitutional Rights

In the specific context of government handling of personal information, courts have recognized that the threat of identity theft occasioned by governmental infringement of privacy rights can support a claim under 42 U.S.C. § 1983. In *Tomblin v. Trevino*, No. SA01CA1160–OG, 2003 WL 24125145 (W.D. Tex. Feb. 19, 2003), a plaintiff argued that a local police force's practice of collecting Social Security numbers during routine

---

[1]   *See, e.g.*, Polzer v. TRW, Inc., 682 N.Y.S.2d 194 (N.Y. App. Div. 1998); Jones v. Alltel Ohio Ltd. P'ship, 06 CV 02332, 2007 WL 1731321 (N.D. Ohio June 14, 2007); Allison v. Aetna, Inc., No. 09-2560, 2010 WL 3719243 (E.D. Pa. Mar. 9, 2010); Reilly v. Ceridian Corp., 664 F.3d 38 (3rd Cir. 2011).

traffic stops was a Fourth Amendment violation. Noting that the use of Social Security numbers was regulated by statute and that dissemination of an individual's Social Security number posed a significant threat of identity theft, the court concluded that an individual could have a reasonable expectation of privacy in the number. A government actor would require a justifiable basis for collecting information, given the Fourth Amendment privacy interest attached to a Social Security number. Based on testimony from the local police chief and the officer involved in the traffic stop, the court concluded that there was not a sufficiently strong government interest to justify collecting the information in the circumstance of an ordinary traffic stop.

2. Remedies for Claims Related to Identity Theft

a. Damages

Although some courts have permitted plaintiffs to proceed with claims arising from identity theft even in the absence of allegations of specific damages resulting from the theft itself, *see, e.g., Shqeirat v. United States Airways Group*, 515 F. Supp. 2d 984, 998 (D. Minn. 2007) (permitting disclosure claim based on injury in form of fear of identity theft), the vast majority of claims are dismissed or disposed of by summary judgment due to an inability by the plaintiffs to demonstrate an actual injury. *See Pisciotta v. Old Nat'l Bancorp*, 499 F.3d 629, 635, 639 (7th Cir. 2007) (discussing lack of precedence for finding a mere risk of identity theft to be a compensable injury); *Reilly v. Ceridian Corp.*, 664 F.3d 38 (3rd Cir. 2011) (rejecting claim for time and money spent on credit monitoring to protect against an increased risk of identity theft). For a successful claim, a plaintiff must prove that the breach of duty by the defendant resulted in both an exposure of personal information and that the exposure resulted in a use of the personal information in a manner that caused an actual injury. Alternatively, but for the same reasons, many such claims have been disposed of for failure to allege an injury-in-fact sufficient to confer Article III standing.[2] This effectively means that most large-scale incidents in which the security of personal information is compromised will not be compensable because it is quite rare that any specific injury can be traced to the breach.

b. Restitution

Actual damages resulting from identity theft are difficult to prove and even if demonstrated, often do not fully compensate victims for costs incurred in correcting the damage to their credit and financial standing. A number of states, therefore, have

---

[2]   *See, e.g., In re* Barnes & Noble PIN Pad Litig., No. 12-cv-8617, 2013 WL 4759588, at *3–6 (N.D. Ill. Sept. 3, 2013) (holding plaintiffs failed to satisfy the elements of Article III standing, and dismissing all five pleaded causes of action: (1) breach of contract, (2) violation of the Illinois Consumer Fraud and Deceptive Business Practices Act (ICFA), (3) invasion of privacy, (4) violation of the California Security Breach Notification Act, and (5) violation of the California Unfair Competition Act) (slip op.).

enacted statutes that require identity thieves to pay restitution to their victims. "Restitution" in this context refers to costs incurred by identity theft victims that are the consequence of the theft, but that do not result directly from the theft. In Delaware, for example, identity thieves may be ordered to pay a victim's lost wages and reasonable attorney fees incurred as a result of the theft.[3] Under Maine law, this may include recovery for costs of acquiring identity theft insurance and fees related to replacing stolen financial account information.[4] Maryland also allows reasonable attorney fees, costs for clearing the victim's credit history, and costs incurred to satisfy debts, judgments, or liens against the victim that resulted from the defendant's actions.[5]

B.   PRETEXTING

"Pretexting" is the act of creating and utilizing an invented scenario (the pretext) to persuade a target to give information or perform an action. Typically, pretexting is more than a simple lie, but usually involves prior research and the use of pieces of known information to establish legitimacy in the mind of the target, so as to increase the likelihood that he or she will reveal the sought after information. Like identity theft, pretexting is not in and of itself a new phenomenon. Mythology is

---

[3]   11 DEL. CODE § 854(e).

[4]   Anderson v. Hannaford Bros. Co., 659 F.3d 151, 167 (1st Cir. 2011).

[5]   MD. CRIM. L. CODE ANN. § 8–301(g).

replete with tales of characters gaining information on the weaknesses of others by posing as an innocent third party. Technology has simply made pretexting far more feasible because of the ease by which it can be accomplished remotely.

Pretexting has been addressed through two major pieces of legislation. Under the Gramm-Leach-Bliley Act (GLB) discussed in Chapter 2,[6] it is illegal to use forged or stolen documents or false statements to obtain customer information from a financial institution or directly from a customer of a financial institution. The GLB also criminalizes the same conduct by intermediaries. Congress recently passed the Telephone Records and Privacy Protection Act (TRPPA) in reaction to the revelation that the management of Hewlett-Packard had employed private investigators who used pretexting to obtain the telephone records of board members and members of the media as part of efforts by Hewlett-Packard's management to investigate leaks of internal discussions.[7] The TRPPA specifically criminalizes making false or fraudulent statements to a telephone service provider or providing false or fraudulent documents to a telephone service provider in an attempt to gain a third party's telephone records.

---

[6]   15 U.S.C. §§ 6801 to 6809.

[7]   Pub. L. No. 109–476, 120 Stat. 3568 (Jan. 12, 2007) (codified as amended at 18 U.S.C. § 1039 (2007)).

C.   PHISHING

"Phishing" is a broad term covering any sort of internet fraud scheme designed to trick the recipient into revealing credit card account information, passwords, Social Security numbers, and other personal information to individuals who intend to use them for fraudulent purposes. Phishing typically involves communications (particularly e-mails) made to appear as if they have come from a reputable source, whether a government agency, such as the IRS, or a commercial source, like the victim's bank. The communications often instruct the recipient to verify or update account information by requesting a reply to the e-mail with updated information, or by providing the recipient with a link to a website where the new information may be entered. Regardless of type, phishing schemes are typically dealt with via traditional laws governing fraud or criminal impersonation. The most commonly encountered types of phishing schemes include:

False e-mail messages: The message appears to be from a company that the target does business with, warning that they need to verify account information and that if the information is not provided the account will be suspended. Customers of eBay and Paypal are two of the most targeted groups for this type of phishing scheme, but the approach can be applied to the customers of any business. Although many companies now specifically warn customers that they do not request personal information via e-mail, this remains the most popular variety of phishing scheme, likely because it is the simplest to execute. Many companies now have phishing watch groups that monitor this area, and upon discovery, immediately notify the ISP where the e-mail originated, as well as any appropriate law enforcement agencies.

False escrow sites: This occurs when items are put up for sale at a legitimate online auction to lure the target into making payments to a fake escrow site rather than through the auction provider's regular payment channel. This scheme is more time consuming and elaborate than a simple e-mail, but it has the potential to collect more information, particularly if the phisher actually sends the merchandise that was ordered so that the target does not associate a later instance of fraud with the transaction where the personal information was collected. eBay has tried to combat this type of scheme by providing its members with written policies that prohibit transactions from being completed outside of eBay.[8]

False charities: The fraudster in this type of phishing scheme poses as a charity and asks for direct monetary donations. These schemes most commonly flourish in the wake of major disasters and around holidays when people are likely to be in a particularly generous spirit. While seemingly the most foolproof scheme, since the targets are usually not expecting to receive anything in return, genuine

---

[8]   *See Offers to Buy or Sell Outside of eBay*, EBAY, http://pages.ebay.com/help/policies/rfe-spam-non-ebay-sale.html (last visited Oct. 24, 2013).

charities vigorously search for evidence of such activities and typically are better able to pressure law enforcement agencies to conduct investigations of suspected charity fraud than individual fraud victims. The substantially higher risk of law enforcement becoming involved causes this type of phishing scheme to remain less popular with fraudsters.

False websites: This scheme uses websites made to look similar to legitimate sites or having web addresses that are sufficiently similar to popular sites that they may be accidentally reached by mistyping an address. In particularly extreme cases, phishers have hacked the websites of legitimate enterprises and reconfigured them so that visitors are redirected to the phishers' false websites. In any of these variants, the websites will typically contain false login screens designed to convince visitors to type in their usernames and passwords. The website may also attempt to download spyware onto the target's computer, whether covertly or by representing that the target needs to download a particular software application to use the site. This type of phishing scheme is often paired with the use of false e-mails to drive traffic to the site, and can include a "man in the middle" attack, which intercepts login information entered into a legitimate website after passing through the phisher's false site. The "man in the middle" attack can also take the form of impersonating legitimate wireless access points. In this form of attack, the bogus access point is commonly setup in a "hotspot," such as a popular coffee shop or café, in order to intercept login information and other sensitive data.

D.   RADIO FREQUENCY INFORMATION DEVICE

1. Technological overview

A Radio Frequency Information Device (RFID) is a system that identifies objects, collects data, and transmits information about the object through a "tag." RFIDs consist of three components: a chip, antenna, and a reader. The chip is typically programmed with relatively simple information, including a specific alphanumeric string of characters. The antenna transmits information from the chip to the reader via radio waves. When the reader comes in close enough proximity to the chip, signals transfer between the two. RFIDs are either active or passive. Passive RFIDs stay inactive until a reader scans the tag. Active RFIDs have energy sources built in, allowing active transmission of information without the need of a reader to initiate the action. The latest generations of these devices, called "extended capability" RFIDs, include the ability to be read at longer distances (up to 500 meters), operate in more extreme environmental conditions, and to be paired with microprocessors on a single chip, enabling much more comprehensive monitoring of the object the RFID is attached to.

The principal purpose of RFIDs is to allow a user to track objects that have been "chipped" or "tagged." In a typical application, the user encodes each RFID chip with an alphanumeric string and then in a separate database the user creates a description of the object that corresponds to that particular alphanumeric string. Each time the "tagged" object is scanned, that alphanumeric string can be relayed from the reader to the database, allowing the user to determine the location of the object at the time of the scan. Depending on the degree of detail in the underlying database, and how distributed its RFID readers are, a user can potentially form a very detailed overview of the object's movements.

2. Privacy implications

RFIDs, in of themselves, pose no privacy issues. An RFID chip cannot record information about its surroundings and they typically are not encoded with information that is of use without also having access to an accompanying database providing the information associated with the object to which the chip was attached. The principal privacy concern raised by RFIDs is that they can potentially allow users to track the movement of individuals by tracking the movement of objects in the individuals' possession. This concern has been particularly raised in the context of RFID chips being embedded in government identification cards, passports, license plates, or similar items. If one assumes a sufficiently distributed network of RFID readers, it would be feasible to monitor the location of the individual who is associated with the identification card, assuming that it remains in the possession of the owner for a substantial part of the time.

Currently, this type of network is speculative, although many nations are introducing RFIDs as part of passport control stations at ports of entry.

Currently, no federal law directly regulates the use of RFIDs. However, Arkansas, California, Michigan, Minnesota, Nevada, New Hampshire, North Dakota, Oklahoma, Rhode Island, Texas, Vermont, Virginia, Washington, and Wisconsin have passed some form of state legislation restricting the use of RFIDs.[9] To avoid further regulation, a number of industries connected to the manufacture and use of RFIDs have formed EPCglobal, an organization intended to promote the development of industry standards for self-regulation on the use of RFIDs in consumer products. As part of this effort, EPCglobal has developed guidelines to help deal with RFID privacy concerns. The guidelines call for products containing RFIDs to be labeled, the RFID tags to be capable of being disabled or discarded, information about RFIDs to be readily available to the consumer, and for any personal information collected in conjunction with the use of RFIDs to be handled in a manner complying with any applicable laws.[10]

The EU is also currently studying RFID technology, led by the members of the Coordinating

---

[9] *State Statutes Relating to Radio Frequency Identification (RFID) and Privacy*, NAT'L CONF. OF STATE LEGS., http://www.ncsl.org/issues-research/telecom/radio-frequency-identification-rfid-privacy-laws.aspx (last updated Sept. 9, 2010).

[10] *EPCglobal Guidelines on EPC for Consumer Products*, EPCGLOBAL, http://www.gs1.org/epcglobal/public_policy/guidelines (last updated June 2013).

European Efforts for Promoting the European RFID Value Chain (CE RFID).[11] The CE RFID members focus on the research and application of RFID technology throughout Europe. Much like EPCglobal, CE RFID has issued a series of guidelines to assist in the implementation of RFID technology.[12]

In response to the growth of the RFID market in Europe, the European Commission has passed two directives and one decision to date that touch on RFID technology.[13] Of these, the first directive, the Radio and Telecommunications Terminal Equipment (R&TTE) Directive remains the most important. Passed in 1999, the R&TTE Directive mandates certain standards for the application of RFID tags. The R&TTE Directive applies to the RFID tag "at the stage of placing on the market." This is important because the R&TTE Directive only applies to the tags and not the product it is embedded in, meaning the ultimate buyer of the product is not required to be informed of the RFID tag.[14].

---

[11]   *Members*,   CE   RFID,   http://www.rfid-in-action.eu/public/members.html (last visited Oct. 24, 2013).

[12]   RFID   Guidelines,   CE   RFID,   http://www.rfid-in-action.eu/public/rfid-knowledge-platform/copy_of_rfid-guidelines.html (last visited Oct. 24, 2013).

[13]   *European Commission Directives and Decisions*, CE RFID, http://www.rfid-in-action.eu/public/rfid-knowledge-platform/standards/application-independet-standards/european-commission-directives-and-decisions.html (last visited Oct. 24, 2013).

[14]   *Passive RFID Tags at the Stage of Placing on the Market and the R&TTE Directive*, ENTER. & INDUS., EUROPEAN COMM'N,

E.   BIOTECHNOLOGY

1. Technological Overview

Biotechnology has made historic leaps in the past several decades, resulting in both promising benefits and unanswered questions. It seems only a few years ago that scientists undertook to *map* the human genome—now scientists are looking to *manipulate* the human genome, among other things. New technologies in biochemistry, genetics, and molecular biology have enlightened our understanding of the underlying causes of disease, enabled the discovery of new pharmaceuticals that specifically target disease, and offered hopes of detecting and preventing disease even before patients become symptomatic.

These new innovations, and the research methods giving rise to them, have led to several diverse privacy concerns. First, much of the biotech research currently conducted requires human tissues, cells, or embryonic materials. This fact, paired with the enormous financial stakes involved, has led to questions over the privacy and ownership rights of tissue donors. Second, advances in biotechnology have enabled the advent of personalized medicine, which seeks to diagnose and treat patients based on their particular genetic make-ups. This individualistic treatment rouses concerns over how personal genetic information will be gathered, stored, and transmitted. Third, with

http://ec.europa.eu/enterprise/sectors/rtte/documents/interpretati on_en.htm#h2-36 (last updated Apr. 18, 2013).

the increasing availability and specificity of genetic disease screening and diagnosis, privacy issues arise over potential discrimination by employers and insurance companies based on genetic predispositions or pre-symptomatic genetic diagnosis. Fourth, with the advent of new methods for genetic disease detection, government surveillance and reporting may increasingly rely on individualist genetic data, rather than on group statistical data, resulting in still other concerns over privacy.

2. Human Tissues and Cells in Research and Commerce

Biotech research and development currently relies heavily on human tissues, cells, and embryonic materials. As a result, there is an increasingly lucrative market in human biological materials. Both of these phenomena implicate privacy concerns.

a. Rights of Tissue Donors

Ultimately, as one commentator noted, "our bodies are the source of all we feel and think" and our treatment of them "must incorporate the dignity and sanctity of the body as the source of all we experience."[15] Indeed, one court noted, in considering a patient's right to refuse medical treatment, that "[e]very human being of adult years and sound mind has a right to determine what shall

---

[15]   Elizabeth E. Appel Blue, *Redefining Stewardship over Body Parts*, 21 J.L & HEALTH 75, 114 (2008).

be done with his own body. . . ."[16] As a result of this intimate connection, the donors of biological materials have a special interest in how their tissues are used. Privacy concerns are implicated by various actions of third parties in this area, including: (1) unauthorized use of biological materials in research; (2) unauthorized sale of biological materials after donation; and (3) profits inuring to third parties rather than to donors, but based on donor samples.

The California Supreme Court, in *Moore v. Regents of the University of California*, considered the legal rights of tissue donors when researchers made unauthorized use of their biological materials. 793 P.2d 479 (Cal. 1990). John Moore (Moore) had been treated for many years at the University of California at Los Angeles Medical Center (UCLA Medical Center) for a unique type of leukemia. He later learned that his doctor had developed and patented an extremely valuable cell line by utilizing his cells—without his knowledge or consent. Moore subsequently sued for damages alleging conversion and basing "ownership" of his biological materials on principles of privacy rights.

The *Moore* court concluded that Moore's doctor breached his fiduciary duties by failing to disclose his financial and research interests prior to obtaining Moore's informed consent. The court, however, declined to find the Regents, researchers,

---

[16]   Bouvia v. Superior Court, 225 Cal.Rptr. 297, 302 (1986) (quoting Schloendorff v. Society of New York Hospital, 105 N.E. 92, 93 (1914)).

and commercial genetics corporations liable on Moore's theory of conversion because of its stifling effect on research. Although the court recognized the lower court's concern that "[a] patient must have the ultimate power to control what becomes of his or her tissues [and] [t]o hold otherwise would open the door to a massive invasion of human privacy and dignity in the name of medical progress," the court declined to find a donor property interest in the materials and held that privacy concerns could be adequately addressed by doctor-patient fiduciary duties and informed consent. *Id.* at 491

Subsequent courts have also declined to find property ownership rights in body parts, following *Moore*.[17] On the other hand, courts have shown a willingness to find property rights in regenerative biological materials, including blood, plasma, and sperm cells—even allowing sale of these materials.[18] Commentators have proposed alternate legal theories to protect the privacy and personal interests of donors, including heightened regulation, trust law, and privacy law principles.

b. Special Considerations Regarding Human Embryos

Courts have dealt with reproductive tissues, especially embryos, differently than other biological

---

[17]   *See* Washington Univ. v. Catalona, 437 F. Supp. 2d 985 (E.D. Mo. 2006); Greenberg v. Miami Children's Hospital Research Inst., 264 F. Supp. 2d 1064 (S.D. Fla. 2003).

[18]   Green v. Commissioner, 74 T.C. 1229, 1980 WL 4486 (1980); Hecht v. Superior Court, 20 Cal.Rptr.2d 275 (Cal. Ct. App. 1993).

materials. The Supreme Court's decision in *Roe v. Wade* provides the primary basis for this differential treatment. In *Roe v. Wade*, the Supreme Court recognized a right to procreate, or not, that was inherent to the right of privacy protected by the Fourteenth Amendment. 410 U.S. 113, 153 (1973). Proponents for special treatment of reproductive tissues rely on the privacy rights of the gamete providers, or "parents," for support, but courts remain split.

In *Davis v. Davis*, the Tennessee Supreme Court considered whether the husband or the wife was entitled to "custody" of preembryos that were cryogenically preserved during the marriage. 842 S.W.2d 588 (Tenn. 1992). The court held that "preembryos are not, strictly speaking, either 'persons' or 'property,' but occupy an interim category that entitles them to special respect because of their potential for human life." *Id.* at 597. The court further held that both gamete providers had equal decision-making authority regarding the disposition of the preembryos and proceeded to balance the individual privacy interests involved, specifically the rights to procreation and to avoid procreation. The wife sought only to donate the preembryos and not to become impregnated and the husband was vehemently opposed to the donation. Thus, the court held that the husband's interest prevailed—at least absent prior agreement to the contrary.

In *Kass v. Kass*, the Court of Appeals of New York considered a near identical issue, but held that the wife's right of privacy was not implicated prior to implantation. 696 N.E.2d 174, 179 (N.Y. 1998). The court declined to decide whether the pre-zygotes were entitled to "special respect" as recognized in *Davis*, and rather than weighing the privacy interests of the gamete providers, held that the consent agreement entered into with the fertility clinic controlled the disposition of the pre-zygotes.

c. Special Considerations Regarding Human Reproductive Tissues

Quite distinct privacy concerns arise in the area of sperm and egg cell, or gamete, donation. Donors and recipients are often complete strangers, but the private information of the donor is highly valuable to the recipient. Worldwide, the sale of gametes has become increasingly lucrative, and the private donor information linked to the gametes drives the value of individual gametes.[19] This donor information traditionally includes: (1) a complete medical and genetic history; (2) general information regarding age, weight, height, educational background, sexual activity, and drug usage; and (3) personal information regarding religion, hobbies, talents, and physical features (including a photograph)—even so far as disclosing "what would send [one] . . . to an ATM at three in the morning."[20] Most, if not all, of this information is available for perusal by potential

---

[19]   *See* Sunni Yuen, Comment, *An Information Privacy Approach to Regulating the Middlemen in the Lucrative Gametes Market*, 29 U. PA. J. INT'L L. 527, 528–29 (2007).

[20]   *Id.* at 535–36, 540.

recipients who subscribe to a gamete broker's services.

The international sale of gametes is virtually unregulated and U.S. regulations focus primarily on gamete collection and screening by sperm and egg banks, neglecting regulations regarding the collection, transfer, and protection of personal donor information.[21] As brokers who deal in gametes do not fall neatly under the HIPAA definition of "covered entities," their duties regarding the protection of donor information are questionable. One commentator proposes a regulatory scheme for protecting donor information administered by the Federal Food and Drug Administration (FDA), which currently regulates sperm and egg banks.

3. Personalized Medicine

Personalized Medicine (PM) refers to the individualized diagnosis and treatment of disease based on one's particular genetic makeup.[22] PM thus involves both genomics, the mapping and study of individual genotypes, and pharmacogenomics, the tailoring of pharmaceuticals to particular genotypes. PM appears to be the wave of the future. Dr. Elias Zerhouni, Director of the National Institutes of Health (NIH), stated in congressional testimony that "[w]e can now clearly envision an era when the treatment paradigm of medicine will increasingly

---

[21]   *See* 21 C.F.R. § 1271.1 (2007).

[22]   Gary E. Marchant, *Personalized Medicine and the Law*, 44 ARIZ. ATT'Y 12, 14 (Oct. 2007).

become   more   *predictive,   personalized   and preemptive.*"[23]

Scientists are becoming more and more aware that the particular genetic makeup of patients and their diseases is directly related to whether and how well they will respond to treatment. The genetic profiling of breast cancer patients, for example, reveals that between five and seven percent of women are unable to metabolize the cancer drug tamoxifen.[24] Genetic testing is thus necessary before the drug is prescribed. Genetic disease profiling also reveals that only tumors exhibiting an over-expression of the HER2 gene are responsive to the drug trastuzumab.[25]

PM represents a powerful tool for the diagnosis, prevention, and treatment of disease, but commentators raise major privacy concerns. There are questions about the regulatory oversight of genetic testing. Any laboratory currently may offer genetic testing without government approval[26] and, although the FDA recently proposed a rule for

---

[23]   Dr. Elias Zerhouni, Testimony Before the House Subcommittee on Labor – HHS –Education Appropriations, United States House of Representatives, 109th Cong. (April 6, 2006), *available at* http://olpa.od.nih.gov/hearings/109/session2/ testimonies/overview.asp.

[24]   *Ability to Metabolize Tamoxifen Affects Breast Cancer Outcomes, Mayo Clinic-Led Study Confirms,* MAYO CLINIC (Dec. 26, 2012), http://www.mayoclinic.org/news2012-rst/7228.html.

[25]   Sandhya Pruthi, *HER2-Positive Breast Cancer: What is it?,* MAYO CLINIC (Apr. 11, 2012), http://www.mayoclinic.com/ health/breast-cancer/AN00495.

[26]   *Genetic Testing,* NAT'L HUMAN GENOME RESEARCH INST., http://www.genome.gov/10002335 (last updated Jan. 10, 2013).

expanding its approval requirements, it was met with considerable opposition, and subsequently revised in 2007.[27] Commentators also raise questions as to how individual genetic information will be collected, maintained, and transmitted.

4. Government Surveillance and Reporting

Privacy law not only protects the ability to make personal choices, which was the aspect of privacy protected by the Supreme Court in *Roe v. Wade*, but must protect the very core of each human's existence. As genetic knowledge expands in breadth and depth, it approaches the very basics of each human. Increased governmental surveillance into our genetic information is especially alarming.

The government has increasingly relied on individually-identified health information to monitor public health—whereas traditionally, group statistical data was collected. This tendency by the government to rely more and more on individualist health data is even more alarming when the data collected is genetic data.

In 1977, the Supreme Court in *Whalen v. Roe* outlined the basic principles for balancing privacy

---

[27] The FDA continues to monitor the growth of the genetic testing industry and has sought advice from the public on how it should regulate laboratory-developed tests (tests developed and administered by the same laboratory) and tests marketed and sold directly to consumers. *See* Jeffrey Shuren, Dir., Ctr. for Devices and Radiological Health, Direct-to-Consumer Genetic Testing and the Consequences to the Public (July 22, 2010), *available at* http://www.fda.gov/NewsEvents/Testimony/ucm219925.htm.

with the police power when maintaining individual public health data. This decision indicates that the government will be granted significant leeway in fashioning reporting schemes that promote or protect public health—even when reporting may involve personal genetic information. One commentator notes, however, that surveillance programs should balance public health concerns with individual privacy and confidentiality rights.[28]

II.   DEVELOPING TECHNOLOGIES

Beyond making traditional challenges to privacy more prevalent, technology is also creating entirely new challenges. Justice Brandeis foresaw this possibility over eighty years ago in his dissent from *Olmstead v. United States*:

> The progress of science in furnishing the government with means of espionage is not likely to stop with wiretapping. Ways may someday be developed by which the government, without removing papers from secret drawers, can reproduce them in court, and by which it will be enabled to expose to a jury the most intimate occurrences of the home. Advances in the psychic and related sciences may bring means of exploring unexpressed beliefs, thoughts and emotions.

---

[28]   Michael A. Stoto, *Public Health Surveillance in the Twenty-First Century: Achieving Population Health Goals While Protecting Individual's Privacy and Confidentiality*, 96 GEO. L.J. 703, 717 (2008).

277 U.S. 438, 474 (Brandeis, J. dissenting). While Brandeis was warning solely against the actions of law enforcement agencies, the same forces that drive the continuously declining cost and increasing ease of use that applies to consumer goods, also applies to technologies that can impact individual privacy. While government actors will likely always remain the largest single threat to privacy interests, technology has "democratized" surveillance in manners never before seen, and that will likely continue to accelerate in the future.

A.   ONLINE TRACKING

Somebody is watching your Internet activity, whether you like it or not. Online tracking is a concept that many of us know about, but few of us care to know its ramifications. In essence, online tracking is the idea that each time users access the Internet they are leaving a trail of information that, over time, is being used to create massive amounts of data about you, the user. This data is then used by businesses and governments to create a "digital fingerprint." This "fingerprint" consists of any sort of information that can be considered "personally identifiable," including IP addresses, user names, credit card numbers, physical addresses, etc. The data in this fingerprint allows businesses to detect spending habits for targeted advertising and governments to know where you have been and even predict where you may go. Over time these digital fingerprints, which can be created consciously by registering an account with a website and unconsciously by simply performing a web search, are combined to construct detailed profiles of users' activities.

1. Technological Overview

Each time a user connects to the Internet, a series of events are set in motion allowing profiling data to be collected. Most methods of connecting to the Internet rely on a process that assigns the user an Internet Protocol (IP) address. From the IP address, an online profiler is usually able to obtain the domain name associated with the users' Internet service provider (ISP)—the organization providing the Internet connection. The web browser used also provides significant profiling data to websites for collection purposes. A web browser's "header" often contains not only the user's IP address, but also the time, pages, and images downloaded, the referring website, form data entered by the user during that browsing session, and any "cookie" data relevant to sites previously visited. Cookie files are stored on a user's computer to collect website specific information, *e.g.*, registration information, user preferences, sites previously visited, customer codes, etc. Technology inherent to, and embedded in, a web browser also facilitates profile data collection. All of this information can theoretically be concealed or otherwise screened by users, but in practice, most users do not take such precautions.

Any data that a user actively and voluntarily provides to a website is further fodder for profiling activity. Web-based forms, registration, and input allow data to be directly transferred to the sponsoring website. Responses to e-mail marketing and advertising campaigns are tracked, not only to gauge success of the campaign, but also to identify the respondent and track their consumption preferences.

2. Privacy Implications

At its most innocuous level, online tracking is a benefit for Internet users. It facilitates targeted advertisements for products that the user is more likely to be interested in, tailors results from search engines to highlight results that fit a user's past preferences, and otherwise enhances a user's interaction with websites. Yet online tracking can also be used to learn information that users may generally prefer to keep private, including political or religious views, sexual interests, or medical conditions. Most parties engaged in online tracking do not attempt to be selective in the information they gather about users. Indeed, being selective would in large part defeat the purpose of online tracking: attempting to extrapolate the user's interests from many disparate pieces of information.

The principal objection to online tracking is the seemingly clandestine nature of the data collection. Although it is now common knowledge that it is possible to track users' online activities, users are rarely aware of which parties are tracking their activities, how extensive or limited that tracking may be, and to what use the collected information will be put. Compounding this problem further is that many websites, particularly commercial sites, are now so heavily dependent on collecting user information that users who have made efforts to anonymize their browsing habits may find the sites unusable. Even sophisticated users often find that they have to compromise on the degree of privacy protection they employ while web surfing.

Attempts to find legal solutions to this issue have been disjointed, but the possibility of some sort of regulation has motivated a number of businesses with strong online presences to form the Network Advertising Initiative (NAI) to push self-regulatory solutions to avoid more rigid government oversight. The NAI describes itself as a "self-regulatory association . . . [which] maintain[s] and enforce[s] high standards for data collection and use for online advertising purposes. Our organization also educates and empowers consumers to make meaningful choices about their experience with online advertising . . . ."[29] Central to the NAI's self-regulatory scheme is consumer education and choice. Online advertisers who adhere to the NAI principles through the NAI's Self-Regulatory Code of Conduct (NAI Code), must agree to ten requirements:

[1]   Transparency: educate consumers about behavioral advertising and choices available to them;

---

[29]   *About   The   NAI*, NETWORK ADVER. INITIATIVE, http://www.networkadvertising.org/about-nai (last visited May 15, 2013).

[2]   Notice: post notice on its website that describes its data collection, transfer, and use practices;

[3]   Choice: providing consumers with an "opt-out" mechanism;

[4]   Use Limitations: information collected shall only be used for marketing purposes;

[5]   Transfer & Service Restrictions: contractually require compliance with the NAI Code for any third parties who have access to information collected;

[6]   Access: provide consumers access to any information collected;

[7]   Reliable Sources: ensure they are obtaining data from reliable sources;

[8]   Security: provide reasonable security for any data collected;

[9]   Data Retention: retain data only for as long as needed to provide the service; and

[10]   Applicable Law: abide by all laws applicable to their business.[30]

The NAI principles have been recognized by the FTC as a "sound baseline for . . . self-regulatory efforts;" however, the FTC has also warned that self-regulation to date has been "too lax" and this

---

[30]   *2008 NAI Principles: The Network Advertising Initiative's Self-Regulatory Code of conduct*, NETWORK ADVER. INITIATIVE 7–10, http://www.networkadvertising.org/sites/default/files/imce/principles. pdf (last visited May 15, 2013).

attempt at self-regulation could be the last if it falls short of "effectively protect[ing] consumers' privacy."[31]

One new private resource for consumers interested in their online privacy has recently emerged, and the results are not good. The website, "Terms of Service; Didn't Read," reviews the privacy policies of popular websites and online services and grades them based on how they gather personal data, how they use the personal data, and with whom they share it. Some of the largest and most frequented websites have received negative reviews, including Amazon, Apple, Facebook, and Google.[32] It is still to be seen whether these companies take notice and attempt to change their policies based on this new service.

Seemingly taking direction from the FTC and the lack of response from these companies on their own initiative, the courts and states are beginning to step in. Ruling against Google's motion to dismiss, a federal judge in California rejected Google's argument that Gmail users have no reasonable expectation of privacy in their e-mail.[33] This

---

[31]   Jon Leibowitz, *Concurring Statement of Commissioner Jon Leibowitz—FTC Staff Report: Self-Regulatory Principles for Online Behavioral Advertising*, FTC 1 (February 2009), http://www.ftc.gov/os/2009/02/P085400behavadleibowitz.pdf.

[32]   TERMS OF SERVICE; DIDN'T READ, (last visited Nov. 3, 2013).

[33]   *See In re* Google Inc. Gmail Litigation, No. 13-MD-02430-LHK, 2013 WL 5423918, at *14 (N.D. Cal. Sept. 26, 2013) ("Google has cited no case that stands for the proposition that users who send emails impliedly consent to interception[ ] and

decision will likely be challenged by Google, but for now, it shows that courts are stepping in to curtail policies that may be considered abusive. The state of California is also getting in on the action. On September 27, 2013, California amended its Online Privacy Protection Act (CalOPPA) to require website operators to disclose how it responds to a user's "do-not-track" preferences and whether third parties may collect PII through their websites.[34] Although CalOPPA only applies to collecting PII from California residents, it should have an impact for all Internet users unless companies choose to create a separate policy for California residents only.

The flipside of this issue is that these same Internet companies are moving to limit the federal government's access to and spying on the data they have collected from consumers. The same giants of the Internet—AOL, Apple, Facebook, Google, Microsoft, and Yahoo—accused of tracking and prying into its users online activity are now banning together to support a bill to prevent the collection of certain PII by the federal government.[35] It will be interesting to see if this concerted action by these companies turns out to be the spark that begins to

---

use of their communications by third parties other than the intended recipient of the email.").

[34]   Act of Sept. 27, 2013, no. 370, CAL. BUS. & PROF. CODE § 22575.

[35]   Craig Timberg & Ellen Nakashima, *Amid NSA Spying Revelations, Tech Leaders Call for New Restraints on Agency*, WASH. POST (Nov. 1, 2013, 7:34 AM), http://www.washingtonpost.com/world/national-security/amid-nsa-spying-revelations-tech-leaders-call-for-new-restraints-on-agency/2013/10/31/7f280aec-4258-11e3-a751-f032898f2dbc_story.html.

change their own practice of tracking and collecting PII.

B.   BIG DATA

We are an online society and that means that information is always being transmitted. "Big data" is a term that can be characterized by the volume, variety, and velocity of this data. Not too long ago, this data was too big, it didn't fit within the structure of conventional databases, and the data moved too fast. Improvements and changes in the way data is handled and processed, most notably with the advent of cloud computing, has allowed big data to be managed and analyzed, otherwise called "mined." The concept of data mining has existed for decades, but was primarily limited to searching for patterns in one database at a time and then cross-referencing results. As a result of these improvements in computer networking and processing power, however, it has become increasingly feasible, particularly for large Internet companies, and even government actors who can compel access to otherwise proprietary databases by law, to consolidate and scrutinize personal information from numerous different sources, allowing a previously unrivaled degree of analysis.

1. Private Use

As alluded to in the earlier discussion on online tracking, the information that users leave behind, and the corresponding use of that information by private entities, while doing seemingly innocuous tasks is surprising. Consider the following example. You open your favorite search engine and type in "best prenatal vitamins" into your search bar. Instantly, thousands of search results are returned, including retailers that carry prenatal vitamins and articles and blogs written about the desired content of good prenatal vitamins. What you may not realize, is that this information is now being collected by your Internet search provider and used to target its advertisements to you. So the next time you open your web e-mail account, you begin to notice advertisements for certain prenatal vitamins and other baby products. Now take this example one step further and assume that you are a parent in a household that shares a computer among members of your family. The next time you go online to enter a search term or check the inbox of your web e-mail account you see advertisements for prenatal vitamins and baby products. You, as a responsible and prudent parent, begin to wonder why advertisements for baby products are popping up because you and your spouse are not expecting another child. Perhaps you think nothing of it at first, but the advertisements continue over the next several weeks until finally you really start to question why advertisements for baby products continue to appear. It then hits you, "Was my daughter searching for prenatal vitamins? Is she pregnant?" You then later find out that she is pregnant and has been using the computer to research prenatal vitamins and other baby products.

This illustration is just to demonstrate the type of information and analysis that can be extracted from a simple Internet search, but it can also occur from something as simple as the loyalty card you carry for your favorite grocery store. Companies use this type of collection and analysis of information to their advantage, and it is a huge business. Take for example Google, one of the largest Internet companies in the world. Google's revenue in 2012 exceeded $50 billion, of which greater than 90 percent was attributable to advertising. The large dollars involved has many companies wanting a piece of the pie, leading them to collect as much information as they can in the hopes they can monetize it. This desire for revenue, however, provides incentives to companies to ignore privacy principles that could lead to real risks for consumers.

The latest installment of advertising based on information collected from consumers is called Targeted Real-Time Advertising. This type of advertising is targeted advertising taken to the extreme. Rather than wait for the information to be collected, analyzed, and presented to you for a future visit, Targeted Real-Time Advertising strives to render advertising in, you guessed it, real-time. This means walking into your current retail store and seeing customized ads based on your shopping patterns or an advertisement for a donut sale at your local donut shop that you pass on your way to work. While some of these scenarios are still a couple of years off, it is currently being tested and marketed for the Internet in the United States. Facebook, for example, was testing this model with one percent of its user base as of late 2013. For

Facebook, this means presenting its users with targeted advertising based on real-time comments and conversations the user is having with other Facebook users. Another company, Zoomph, brings this type of technology to all social media networks, like Twitter and Instagram. If the testing of these programs is successful in 2013, real-time advertising could become a reality in all of our online communications.

2. Government Use

Although the volume of information collected by private organizations is astounding, government access to, and collection of, information is perhaps even greater. Revelations from Edward Snowden, a former National Security Agency (NSA) contractor, show the potential for abuse by governments in collecting vast amounts of data and the means by which they can go about that collection. The impact of Snowden's disclosures will be felt for years.

The US laws at the center of this issue are Executive Order 12333 (Order 12333), the Foreign Intelligence Surveillance Act (FISA), and the FISA Amendments Act of 2008 (FAA).

- Order 12333 was implemented in 1981 by then-President Ronald Reagan. The stated goal of Order 12333 was to develop intelligence of foreign nations, persons, and organizations for better national security. The order specifically directs the intelligence agencies of the United States to collect such information vigorously;

however, it also states that measures should be taken to protect "individual interests." [36]

- FISA, which became effective in 1978, authorizes electronic surveillance for the collection of "foreign intelligence information" between "foreign powers" and "agents of foreign powers." FISA has been amended several times since 2001 after the attacks on September 11, including the PATRIOT Act. Under FISA, probable cause must be shown that the "target of the surveillance is a foreign power or agent of a foreign power." An important limitation of FISA is that it is not applicable outside the United States, so the gathering of intelligence on foreign soil is not bound by this law.[37]

- The FAA allows U.S. intelligence to target persons outside of the United States and monitor their electronic communications. The FAA does not permit targeting of any person known to be located in the United States, nor does it permit the targeting of any U.S. person.[38]

---

[36]   Exec. Order No. 12333, 3 C.F.R. 200 (1981).

[37]   Foreign Intelligence Surveillance Act of 1978, 50 U.S.C. § 1801 *et seq.*

[38]   FISA Amendment Act of 2008, Pub. L. No. 110-261 (codified as amended in 50 U.S.C.).

Today, the content of the documents Snowden released are driving a change in how citizens around the world view their government and its intrusiveness into their private lives. Public rallies have been held demanding an end to government spying. Foreign leaders, including U.S. allies caught up in the spying allegations, are calling for change.[39] The Internet community is also voicing its outrage. In documents revealed by Snowden, the NSA appeared to have infiltrated company networks, such as Google and Yahoo, and copied information from millions of users, most of whom were innocent American citizens. Although the NSA responded by stating it did not keep all of the information it copied and only focused on discovering "intelligence about valid foreign intelligence targets,"[40] the practice sparked public outrage. In direct response to these allegations, Google and Yahoo both stated publicly that they have never authorized free access to their networks and urged that action from Congress is necessary to curtail this activity. Given the unified stance of

---

[39]   One such foreign leader caught in the NSA's web of spying activity was German Chancellor Angela Merkel, whose personal mobile phone was alleged to have been monitored. *See, e.g.*, Mark Mazzetti & David E. Sanger, *Tap on Merkel Provides Peek at Vast Spy Net*, N.Y. TIMES, Oct. 31, 2013, at A1, *available at* http://www.nytimes.com/2013/10/31/world/europe/tap-on-merkel-provides-peek-at-vast-spy-net.html.

[40]   *NSA Statement on Washington Post Report on Infiltration of Google, Yahoo Data Center Links*, WASH. POST (Oct. 30, 2013), http://www.washingtonpost.com/world/national-security/nsa-statement-on-washington-post-report-on-infiltration-of-google-yahoo-data-center-links/2013/10/30/5c135254-41b4-11e3-a624-41d661b0bb78_story.html.

private citizens, foreign governments, and private organizations to change the laws to prevent this type of data collection and mining, some type of reform may be a possibility.

C. DATA BROKERS

With so much data being transmitted, where is it all kept? Each company you provide information to, whether to enter a sweepstakes or to apply for a loan, uses that information for its intended purpose, but also to update its own records so that it may possibly use that information to target advertising to you in the future. The average consumer understands this. But what happens when a company seeks out this type of information from every type of source you can think of—online social networks, banks, retail stores, and so on—for the sole purpose of creating the most detailed profile about individual consumers that it can. Enter the data broker, a business that collects vast amounts of information, packages it, and then sells that information to other businesses for a profit. Companies in this business accumulate over 1,500 pieces of data per individual, covering over half a billion people worldwide.[41] The largest data brokers today have annual revenues in the billions of dollars. With this much money to be made, it is no

---

[41]   A company in the data broker industry may use as many as ten to twenty elements (of the 1,500 pieces of data) to describe an individual's age.

wonder that there are over 250 data brokers today taking their slice of the pie.[42]

1. Privacy Implications

It is not hard to imagine why a company that houses so much information about individuals presents unique privacy risks. Most immediately, they are easy targets for criminals. If a sophisticated criminal wanted to gather the most information with one hack, a data broker would be at the top of the list. Unfortunately, this has already occurred and will continue to occur so long as such inviting repositories of information are maintained.[43]

The more immediate concern, however, is how these data brokers are collecting, using, and selling the information. Laws regulating this type of practice are minimal, with the primary source being the Fair Credit Reporting Act (FCRA).[44] The FCRA requires entities that collect consumer information, such as employment history, do so in a manner that ensures accuracy. The FTC, which is responsible for enforcement, has taken an increasing interest in the practices of data brokers. In December 2012, the

---

[42]   *Online Data Vendors: How Consumers Can Opt Out of Directory Services and Other Information Brokers*, PRIVACY RIGHTS CLEARINGHOUSE, https://www.privacyrights.org/online-information-brokers-list (last updated Mar. 2013).

[43]   *See, e.g.*, Brian Krebs, *Data Broker Giants Hacked by ID Theft Service*, KREBS ON SECURITY (Sept. 25, 2013, 12:02 AM), http://krebsonsecurity.com/2013/09/data-broker-giants-hacked-by-id-theft-service/.

[44]   Fair Credit Reporting Act, 15 U.S.C. § 1681 *et seq.* (2012).

FTC began an investigation into the subject when it issued orders to nine of the largest data brokers to study how these companies collect and use the information they collect.[45] One of the early results from this study is a proposed "Reclaim Your Name" initiative, with the aim of getting the data brokers to make the information they have transparent to the consumer. In response to this suggestion by the FTC, Acxiom, one of the largest data brokers in the world, unveiled in 2013 a new website that would allow a consumer to see what information has been collected by it and how the information is being used, as well as providing an opt-out option from Acxiom's marketing services, and even allow corrections to be made through the website.[46] In a statement by Acxiom's CEO, the company acknowledged that this website was both an attempt to empower the individual consumer and appear friendly to any impending legislation.[47] Unless more data brokers take similar steps, however, it seems unlikely that the industry will be able to avoid some degree of formal legislation.

---

[45]   *FTC to Study Data Broker Industry's Collection and Use of Consumer Data*, FTC (Dec. 12, 2012), http://www.ftc.gov/opa/2012/12/databrokers.shtm.

[46]   ABOUTTHEDATA.COM,   https://aboutthedata.com/   (last visited Nov. 8, 2013).

[47]   Natasha Singer, *A Data Broker Offers A Peak Behind the Curtain*, N.Y. TIMES, Sept. 1, 2013, at BU1, *available at* http://www.nytimes.com/2013/09/01/business/a-data-broker-offers-a-peek-behind-the-curtain.html?_r=0.

D.   GEO TRACKING

"Geo tracking" refers to the ability of a third party to track and pinpoint the location of an individual or thing through global navigation satellite systems. This tracking most often results from purposefully revealing your location information. Examples of this include typing your current location into your personal navigation system equipped in your car or on your phone for purposes of getting driving directions, or by placing some type of tracking tag on a product that allows shipping companies to monitor the progress of cargo. Location information may also be collected, however, without individuals even knowing that their location information is being transmitted to a third party. Privacy concerns related to geo tracking center around this latter type of geo tracking: the involuntary and hidden collection and recording of a person's location and how this location information is being used.

1. Technological Overview

The term "global navigation satellite system" refers to any system that relies on a network of orbiting satellites to determine the geographic position of a radio beacon. The first fully deployed global navigation satellite system was the U.S. Global Positioning System (GPS), but several other such systems have become operational or under development since the GPS first became operational in 1994.[48] The GPS is currently composed of thirty-

---

[48]   These other systems include the Russian GLONASS (became fully operational in 2011); the E.U. Galileo system

one satellites that each orbit the Earth twice daily. The orbits of the satellites are structured so that four satellites are above the horizon relative to any point on Earth at any given time. Each GPS satellite has an atomic clock and continually transmits a signal containing the current time at the start of the message and information concerning its location in the orbital pattern. A GPS receiver intercepts the satellites' signals. The receiver computes the difference in time between when each signal was transmitted and when it arrived, allowing it to extrapolate the receiver's position relative to each of the satellites. Collating this information from all the satellites allows the receiver to determine its latitude, longitude, and altitude to a high degree of accuracy.

GPS receivers can be very compact. Commercially available GPS processing chips as small as 5 cubic millimeters have been developed, although display screens, user interfaces, and other features that make the GPS receiver's information usable to human operators inevitably make the devices larger. Once limited to military and high-value commercial use, it has become routine for GPS receivers to be installed in automobiles, cellular phones, and other consumer electronics. The main limitations on the use of GPS receivers is that they are susceptible to having the signal disrupted on a local level by electromagnetic interference or

(scheduled to become fully operational in 2019); the Chinese COMPASS (scheduled to become fully operational in 2020); and the Indian IRNSS (scheduled to become operational in the Indian subcontinent by 2014).

physical obstacles, and they must have a power source to be able to process signal data from the GPS satellites.

2. Privacy Implications in the Courtroom

The major privacy concern with GPS receivers is that, when paired with a computer capable of recording GPS position information, they are able to produce extremely accurate records of the movement of a vehicle or individual carrying the device. While the privacy implications of the use of GPS have been litigated in both the criminal and civil context, it was not until recently that the United States Supreme Court changed its view on the use of GPS and its application under the Fourth Amendment.

Prior to 2012, the common thread in these cases was a reliance on the United States Supreme Court's ruling in *United States v. Knotts*, 460 U.S. 276 (1983). *Knotts* predated public access to GPS (although military applications of the system were already being made), and instead concerned the use of a radio tracking device installed on a drum of chemicals as part of a police sting operation. The Supreme Court found that no Fourth Amendment violation resulted from the tracking because a "person traveling in an automobile on public thoroughfares has no reasonable expectation of privacy in his movements from one place to another." 460 U.S. at 281. Subsequent cases concerning GPS tracking applied the reasoning of *Knotts* to both criminal and civil cases to find that the use of GPS did not present actionable privacy concerns.[49] Recently, however, the United States Supreme Court addressed the use of GPS tracking directly in *United States v. Jones*.[50] In *Jones*, the Court considered whether the attachment of a GPS device to a vehicle and monitoring of that device constituted a search or seizure under the Fourth Amendment. Relying on the settled conclusion that a vehicle is an "effect" as that term is used in the Fourth Amendment, the Court found that installation of a GPS device on a target's vehicle, and subsequent monitoring of that device, constituted a "search."[51] Following the *Jones* decision, courts have been forced to revisit the use of GPS devices and its application under the Fourth Amendment's protections against unreasonable searches.[52]

---

[49]   *See, e.g.*, United States v. Garcia, 474 F.3d 994, 996–98 (7th Cir. 2007) (finding no Fourth Amendment violation where GPS receiver was placed on vehicle by law enforcement agents); Elgin v. St. Louis Coca-Cola Bottling Co., Case No. 4:05CV970–DJS, 2005 WL 3050633, *3 (E.D. Mo. Nov. 14, 2005) (rejecting claim for tort of intrusion based on placement of GPS receiver on vehicle by employer).

[50]   132 S.Ct. 945 (2012).

[51]   *Id.* at 949.

[52]   *See, e.g.*, United States v. Sparks, 711 F.3d 58 (1st Cir. 2013) (finding that settled, binding circuit precedent that use of a tracking device on a target's vehicle did not implicate Fourth Amendment protections was abrogated by Supreme Court's decision in *Jones*); United States v. Pineda-Moreno, 688 F.3d 1087 (9th Cir. 2012) (holding that installation of GPS tracking device was not subject to exclusionary rule due to reasonable reliance on existing binding precedent that stated use of GPS device to track movement did not constitute a search under the Fourth Amendment).

3. Privacy Implications to the Public at Large

Although the issue of geo tracking in the courtroom is important, and will certainly continue to evolve as the technology continues to improve, it is the use of geo tracking for individual consumers by private entities that is raising the most eyebrows. Much of this concern is linked to the rapid expansion of the smartphone market. Since 2007, smartphone sales have steadily been increasing, but 2013 was the first year that smartphone sales eclipsed standard mobile phones in sales.[53] This means that more than half of the nearly 500 million mobile phone consumers are now at an increased risk of geo tracking. Smartphone geo tracking can arguably be more precise than GPS because smartphones connect and disconnect to cell towers and WiFi hotspots everywhere they go. This can lead to a very detailed map of where the smartphone holder was at different times of the day, even including what floor and office the holder was in a particular building.

There is no doubt that geo tracking has its benefits to the average consumer. Millions of smartphone applications are now available that use geo tracking software to deliver an enhanced consumer experience. These experiences range from receiving discounts at a favorite restaurant courtesy of a Foursquare check-in to keeping children safe by

---

[53] Eric Zeman, *Smartphone Sales Beat Feature Phones, InformationWeek* (Aug. 14, 2013, 10:50 AM), http://www. informationweek.com/mobility/smart-phones/smartphone-sales-beat-feature-phones/240159950.

monitoring the movement of their smartphones. However, these benefits are a double-edged sword. These same, good-intended applications may provide sexual predators access to information regarding a vulnerable child's location, or facilitate a stalker's pursuit of its victim. Beyond these most serious concerns, there is the question of what use private companies may make of this information on a day-to-day basis. Insurance companies are considering using geo tracking information to help inform them of an applicant's medical and financial tendencies. For instance, an insurance company may use frequent online check-ins at fast food restaurants to determine whether an insured's dietary habits place them at a higher risk of health problems in the future.

The FTC is the government agency principally responsible for ensuring that companies abide by their own privacy policies and do not mislead consumers. Section 5 of the FTC Act is the law most used by the FTC in these types of cases and prohibits "unfair or deceptive acts or practices in or affecting commerce."[54] The FTC is making a concerted effort to crack down on geo tracking violators. One such example is a series of orders the FTC handed out in 2013 to settle charges of computer spying.[55] The orders prohibit the subject companies from using "geophysical location tracking

---

[54]   Federal Trade Commission Act § 5, 15 U.S.C. § 45 (2012).

[55]   *FTC Approves Final Order Settling Charges Against Software and Rent-to-Own Companies Accused of Computer Spying*, FTC (Apr. 15, 2013), http://www.ftc.gov/opa/2013/04/designerware.shtm.

without consumer consent and notice." The FTC has also issued recommendations to companies operating in the mobile space that are intended to better inform consumers. These recommendations include requiring affirmative consent before collecting location information, offering an easy to use interface to allow consumers to review what information is being collected, implementing a privacy by design policy, and offering smartphone users a "Do Not Track" mechanism.[56]

The FTC's efforts have no doubt caught the attention of companies operating in the geo tracking market. Perhaps fearing a broad legislative scheme specifically directed at mobile privacy, a group of geo tracking companies has banded together in an effort to self-regulate by publishing the Mobile Location Analytics (MLA) Code of Conduct (the "Code").[57] This Code declares seven principles that MLA companies should incorporate into their business practices. These principles are:

[1] Notice: "[P]rovide consumers with privacy notices that are clear, short, and standardized . . . ."

---

[56] *FTC Staff Report Recommends Ways to Improve Mobile Privacy Disclosures*, FTC (Feb. 1, 2013), http://www.ftc.gov/ opa/2013/02/mobileprivacy.shtm. The full FTC report is available at http://www.ftc.gov/os/2013/02/130201mobileprivacyreport.pdf. Privacy by Design (PbD) is the idea that privacy should be built into products at every stage of development.

[57] *Mobile Location Analytics Code of Conduct*, FUTURE OF PRIVACY FORUM (Oct. 22, 2013), http://www.futureofprivacy.org/ wp-content/uploads/10.22.13-FINAL-MLA-Code.pdf.

[2]   Limited Collection: "MLA Companies . . . shall limit the data collected for analysis to information needed to provide analytics services."

[3]   Choice: "MLA Companies shall provide consumers with the ability to decline to have their mobile devices used to provide retail analytics services."

[4]   Limitation on Collection and Use: "MLA [d]ata should not be collected or used in an adverse manner . . . ."

[5]   Onward Transfer: "MLA Companies . . . shall contractually provide that third party use of MLA [d]ata must be consistent with [these principles]."

[6]   Limited Retention: "MLA Companies shall set [ ] policies for data retention and deletion . . . [and provide the] data retention policy in their privacy notice."

[7]   Consumer Education: "MLA Companies shall participate in education efforts to help inform consumers about the use of MLA services."

III.   FUTURE TRENDS

Over the next ten to twenty years, continuing improvements in computing power combined with the proliferation of Internet-capable wireless devices will cause many of the technologies discussed above to become ever cheaper and more widely distributed.

In turn, as ever-greater volumes of information are collected, whether by fair or foul means, data mining from that information will become an increasingly powerful tool for both monitoring and manipulating individuals. The following topics provide a few examples of the future technological challenges that privacy will face.

Ubiquitous Observation: The term "ubiquitous observation" has been coined to describe programs that focus on prolonged surveillance of individuals and geographic areas. The starting point of ubiquitous observation begins with broad area surveillance as well as "birth-to-death" tracking and identification of critical targets. This ever-present observation is facilitated using both existing technologies and anticipated near-future improvements in them. Many of the technologies required for ubiquitous observation, *e.g.*, wireless microcameras, facial recognition software, RFID-enabled identification cards, "always on" GPS receivers in cell phones and automobiles, are already available on the consumer market. The key to moving from these many scattered components to an integrated surveillance system will be improvements in networking and data management so that information from many thousands of separate collection points can be collated and searched within a reasonable time frame. Ubiquitous observation will effectively be Jeremy Bentham's Panopticon made real, except that instead of consisting of a single building, it will exist as an overlay on cityscapes.

No full-scale ubiquitous observation system is yet in use, but the United Kingdom is rapidly progressing in that direction through the deployment of increasingly sophisticated networks of closed-circuit television cameras and listening devices. The U.S. military is also experimenting with developing these systems in hopes they may predict danger before it happens. The system, known as the Cognitive Engine, is an artificial visual intelligence system that can identify and notify officials if it recognizes anomalous behavior. One such application could be in crowded transportation hubs, notifying officials if abandoned bags are left unattended for more than a few minutes.

Genetic Testing: Genetic testing is the process of testing an individual's DNA to determine vulnerability to certain diseases and conditions. Genetic testing raises privacy concerns in two principal areas: employment and medical insurance. Congress addressed both of these concerns with the passage of GINA in 2008; however, it is still uncertain what role genetic testing will play in other areas of our life. As mentioned above, GINA does not extend to other types of insurance, such as life, disability, or long-term care insurance. Furthermore, GINA was meant to protect the individual consumer from discrimination by employers and health insurance providers, but what about consumers who attempt to "game the system" by purchasing insurance coverage on favorable terms when an individual knows that an elevated risk of a particular condition exists? If this practice becomes widespread, it will undoubtedly affect insurers' bottom lines and may lead insurance companies to pursue more favorable federal regulation.

As noted in Chapter 1, it has been said that "[c]ivilization is the progress toward a society of privacy."[58] In these times of rapid technological developments, the accuracy of this statement will likely be tested as never before during the coming decades. If history is any guide, however, the cause of privacy protection will likely advance in certain areas, while retreating in others.

---

[58]   AYN RAND, *The Soul of an Individualist, in* FOR THE NEW INTELLECTUAL 84 (1961).

INDEX

References are to Pages